Then Opened He Their Understanding

A Confirmation Review for the Episcopal Church

Confirmand Reference Book

First edition

By

Charles R. Lundelius, Jr., CPA/ABV/CFF

Lundelius & Associates, Incorporated

Bethesda, Maryland

Confirmand Reference Book   First Edition

Copyright @ 2021 by Charles R. Lundelius, Jr.

The purpose of the copyright is to protect the writer's intellectual property and encourage others to do so as well. Should you need to reproduce any part of this book, other than for a book review or other permitted use, please obtain permission by contacting the author at charles.lundeliusjr@gmail.com.

ISBN: 978-1-7355517-1-5

Dedication

Without three children, I likely would not have been brought into the work of becoming a Confirmation Class Instructor. My eternal thanks to Alexandria, Christina, and Trey, and to their mother, Patricia.

Acknowledgements

Special thanks to Dani Thorne for extensive editing and very insightful comments. Her questions prompted several useful annotations to the course material. Additional thanks to my sister, Carolyn Doeren, for guidance in compiling teacher outlines for the Confirmation course. I am also grateful to Spencer Ritchie for assistance with copyrights. I wish to thank the parents and their children who took my course and gave me invaluable feedback, and I especially wish to thank Debbie Hokansen and Janice Genter, the Sunday School Directors who gave me the opportunity to teach Confirmation Class.

Disclaimer

For the sake of clarity and avoidance of doubt, the course discussed in this student reference, like several others available on the market today, has not been authorized or approved by the Episcopal Church of the United States of America, or by any diocese or parish within that Church. This course and the accompanying student reference are merely the product of a confirmation instructor who had success using the approach described in this book. I leave it to you, the reader, to determine if it is of any value.

Cover art: *The Appearance to the Apostles* by Duccio di Buoninsegna ca. 1255 – 1319. Public domain.

Confirmand Reference Book First Edition

Table of Contents

Table of Contents 3
A Note for Those New to This Material 7
Introduction to the Reference 7
    A.   Scripture Focus 8
    B.   Question and Answer Format 8
    C.   Materials to Accompany this Reference Book 10
    D.   How to Use this Reference Book 11
I.   From Baptism to Confirmation 12
    A.   Why are you here? 12
    B.   Baptismal Covenant 14
    C.   How Confirmation Used to be Taught 16
II.   Human Nature 22
    A.   God's Plan of Redemption 22
    B.   The Way God Wanted Things To Be And The Way Things Will Be 27
    C.   Separation of Man from God 33
        a.   Tree of Knowledge of Good and Evil 33
        b.   Abrahamic Covenant 35
    D.   The Way Out of This Mess 35
III.   The Old Covenant – Abraham to the Early Tabernacle 38
    A.   Promise to a Righteous Man 38
    B.   Abraham to Jesus 40
    C.   The Early Tabernacle 44
IV.   The Old Covenant - Temple History and The Law 57
    A.   First and Second Temples 57
    B.   The Old Testament Law 64
V.   The New Covenant – Rights, Sin and Redemption 74
    A.   Our Rights under the New Covenant 74
        a.   Blessings and Curses 74
        b.   Faith and Scripture as Keys to Our Rights as Christians 77
    B.   Sin and Jesus' Role in Redemption 82

	a.	The Nature of Sin	82
	b.	Confession and Forgiveness	86
	c.	Jesus as Great High Priest	91
VI.	The Trinity		98
	A.	The Third Creed	98
	B.	God the Father	102
	C.	God the Son	106
		a. Prophecies	106
		b. Love goes to the cross	108
VII.	The Gifts of the Holy Spirit		112
	A.	God dwelling in us	112
	B.	Early Church: for Jews only?	115
	C.	Gifts of the Spirit	121
VIII.	Christian Apologetics within and without Scripture		133
	A.	Authority of the Scriptures	133
		a. God-breathed Scriptures	133
		b. Development of the Canon	135
	B.	Extra-Biblical Texts and the Resurrection	138
IX.	C.S. Lewis and "Inside Information"		167
X.	The Church		178
	A.	The Rise of Reason	180
	B.	Christianity and "Religious Capitalism"	183
	C.	Apostolic Succession	189
	D.	The Protestant Reformation	193
	E.	The American Revolution	195
	F.	The Protestant Episcopal Church in the USA	200
XI.	The Creeds and the Sacraments		203
	A.	The Nicene Creed	203
	B.	The Apostles' Creed	211
	C.	The Sacraments	219
		a. Holy Baptism	219
		b. Holy Eucharist	224
		c. Other Sacramental Rites	227

Confirmand Reference Book First Edition

XII.	Worship	**233**
	A. Rite One and Rite Two	233
	B. Varieties of Services	234
	C. The Word in the Holy Eucharist	236
	D. Preparation for Holy Communion	242
XIII.	The Christian Hope	**248**
XIV.	Next Steps	**258**
	A. The Baptismal Covenant in Action	258
	B. Beyond This Course	259

About the Author

Charles Lundelius is a Certified Public Accountant, Accredited in Business Valuation and Certified in Financial Forensics by the American Institute of Certified Public Accountants ("AICPA"). In his forty-year professional career as a forensic accountant, he has led investigations of major financial frauds and testified as an expert witness in federal and state courts on numerous accounting and financial matters. When asked to teach Confirmation Class at his church for his three children, Charles applied the same investigative approach to development of the course curriculum contained in this manual. He ended up teaching Confirmation Class for over ten years and, in 2015, became a Licensed Catechist.

On behalf of Montgomery County (Maryland) Public Schools, a school system in the Washington, D.C. suburbs with over 120 schools and an annual operating budget in excess of $100 million, the superintendent appointed Charles to various positions on the superintendent's Budget Review Committee over a four-year period. On that committee, Charles worked extensively with school administrators, teachers and principals on many issues relating to teaching methods, teacher education, and classroom support. Charles also served as PTA president and was active in several learning initiatives.

Charles has written two previous books. In 2003, he authored *Financial Reporting Fraud: A Practical Guide to Detection and Internal Control*, peer-reviewed and published by the AICPA, which has been used as a textbook in academic and professional courses. The second edition of the book was released in July, 2010.

For a major Episcopal Diocese, Charles has served on finance and audit committees overseeing financial reporting, internal controls, investment management and policy, and operational issues. For a large Episcopal Church congregation, he analyzed investment objectives and operating cash requirements to develop long-term investment policy, as well as processes to monitor performance. For another congregation, as chair of the finance committee, Charles analyzed internal control, supervised the change in accounting systems, revised administrative and investment policies, and updated budgeting processes. Currently, Charles serves as the Audit Committee Chair for a major Episcopal Diocese, overseeing internal control for the multi-million-dollar operating budget for the diocese and its endowment funds. Charles also has served on the Diocesan Finance Committee and as a seminar instructor to church treasurers on Not-For-Profit accounting and internal control issues, and he has consulted with the diocese on audit and accounting issues relating to diocesan financial statements.

Confirmand Reference Book First Edition

A Note for Those New to This Material

This is a reference designed to serve as a review for teenage confirmands who have completed the companion classroom confirmation course titled, *Did Not Our Heart Burn Within Us?* This book, then, provides a summary of material covered in that course's curriculum, but if you did not take the course, you should still be able to follow the material presented here.[1] In addition, this reference provides an excellent means for parents of teenage confirmands to gain insight into what their children learned from the course.

Introduction to the Reference

Congratulations on your Confirmation! You took a huge step in your personal faith journey and made a truly **adult** decision.

This reference book is for you, the confirmand, who has **completed** Confirmation Class taught from materials in the course manual titled, *Did Not Our Heart Burn Within Us?* The reference's purpose is to provide you with a tool to build your faith in future years. The course itself is packed with information that, by design, comes at you fast and moves quickly to give you a broad overview. This reference, also by design, is intended to help you re-examine what you heard in class while proceeding at your chosen pace to ponder the details as you see fit. In addition, if your class teacher had to truncate or eliminate some sections of the course, this reference will fill in the gaps.

The course you took was intended to help you as a teenage confirmand make the personal decision to commit your life to Jesus Christ and state that "with God's grace I will follow him as my Savior and Lord".[2] The course, though, was a little different from most in that it was grounded in Scripture. Why? Because I believe that to lead confirmands to commit their lives to Jesus Christ, Scripture reveals the Son of God. Indeed, our Catechism states:

Q.   Where may we find what Christians believe about Christ?

A.   What Christians believe about Christ is found in the Scriptures and summed up in the creeds.[3]

And the course covered all three creeds, as well (remember from the course, the origins of the Episcopal Church can be traced back to three creeds, not just two, all explained in this reference).

---

[1] This book does condense or omit subjects covered more fully in the classroom manual, though. If you are trying to evaluate the suitability of this course for your parish, I urge you to make that determination from the companion publication, *Did Not Our Heart Burn Within Us?*

[2] Book of Common Prayer, 2007, p. 415. All cites to the Book of Common Prayer, abbreviated as "BCP", are from the 2007 edition, unless otherwise noted. If your church still uses the 1979 edition, the page references are the same (only the Lectionary was changed), so do not fret about which edition you have available for this course.

[3] BCP, p. 851.

A. Scripture Focus

If there is a secret to the success of this course, it is no secret to those who live by Scripture: there is great power in the Word of God, and it is my prayer that the use of Scripture in this course drew you into a closer relationship with God. Make no mistake, I believe, with St. Paul, that "[a]ll Scripture is given by inspiration of God, and is profitable for doctrine, for reproof, for correction, for instruction in righteousness".[4] In addition, as explained in the Catechism, Scripture leads us into all truth through the workings of the Holy Spirit:[5]

Q. How is the Holy Spirit revealed in the New Covenant?
A. The Holy Spirit is revealed as the Lord who leads us into all truth and enables us to grow in the likeness of Christ.

...

Q. How do we recognize the truths taught by the Holy Spirit?
A. We recognize truths to be taught by the Holy Spirit when they are in accord with the Scriptures.

This course covers the salient points of the Catechism, labeled as "An Outline of the Faith" in the Book of Common Prayer ("BCP"), pp. 845-862, though not in a structured way. For example, Section II, Human Nature, will cover four Catechism topics, as shown at the end of sub-section A. You will find many other references to the Catechism in footnotes. For many Episcopalians of my generation (Baby Boomers), we studied for Confirmation by rote memorization of the Catechism, which you will see in Sec. I.C. is a teaching method that dates back to the sixteenth century. In a personal sense, this course is my attempt to update that teaching method!

B. Question and Answer Format

Both this reference and the course are in a format whereby the teacher poses a question and the confirmand answers. That format is called the Socratic Method, after the Greek philosopher Socrates. Here is how the Stanford University Newsletter on Teaching describes this method:

> Socratic inquiry is emphatically not "teaching" in the conventional sense of the word. The leader of Socratic inquiry is not the purveyor of knowledge, filling the empty minds of largely passive students with facts and truths acquired through years of study. As the people in [Stanford's] School of Education would say, the Socratic teacher is not "the sage on the stage." In the Socratic method, there are no lectures and no need of rote memorization. But neither, as you might expect, is the Socratic teacher "the guide on the side." In the Socratic method, the classroom experience is a shared dialogue between teacher and students in which both are responsible for pushing the dialogue forward through questioning. The "teacher," or leader of the dialogue, asks probing questions in an effort to expose the values and beliefs which frame and support the thoughts and statements of the participants in the inquiry. The students

---

[4] II Timothy 3:16.
[5] BCP, pp. 852-853.

ask questions as well, both of the teacher and each other. The inquiry progresses interactively, and the teacher is as much a participant as a guide of the discussion.[6]

The Socratic Method, then, is a process in which the teacher asks questions that guide the discussion to where students' answers trigger learning. This reference book actually scripts out questions and answers so that you can see the Socratic Method in action.[7] The teacher's statements begin with a "T" and are in black ink; the confirmands' anticipated answers, answers that I collected over my years of teaching, begin with a "C" and are in blue ink. The Q&A exchange is contained in a box to separate it from general instructions and commentary. Also, at the beginning of major sections, I provide a summary of learning objectives to show you where the discussion is headed (kind of a sneak preview). Interestingly, the earliest Catechism, which provided the skeletal outline of our Faith used to teach confirmands today, was in a question and answer format.[8]

The title of the course manual, *Did Not Our Heart Burn Within Us?*, reflects the course's approach and emphasis. The title is a question posed by two disciples after encountering Jesus shortly after the Resurrection as they traveled the road to Emmaus: "Did not our heart burn within us, while he talked with us by the way, and while he opened to us the Scriptures?"[9] Jesus had walked with the disciples along the road, though they did not recognize Him at first, and explained why the Messiah had to suffer death and then rise from the dead, and "beginning at Moses and all the prophets, he expounded unto them in all the Scriptures the things concerning himself."[10] The discussion started with questions from the disciples about events in Jerusalem that day and ended with Jesus drawing upon the Scriptures to explain those events. When Jesus finally revealed Himself before disappearing from their sight, the disciples exclaimed, "Did not our heart burn within us?" In the same manner, the Confirmation course uses Scripture to answer confirmands' questions in a dialogue format, just like Jesus talking to the disciples on the road to Emmaus.

The title of this reference book, *Then Opened He Their Understanding*, reflects the events that took place after Jesus disappeared from the presence of the disciples on the road to Emmaus. Those disciples then turned around to return to Jerusalem, linked up with the other disciples there and explained what had happened on the road to Emmaus. As they were speaking, Jesus suddenly appeared in their midst and, as told by St. Luke, "[t]hen opened he

---

[6] "The Socratic Method: What it is and How to Use it in the Classroom," *Speaking of Teaching*, Stanford University, FALL 2003 Vol.13, No. 1.

[7] The Stanford publication goes on to say that, under the Socratic Method, "[t]here is no pre-determined argument or terminus to which the teacher attempts to lead the students." A true Socratic Method course, therefore, does not have a script, but in order to be sure we covered the necessary material, I had to develop one. My apologies to Socrates!

[8] The next section discusses the Confirmation requirements set forth in the first Book of Common Prayer published in 1549. The authors of that prayer book wrote a catechism in question and answer format, which can be viewed at http://justus.anglican.org/resources/bcp/1549/Confirmation_1549.htm. I should point out, though, that our Anglican forbearers were influenced by Martin Luther when he published his "Small Catechism" twenty years earlier, and Luther's catechism was in Q & A format. For a more comprehensive timeline of the development of the catechism, see *Anglican Foundations, A Handbook to the Source Documents of the English Reformation* by Tim Patrick (The Latimer Trust, 2018), Chapter 4.

[9] Luke 24:32.

[10] Luke 24:27.

Confirmand Reference Book First Edition

their understanding, that they might understand the scriptures."[11] That is, Jesus explained why the Messiah had to suffer on the cross and rise again, again drawing upon the Scriptures. This reference book serves a purpose similar to Jesus' reappearance: it allows you, the confirmand, to encounter for a second time, after having completed the Confirmation course, the knowledge needed to understand our Faith based upon the Scriptures.

C. Materials to Accompany this Reference Book

In terms of Bible coverage, the Confirmation course literally began at Genesis and went to Revelation. In addition, the course followed the development of the early Church during the Roman Empire, then moved through the Middle Ages to the Protestant Reformation, and from there to the American Revolution. To gain better context for those periods, the course utilized a remarkable chart of human history developed by a geologist named Edward Hill and first published in 1890. A century later, the chart was re-published as *The Timechart History of the World* and is in its sixth edition by Third Millennium Press Limited. This chart consists of eighteen continuous panels with a width of one foot each. If you are able to get a copy for your own use with this reference book, that would be preferred but is not necessary. The *Timechart* is available through on-line book sellers, but be sure to order the full timeline version subtitled "Over 6000 Years of World History Unfolded". The same publisher also produces other versions, such as the *The Timechart of Biblical History*, but that version stops shortly after the first century A.D.,[12] which omits important events in the history of the early Church.

This reference book also provides quotes from the King James Version of the Bible, so you do not need a Bible. If, however, you wish to use a more modern translation of the Bible, feel free to do so. This reference also provides all quotes needed from the Book of Common Prayer ("BCP"), but if you want to be able to compare different sections of the BCP when the teacher makes comparisons or just to follow along with the discussion as the teacher refers to specific pages, then see if you can borrow or buy a copy.[13] Alternatively, you can download a BCP at https://www.episcopalchurch.org/files/book_of_common_prayer.pdf.

Also, for this reference book, you will need access to the following:

- **Mere Christianity**, by C.S. Lewis
Hopefully, you got to keep your copy used in the Confirmation course! If not, Harper Collins has published several versions available through most on-line booksellers. Mr.

---

[11] Luke 24:45.

[12] I use the term A.D., from the Latin *anno Domini* and is translated "in the year of the Lord", instead of the term more popular in academia, the "Common Era" or C.E. For a book such as this, written by a Christian for fellow Christians, the use of A.D. is more appropriate. For the same reason, I use B.C., for "Before Christ", instead B.C.E., for "Before the Common Era". Indeed, due to the use of A.D. and B.C., instead of their secular counterparts, in popular videogames such as Sid Meier's *Civilization*, I suspect you will be more familiar with the Christian notation!

[13] The Book of Common Prayer was amended to use the Revised Common Lectionary in 2006 and released in 2007. I have adjusted the curriculum for the few changes that impact course material, though, so there is no need to obtain new prayer books for this reference if you are still using the 1979 edition.

Confirmand Reference Book   First Edition

Lewis' widely recognized work, *Chronicles of Narnia: The Lion, the Witch and the Wardrobe*, is optional, but you may wish to order it if you have never read it. Note: optional material will appear in green type in this reference.

- **The Victory of Reason: How Christianity Led to Freedom, Capitalism and Western Success,** by Rodney Stark (Random House, 2005)
Hopefully, you got to keep your copy used in the Confirmation course as well. If not, this book is available through the same sources as *Mere Christianity*. Be aware, though, that Professor Stark is a prolific writer, so be sure to order this specific book by name.

D. How to Use this Reference Book

At the beginning of each section or major topic, I provide a list of Learning Objectives. The purpose of these objectives is simply to direct you as to where the discussion is headed. As I stated earlier, the course itself is set out in a Q & A format, and you can literally follow the development of the logic used to reach each Learning Objective. Note that key concepts are highlighted in blue in this text.

For those who took this Confirmation course, I want to make a prediction and see if I am right. After your instructor handed you this reference book, I suspect you did not open the book and read it (to this point) until your last year in high school or as you just entered college or the workforce. If I am wrong, email me at charles.lundeliusjr@gmail.com and tell me how far off my prediction was! This statement is not meant to be derogatory but to illustrate that there are certain points in your spiritual development where old questions will arise anew and cause you to want to seek out the answers again and do so in a more thorough manner. Going to college or preparing to enter the workforce are chances for you to reassess the origins of your faith. That is the primary reason for this reference book!

Now, as you start the first section, From Baptism to Confirmation, picture yourself back in a class setting as you are about to see and listen to a dialogue between the teacher and the confirmands. As you do, it is my heartfelt prayer that this reference book opens your mind and heart to the knowledge and love of Christ!

Confirmand Reference Book First Edition

I. From Baptism to Confirmation

<u>Learning Objectives</u>

1. Confirmands will understand that Confirmation is a choice to be made by each of them, and that choice reaffirms the promises made by their parents and godparents who may have spoken for them at Baptism.
2. Confirmands will understand the importance of the Baptismal Covenant, said at both their Baptism and at their Confirmation, as well as the promises made at their Baptism.
3. Examining the instructions for Confirmation in the first prayer book, Confirmands will know the foundations laid in the sixteenth century for this course and the sacrament in which they will partake.

A. Why are you here?

T: An event took place when you were younger, probably so young that you do not remember, that brings you to Confirmation Class today. What event could that be?

C: Holy Baptism

T: And what took place at your baptism?

C: I got splashed with water and cried.

T: Who was there?

C: Parents and godparents…,

T: … sometimes referred to as "Sponsors" in the Book of Common Prayer in use today. And what promises did they make on your behalf?

C: They made promises?

T: Yes. Open the Book of Common Prayer to pp. 302-303:

When all have been presented the Celebrant asks the parents and godparents

Will you be responsible for seeing that the child you present is brought up in the Christian faith and life?

Parents and Godparents

I will, with God's help.

Celebrant

Will you by your prayers and witness help this child to grow into the full stature of Christ?

Parents and Godparents

I will, with God's help.

Then the Celebrant asks the following questions of the candidates who can speak for themselves, and of the parents and godparents who speak on behalf of the infants and younger children

Question	Do you renounce Satan and all the spiritual forces of wickedness that rebel against God?
Answer	I renounce them.
Question	Do you renounce the evil powers of this world which corrupt and destroy the creatures of God?
Answer	I renounce them.
Question	Do you renounce all sinful desires that draw you from the love of God?
Answer	I renounce them.
Question	Do you turn to Jesus Christ and accept him as your Savior?
Answer	I do.
Question	Do you put your whole trust in his grace and love?
Answer	I do.
Question	Do you promise to follow and obey him as your Lord?
Answer	I do.

T: Now, keep your finger on that page and flip to page 415. This is part of the Confirmation service you will soon attend, and these are questions the Bishop will ask you:

The Bishop asks the candidates

Do you reaffirm your renunciation of evil?

Candidate I do.

Bishop

Do you renew your commitment to Jesus Christ?

Candidate

I do, and with God's grace I will follow him as my Savior and Lord.

T: Why is the Bishop asking you to "reaffirm your renunciation of evil" and "renew your commitment to Jesus Christ"? When did you first renounce evil and commit to Jesus?

C: [A wide range of answers is possible, or utter silence!]

T: Look at the bottom half of p. 302. The first three questions start with what?

C: "Do you renounce ...."

T: And each question deals with some aspect of evil. So that's what the Bishop means when asking you to "reaffirm your renunciation of evil". What does the Bishop mean when asking you to "renew your commitment to Jesus Christ"?

C: That refers to the next three questions. [pp.302-303]

T: Correct, but why, then, is it necessary for you to reaffirm during your Confirmation the answers to questions your parents and godparents gave on your behalf when you were younger?

C: Because we are now old enough to answer for ourselves.

B. Baptismal Covenant

T: Now flip back to p. 304 and what do you see?

C: The Baptismal Covenant ...

T: ... that's the covenant said by your parents and godparents at your Baptism:

The Baptismal Covenant

Celebrant Do you believe in God the Father?
People I believe in God, the Father almighty,
creator of heaven and earth.

Celebrant Do you believe in Jesus Christ, the Son of God?
People I believe in Jesus Christ, his only Son, our Lord.
He was conceived by the power of the Holy Spirit
and born of the Virgin Mary.
He suffered under Pontius Pilate,
was crucified, died, and was buried.
He descended to the dead.
On the third day he rose again.
He ascended into heaven,
and is seated at the right hand of the Father.
He will come again to judge the living and the dead.

Celebrant Do you believe in God the Holy Spirit?
People I believe in the Holy Spirit,
the holy catholic Church,
the communion of saints,

> These three paragraphs, up to th[is] point, constituted the Apostles' Creed, one of the **three** creeds o[f] our faith. We will learn more abo[ut] these creeds later.

Confirmand Reference Book First Edition   Page 15

> the forgiveness of sins,
> the resurrection of the body,
> and the life everlasting.

Celebrant Will you continue in the apostles' teaching and fellowship, in the breaking of bread, and in the prayers?
People I will, with God's help.

Celebrant Will you persevere in resisting evil, and, whenever you fall into sin, repent and return to the Lord?
People I will, with God's help.

Celebrant Will you proclaim by word and example the Good News of God in Christ?
People I will, with God's help.

Celebrant Will you seek and serve Christ in all persons, loving your neighbor as yourself?
People I will, with God's help.

Celebrant Will you strive for justice and peace among all people, and respect the dignity of every human being?
People I will, with God's help.

> Now the Celebrant asked everyone at your baptism to make a series of promises. Take note of these! These promises are an important part of your Christian commitment, and we will revisit these later in the course.

T: Now jump back to p. 416. You are now in the Confirmation service, and what do you see?

C: The Baptismal Covenant

T: That is the identical covenant said in your Baptism service. Why do we repeat that covenant at your Confirmation?

C: Because we are now old enough to answer the questions for ourselves.

T: So, let's see what your parents and godparents promised in order to get you to the point where you will be confirmed. Refer back to the questions and answers on BCP pp. 302-303. These are questions put to your parents and godparents at your baptism. Read each question and write out a short paraphrase on your white boards.

After paraphrasing the six questions, associate them with the two questions the Bishop asks on the bottom of p. 415:

Answer Key

	From BCP pp. 302-303	From BCP p. 415
1.	renounce Satan and all the spiritual forces of wickedness,	Do you reaffirm your renunciation of evil?
2.	renounce the evil powers of this world,	
3.	renounce all sinful desires,	
4.	turn to Jesus Christ and accept Him as your Savior,	Do you renew your commitment to Jesus Christ?
5.	put your whole trust in His grace and love, and	
6.	promise to follow and obey Him as your Lord.	

Confirmand Reference Book First Edition

C. How Confirmation Used to be Taught

T: At this point, I do not expect you to understand much about any of these renunciations and promises. The purpose of this course is to help you understand what these terms mean so that you can make an informed choice.

T: Let's take a few minutes to see how I was taught in Confirmation Classes of old. Turn to p.845 in the Book of Common Prayer, flip through to page 862. Though labeled "An Outline of the Faith", this section is more frequently referred to as the "Catechism". You'll see the Catechism is a series of questions and answers, organized by topic. A typical confirmation class, back before the internet, required that the confirmand, that's what your designation is when taking this course, memorize the answers to the questions for a given section of the Catechism. The person conducting the course would then randomly call upon a confirmand, read one of the questions, and expect the confirmand to recite the correct answer by memory. This was repeated, class after class. Fortunately for you, we will not be doing that here!

C: [Sighs of relief!]

T: But let's travel back nearly 600 years and see how the early Anglican Church treated Confirmation. This handout [#1] is a reprint of the Confirmation service from the very first Book of Common Prayer published in England in 1549.

This is the first reading from original texts and is actually a re-configured reprint in that modern-day transcribers copied letters from the original book (see the actual reproductions below) into modern (ASCII-compliant) type so that you can read it more easily. To appreciate the difference, try reading from the original texts that follow the modern typeset in the handout!

Handout #1

1549 Book of Common Prayer, the first Book of Common Prayer

CONFIRMACION,

WHERIN IS CONTEINED A CATECHISME FOR CHILDREN.

To thende that confirmacion may be ministred to the more edifying of suche as shall receive it (according to Saint Paules doctrine, who teacheth that all thynges should be doen in the churche to the edificacion of the same) it is thought good that none hereafter shall be confirmed, but suche as can say in theyr mother tong, tharticles of the faith the lordes prayer, and the tenne commaundementes; And can also aunswere to suche questions of this shorte Catechisme, as the Busshop (or suche as he shall appoynte) shall by his discrecion appose [=examine] them in. And this ordre is most convenient to be observed for divers consideracions.

> You can see here why Confirmation Classes of old consisted of much memorization.

> Even to this day, it is the Bishop's prerogative to examine confirmands, so listen and learn!

> And today, by your "owne consent", will you be confirmed.

¶ First because that whan children come to the yeres of discrecion and have learned what theyr Godfathers and Godmothers promised for them in Baptisme, they may then themselfes with their owne mouth, and ==with theyr owne consent==, openly before the churche ratifie and confesse the same, and also promise that by the grace of God, they will evermore endevour themselves faithfully to observe and kepe such thinges, as they by theyre owne mouth and confession have assented unto.

¶ Secondly, for asmuch as confirmacion is ministred to them that be Baptised, that by imposicion of handes, and praier they may receive strength and defence against all temptacions to sin, and ==the assautes of the worlde==, and the devill: it is most mete to be ministred, when children come to that age, that partly by the frayltie of theyr owne fleshe, partly by the assautes of the world and the devil, they begin to be in daungier to fall into sinne.

¶ Thirdly, for that it is agreeable with the usage of the churche in tymes past, wherby it was ordeined, that Confirmacion should bee ministred to them that were of perfecte age [i. e., an adult], that they beyng instructed in Christes religion, should openly professe theyr owne fayth, and promise to be obedient unto the will of God.

> The second and third "consideracions" are essentially the arguments for youth confirmation. The "assautes of the world" are coming at you, and you need to be prepared. You will find your beliefs challenged in high school, and especially in college. This course will help you to better understand and. if you choose. defend those beliefs.

> There is no "detrimente" to any person who defers Confirmation. Also, Confirmation is not necessary to salvation, but the training can help you understand why you are saved.

==And that no manne shall thynke that anye detriment shall come to children by differryng of theyr confirmacion==: he shall knowe for trueth, that it is certayn by Goddes woorde, that children beeyng Baptized (if they departe out of thys lyfe in theyr infancie) are undoubtedly saved.

The curate of every parish once in sixe wekes at the least upon warnyng by him geven, shal upon some Soonday or holy day, <mark>half an houre before evensong</mark> openly in the church instructe and examine so many children of his parish sent unto him, as the time wil serve and as he shal thinke conveniente, in some parte of this Cathechisme. And all fathers, mothers, maisters, and dames, shall cause theyr children, servountes, and prentises (whiche are not yet confirmed), to come to the churche at the daie appoynted, and obediently heare and be ordered by the curate, until suche time as they have learned all that is here appointed for them to learne.

> Confirmands were to attend class held at least every "sixe wekes", taught 30 minutes before the Evensong service. Younger children to comes as well to start their preparation.

> To this day, the head priest at each parish, usually called a "rector", sponsors the confirmands. It is his or her responsibility to make sure you are prepared.

And whansoever the Bushop shal geve knowlage for children to be brought afore him to any convenient place, for their confirmacion: <mark>*Then shal the curate of every parish either bring or send in writing, ye names of al those children of his parish which can say tharticles of theyr faith, the lordes praier, and the ten commaundementes. And also how many of them can answere to thother questions contened in this Cathechisme.*</mark>

<mark>*And there shal none be admitted to the holye communion: until suche time as he be confirmed.*</mark>

> This requirement since changed to allow all <u>baptized</u> persons to receive communion.*

* Some dioceses allow any person to receive communion (i.e., "open communion"), but this response comports with The Episcopal Church website at https://episcopal-church.org/communion.

Source: © Chad Wohlers, Used With Permission, found at http://justus.anglican.org/resources/bcp/1549/Confirmation_1549.htm.

Note: *Handout #1* continues with reproductions of the 1549 Book of Common Prayer on the following two pages.

Confirmand Reference Book First Edition   Page 19

> Two pages from the Confirmation service, 1549 Book of Common Prayer.

Confirmacion.

of al goodnesse to sende his grace vnto me, and to all people, that we may wurship hym, serue hym, and obey hym, as we ought to doe. And I praye vnto God, that he will sende vs al thynges that be nedeful both for our soules, and bodies: And that he wil bee mercifull vnto vs & forgeue vs our sinnes: And that it will please him to saue & defende vs in al daungers gostly and bodily: And that he wil kepe vs from al sinne and wickednes, & from our gostly enemye, and from euerlastyng death. And this I truste he wil do of his mercie and goodnes, through our lorde Jesu Christe. And therefore I say. Amen. So be it.

¶ So soone as the children can say in theyr mother tongue tharticles of the faith, the lordes praier, the ten commaundementes, and also can aunswere to such questions of this short Cathechisme as the Bushop (or suche as he shall appointe) shal by hys discrecion appose them in: then shall they bee brought to the Bushop by one that shaldbe his godfather or godmother, that euerye childe maye haue a wittenesse of hys confirmacion.

¶ And the Bushop shal confirme them on this wyse.

Confirmacion.

Our helpe is in the name of the Lorde.
Answere.
whiche hath made both heauen and yearth.
Minister.
Blessed is the name of the lorde.
Answere.
Henceforth worlde without ende.
Minister.
The lorde be with you.
Answere.
And wyth thy spirite.

Let vs praye.

Almighty and euerliuing God, who hast vouchesafed to regenerate these thy seruauntes of water & the holy goste: And haste geuen vnto them forgeuenesse of all

Confirmation. Fol. xii.

all their sinnes: Sende downe from heauen we beseche thee (O lorde) vpon them thy holy goſt the coumforter, with the manifold giftes of grace, the spirite of wisdom and vnderſtandyng: The spirite of counsell and goſtly strength: The spirite of knowledge and true godlinesse, and fulfil them (o lord) with the spirite of thy holy feare.

Answere.

Amen.

Minister.

Signe them (o lorde) and marke them to be thyne for euer, by the vertue of thy holye croſſe and paſſion. Confirme and strength them with the inward vnction of thy holy goſt, mercifully vnto euerlaſting life. Amen.

Then the Bishop shal crosse them in the forehead and ley his handes vpon their heades saying.

N. I signe thee with the signe of the croſſe, and laye my hande vpon thee. In the name of the father, and of the sonne, and of the holy goſt. Amen.

And thus shall he doe to euery childe one after an other. And whan he hath layed hys hande vpon euery chylde, then shall he say.

The peace of the lorde abide with you.

Answere.

And with thy spirite.

¶ Let vs pray.

Almightie euerliuing god, which makeſt vs both to will and to doe thoſe thinges that bee good and acceptable vnto thy maieſtie: we make our humble supplications vnto thee for theſe children, vpon whome (after thexample of thy holy Apoſtles) we haue laied our handes, to certifie them (by this signe) of thy fauour and gracious goodnes toward them: leat thy fatherly hand (we beseche thee) euer be ouer them, let thy holy spirite euer bee with them, and so leade them in the knowledge and obedience of thy woord, that in the end they may obtein the life euerlaſting, through our lord Jeſus Chriſt, who with thee and the holy goſte liueth and reyneth one god world without ende. Amen.

The

Author's Note

Background on the 1549 Book of Common Prayer:

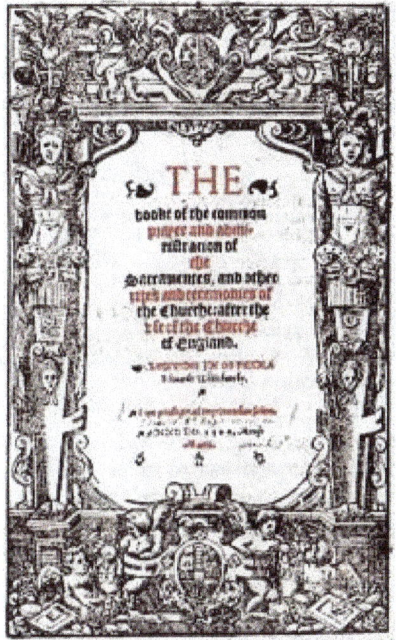

The First Book of Common Prayer

Although a formal break with the Papacy came about during the time of Henry VIII, the Church of England continued to use liturgies in Latin throughout his reign, just as it always had. However, once Henry died and the young Edward VI attained the throne in 1547, the stage was set for some very significant changes in the religious life of the country. And so a consultation of bishops met and produced the first Book of Common Prayer. It is generally assumed that this book is largely the work of Archbishop Thomas Cranmer, but, as no records of the development of the prayer book exist, this cannot be definitively determined.

This Book of Common Prayer was not created in a vacuum, but derives from several sources. First and foremost was the Sarum Rite, or the Latin liturgy developed in Salisbury in the thirteenth century, and widely used in England. Two other influences were a reformed Roman Breviary of the Spanish Cardinal Quiñones, and a book on doctrine and liturgy by Hermann von Wied, Archbishop of Cologne.

This prayer book was in use only for three years, until the extensive revision of 1552. However, much of its tradition and language remains in the prayer books of today, as may be seen by even a cursory examination of the text.

© Chad Wohlers, Used With Permission, found at http://justus.anglican.org/resources/bcp/1549/BCP_1549.htm

II. Human Nature

Learning Objectives

1. Confirmands will learn that God had a plan to restore Man to a right relationship after Man turned away from God.
2. Confirmands will learn how evil came into the world and how God conquers evil.
3. Confirmands will be introduced to the world yet to come, after the return of Jesus.
4. Confirmands will be introduced to the concept of "God is light", which will be used throughout this course.

A. God's Plan of Redemption

Author's Note

This entire subsection contains important background material, which will be incorporated into the next three subsections.

When Adam and Eve disobeyed God's instructions and ate from the Tree of Knowledge of Good and Evil in the Garden of Eden, they introduced evil into the world, contrary to God's intent, and that evil brought upon mankind the human misery that fills our history books to this day (Genesis 3:8-24).[14] God, though, was not going to leave us in this pitiful state. His plan was to send a Redeemer who would satisfy the judgment for our sins so that we would not have to pay for them, and He set that plan in motion soon after Adam and Eve ate the fruit of the tree (Genesis 3:14-15). God had an obstacle, though, in that He had given dominion over the earth to Man:[15]

> Genesis 1
>
> 26 And God said, Let us make man in our image, after our likeness: and let them have dominion over the fish of the sea, and over the fowl of the air, and over the cattle, and over all the earth, and over every creeping thing that creepeth upon the earth.
>
> 27 So God created man in his own image, in the image of God created he him; male and female created he them.

---

[14] C.S. Lewis reached an interesting conclusion from the Genesis accounts of Creation and the Fall of Man: "God saw the crucifixion in the act of creating the first nebula." *The Problem of Pain* by C.S. Lewis © copyright CS Lewis Pte Ltd 1940, p. 80. Extract reprinted by permission. In other words, as God created the universe, He foresaw that the Man He would create for that universe to freely love Him would instead turn against Him and then need a way back.

[15] The writer of Hebrews makes the same point quoting Psalm 8: "thou crownedst [Man] with glory and honour, and didst set him over the works of thy hands." Hebrews 2:7, quoting Psalm 8:5-6. Why God gave Man dominion over the Earth is not stated in Scripture, but the gift of dominion is a clear sign of God's love for Man. It also served as a backup plan: when Man disobeyed God in the Garden of Eden and was kicked out, at least Man had someplace to go!

Note that in verse 27, "Man" is defined as the male and female made in God's image. This point is reinforced in Genesis 5:2: "Male and female created he them; and blessed them, and called their name Adam [Hebrew for "Man"], in the day when they were created." I will use the term "Man", similarly, to refer to this combination of both male and female humans throughout this book.

So God could not just force His way back into the Earth and bring about the change He wanted. God, instead, would have to work with people who believed in Him and, in a very literal sense, give Him permission to introduce a Redeemer by entering into a covenant between God and Man. The first person to do so was Abraham, followed by Moses and other Israelite prophets, whose promises and agreements pointed to the coming of Jesus, the Redeemer. St. Paul described how the plan of redemption unfolded in his letter to the Romans:

> Romans 16
>
> 25 Now to him that is of power to stablish you according to my gospel, and the preaching of Jesus Christ, according to the revelation of the mystery, which was kept secret since the world began,
>
> 26 But now is made manifest, and by the scriptures of the prophets, according to the commandment of the everlasting God, made known to all nations for the obedience of faith:
>
> 27 To God only wise, be glory through Jesus Christ for ever. Amen.

That plan was a mystery but was "made manifest" by St. Paul's epistle and by the "preaching of Jesus Christ", as well as "by the scriptures of the prophets".

Until Jesus' arrival, God instituted a stop-gap measure to deal with the sin that separated Man from God: the Israelites, through their High Priests, would offer a sacrifice once a year that would absolve their sins for that year and then need to be repeated. (The annual sacrifice was in addition to daily sacrifices offered by the priests and lay people for specific sins.) This measure was far from ideal in that forgiveness was limited to those Israelites who followed the practice, and it was temporary; however, the annual sacrificial practice did continually remind the Israelites of the need for redemption. But Jesus' sacrifice[16] on the cross satisfied the requirements for redemption and brought an end to the need for further sacrifices:

> Hebrews 7
>
> 25 Wherefore [Jesus] is able also to save them to the uttermost that come unto God by him, seeing he ever liveth to make intercession for them.

---

[16] You may ask why sacrifices were necessary at all, suggesting that God could have fixed the sin problem some other way. Without going into "what if" scenarios, I would say that the sacrifice of Jesus provided the opportunity for Jesus' ultimate demonstration of love: "Greater love hath no man than this, that a man lay down his life for his friends." (John 15:13.)

26 For such an high priest [as Jesus] became us, who is holy, harmless, undefiled, separate from sinners, and made higher than the heavens;

27 Who needeth not daily, as those [other] high priests, to offer up sacrifice, first for his own sins, and then for the people's: for this [Jesus] did once, when he offered up himself.

God's Plan, though, was not complete with the sacrifice, and subsequent resurrection, of Jesus. We, His followers, need to spread the Good News of redemption through Jesus, following the examples of His apostles (e.g., Acts 20:24). Finally, after some really tough times and scary events as evil has its last days, God will restore His Kingdom on Earth for all of us who have died and risen with Christ, as told in the book of Revelation. God's Restored Kingdom, though, has interesting similarities to the Garden of Eden, and we explore those similarities in this session, using an exercise to give you a high-level view of God's Plan of Redemption.

For background, you can piece together much of God's Plan of Redemption from the Catechism, BCP pp. 845-862:

Human Nature

Q. What are we by nature?
A. We are part of God's creation, made in the image of God.

Q. What does it mean to be created in the image of God?
A. It means that we are free to make choices: to love, to create, to reason, and to live in harmony with creation and with God.

Q. Why then do we live apart from God and out of harmony with creation?
A. From the beginning, human beings have misused their freedom and made wrong choices.

Q. Why do we not use our freedom as we should?
A. Because we rebel against God, and we put ourselves in the place of God.

Q. What help is there for us?
A. Our help is in God.

Q. How did God first help us?
A. God first helped us by revealing himself and his will, through nature and history, through many seers and saints, and especially through the prophets of Israel.

Sin and Redemption

Q. What is sin?
A. Sin is the seeking of our own will instead of the will of God, thus distorting our relationship with God, with other

people, and with all creation.

Q. How does sin have power over us?
A. Sin has power over us because we lose our liberty when our relationship with God is distorted.

Q. What is redemption?
A. Redemption is the act of God which sets us free from the power of evil, sin, and death.

Q. How did God prepare us for redemption?
A. God sent the prophets to call us back to himself, to show us our need for redemption, and to announce the coming of the Messiah.

Q. What is meant by the Messiah?
A. The Messiah is one sent by God to free us from the power of sin, so that with the help of God we may live in harmony with God, within ourselves, with our neighbors, and with all creation.

Q. Who do we believe is the Messiah?
A. The Messiah, or Christ, is Jesus of Nazareth, the only Son of God.

God the Son

Q. What do we mean when we say that Jesus is the only Son of God?
A. We mean that Jesus is the only perfect image of the Father, and shows us the nature of God.

Q. What is the nature of God revealed in Jesus?
A. God is love.

Q. What do we mean when we say that Jesus was conceived by the power of the Holy Spirit and became incarnate from the Virgin Mary?
A. We mean that by God's own act, his divine Son received our human nature from the Virgin Mary, his mother.

Q. Why did he take our human nature?
A. The divine Son became human, so that in him human beings might be adopted as children of God, and be made heirs of God's kingdom.

Q. What is the great importance of Jesus' suffering and death?
A. By his obedience, even to suffering and death, Jesus made the offering which we could not make; in him we are freed from the power of sin and reconciled to God.

Q. What is the significance of Jesus' resurrection?

A. By his resurrection, Jesus overcame death and opened for us the way of eternal life.

Q. What do we mean when we say that he descended to the dead?
A. We mean that he went to the departed and offered them also the benefits of redemption.

Q. What do we mean when we say that he ascended into heaven and is seated at the right hand of the Father?
A. We mean that Jesus took our human nature into heaven where he now reigns with the Father and intercedes for us.

Q. How can we share in his victory over sin, suffering, and death?
A. We share in his victory when we are baptized into the New Covenant and become living members of Christ.

The Christian Hope

Q. What is the Christian hope?
A. The Christian hope is to live with confidence in newness and fullness of life, and to await the coming of Christ in glory, and the completion of God's purpose for the world.

Q. What do we mean by the coming of Christ in glory?
A. By the coming of Christ in glory, we mean that Christ will come, not in weakness but in power, and will make all things new.

Q. What do we mean by heaven and hell?
A. By heaven, we mean eternal life in our enjoyment of God; by hell, we mean eternal death in our rejection of God.

Q. Why do we pray for the dead?
A. We pray for them, because we still hold them in our love, and because we trust that in God's presence those who have chosen to serve him will grow in his love, until they see him as he is.

Q. What do we mean by the last judgment?
A. We believe that Christ will come in glory and judge the living and the dead.

Q. What do we mean by the resurrection of the body?
A. We mean that God will raise us from death in the fullness of our being, that we may live with Christ in the communion of the saints.

Q. What is the communion of saints?
A. The communion of saints is the whole family of God, the living and the dead, those whom we love and those

whom we hurt, bound together in Christ by sacrament, prayer, and praise.

Q. What do we mean by everlasting life?
A. By everlasting life, we mean a new existence, in which we are united with all the people of God, in the joy of fully knowing and loving God and each other.

Q. What, then, is our assurance as Christians?
A. Our assurance as Christians is that nothing, not even death, shall separate us from the love of God which is in Christ Jesus our Lord. Amen.

B. The Way God Wanted Things To Be And The Way Things Will Be

Author's Note

Picture the class divided into two groups: one group called "Genesis"; the other called "Revelation". The Genesis team will read Genesis 2:7-25 and then draw on their white boards their interpretation of the scene described in verses 8-10. The Revelation team will read all of Revelation 21 and Revelation 22:1-5 and draw the scene in verses 22:1-2. Hopefully, the confirmands are familiar with the Creation Story given in the book of Genesis and the events surrounding the Garden of Eden. Revelation, though, may need some introduction.

The book of the Revelation to St. John is largely a prophecy told in visions given to John of Patmos. It is not clear whether this John was John the Apostle who wrote one of the gospels and some or all of the three epistles or a reference to another John, though current scholarly work attributes Revelation to John the Apostle, who, at a minimum, also wrote the Gospel bearing his name and I John.[17] The author, though, whoever he was, was well-versed in the Old Testament prophets who described various aspects of the end of the world, and his message was initially directed to seven churches in what is now modern-day Turkey (the island of Patmos is off the coast of Turkey). Recent scholarship places the time of writing around 70 A.D., which was "just before or shortly after the destruction of the Temple"[18] in Jerusalem by the Roman army in the process of quelling a major rebellion in Israel. Nero, who sadistically persecuted the early Christian church (a subject we explore in Section VIII.B. later), died a year or two earlier in 68 A.D. So contemporary Christian readers of Revelation had the raw memories of Nero's terror and perhaps the sight of four Roman legions laying siege to Jerusalem. Put in that context, Revelation's warnings of earth-shaking calamities are not so unreasonable. For purposes of this course, though, we will focus on the more-upbeat ending chapters, not because they are less scary, but because they point to the Christian Hope of the world God intends to restore on Earth. We will then return to the Christian Hope in Section XIII.

---

[17] See Leighton Pullan's commentary, which can be found at http://biblehub.com/library/pullan/the_books_of_the_new_testament/chapter_xxv_the_revelation_of.htm. As to the authorship of II John and III John, an elder named John who was associated with Jesus' ministry is a likely choice: see http://www.ncregister.com/blog/jimmy-akin/pope-benedict-on-the-mystery-of-john-the-presbyter.
[18] *The Apocalypse: A Brief History*, Martha Himmelfarb, 2010, Chronology.

Drawing Exercise

Imagine the class divided into two groups: one group called "Genesis"; the other called "Revelation". The Genesis team will read Genesis 2:7-25 and then draw on white boards their interpretation of the scene described in verses 8-10. The Revelation team will read all of Revelation 21 and Revelation 22:1-5 and draw the scene in verses 22:1-2.

Texts for the Genesis group, with verses for drawing in bold:

Genesis 2

7 And the LORD God formed man of the dust of the ground, and breathed into his nostrils the breath of life; and man became a living soul.

8 And the LORD God planted a garden eastward in Eden; and there he put the man whom he had formed.

9 And out of the ground made the LORD God to grow every tree that is pleasant to the sight, and good for food; the tree of life also in the midst of the garden, and the tree of knowledge of good and evil.

10 And a river went out of Eden to water the garden; and from thence it was parted, and became into four heads.

11 The name of the first is Pison: that is it which compasseth the whole land of Havilah, where there is gold;

12 And the gold of that land is good: there is bdellium and the onyx stone.

13 And the name of the second river is Gihon: the same is it that compasseth the whole land of Ethiopia.

14 And the name of the third river is Hiddekel: that is it which goeth toward the east of Assyria. And the fourth river is Euphrates.

15 And the LORD God took the man, and put him into the garden of Eden to dress it and to keep it.

16 And the LORD God commanded the man, saying, Of every tree of the garden thou mayest freely eat:

17 But of the tree of the knowledge of good and evil, thou shalt not eat of it: for in the day that thou eatest thereof thou shalt surely die.

Confirmand Reference Book First Edition

18 And the LORD God said, It is not good that the man should be alone; I will make him an help meet for him.

19 And out of the ground the LORD God formed every beast of the field, and every fowl of the air; and brought them unto Adam to see what he would call them: and whatsoever Adam called every living creature, that was the name thereof.

20 And Adam gave names to all cattle, and to the fowl of the air, and to every beast of the field; but for Adam there was not found an help meet for him.

21 And the LORD God caused a deep sleep to fall upon Adam, and he slept: and he took one of his ribs, and closed up the flesh instead thereof;

22 And the rib, which the LORD God had taken from man, made he a woman, and brought her unto the man.

23 And Adam said, This is now bone of my bones, and flesh of my flesh: she shall be called Woman, because she was taken out of Man.

24 Therefore shall a man leave his father and his mother, and shall cleave unto his wife: and they shall be one flesh.

25 And they were both naked, the man and his wife, and were not ashamed.

Here are the texts for the Revelation group, with verses for drawing in bold:

Revelation 21

1 And I saw a new heaven and a new earth: for the first heaven and the first earth were passed away; and there was no more sea.

2 And I John saw the holy city, new Jerusalem, coming down from God out of heaven, prepared as a bride adorned for her husband.

3 And I heard a great voice out of heaven saying, Behold, the tabernacle of God is with men, and he will dwell with them, and they shall be his people, and God himself shall be with them, and be their God.

4 And God shall wipe away all tears from their eyes; and there shall be no more death, neither sorrow, nor crying, neither shall there be any more pain: for the former things are passed away.

5 And he that sat upon the throne said, Behold, I make all things new. And he said unto me, Write: for these words are true and faithful.

6 And he said unto me, It is done. I am Alpha and Omega, the beginning and the end. I will give unto him that is athirst of the fountain of the water of life freely.

7 He that overcometh shall inherit all things; and I will be his God, and he shall be my son.

8 But the fearful, and unbelieving, and the abominable, and murderers, and whoremongers, and sorcerers, and idolaters, and all liars, shall have their part in the lake which burneth with fire and brimstone: which is the second death.

9 And there came unto me one of the seven angels which had the seven vials full of the seven last plagues, and talked with me, saying, Come hither, I will shew thee the bride, the Lamb's wife.

10 And he carried me away in the spirit to a great and high mountain, and shewed me that great city, the holy Jerusalem, descending out of heaven from God,

11 Having the glory of God: and her light was like unto a stone most precious, even like a jasper stone, clear as crystal;

12 And had a wall great and high, and had twelve gates, and at the gates twelve angels, and names written thereon, which are the names of the twelve tribes of the children of Israel:

13 On the east three gates; on the north three gates; on the south three gates; and on the west three gates.

14 And the wall of the city had twelve foundations, and in them the names of the twelve apostles of the Lamb.

15 And he that talked with me had a golden reed to measure the city, and the gates thereof, and the wall thereof.

16 And the city lieth foursquare, and the length is as large as the breadth: and he measured the city with the reed, twelve thousand furlongs. The length and the breadth and the height of it are equal.

17 And he measured the wall thereof, an hundred and forty and four cubits, according to the measure of a man, that is, of the angel.

18 And the building of the wall of it was of jasper: and the city was pure gold, like unto clear glass.

19 And the foundations of the wall of the city were garnished with all manner of precious stones. The first foundation was jasper; the second, sapphire; the third, a chalcedony; the fourth, an emerald;

20 The fifth, sardonyx; the sixth, sardius; the seventh, chrysolite; the eighth, beryl; the ninth, a topaz; the tenth, a chrysoprasus; the eleventh, a jacinth; the twelfth, an amethyst.

21 And the twelve gates were twelve pearls; every several gate was of one pearl: and the street of the city was pure gold, as it were transparent glass.

22 And I saw no temple therein: for the Lord God Almighty and the Lamb are the temple of it.

23 And the city had no need of the sun, neither of the moon, to shine in it: for the glory of God did lighten it, and the Lamb is the light thereof.

24 And the nations of them which are saved shall walk in the light of it: and the kings of the earth do bring their glory and honour into it.

25 And the gates of it shall not be shut at all by day: for there shall be no night there.

26 And they shall bring the glory and honour of the nations into it.

27 And there shall in no wise enter into it any thing that defileth, neither whatsoever worketh abomination, or maketh a lie: but they which are written in the Lamb's book of life.

Revelation 22

1 And he shewed me a pure river of water of life, clear as crystal, proceeding out of the throne of God and of the Lamb.

2 In the midst of the street of it, and on either side of the river, was there the tree of life, which bare twelve manner of fruits, and yielded her fruit every month: and the leaves of the tree were for the healing of the nations.

3 And there shall be no more curse: but the throne of God and of the Lamb shall be in it; and his servants shall serve him:

4 And they shall see his face; and his name shall be in their foreheads.

5 And there shall be no night there; and they need no candle, neither light of the sun; for the Lord God giveth them light: and they shall reign for ever and ever.

The two groups should produce drawings that contain the following elements:

Element	Genesis Group	Revelation Group
River	X	X
Tree of Life	X	X
Tree of Knowledge of Good and Evil	X	

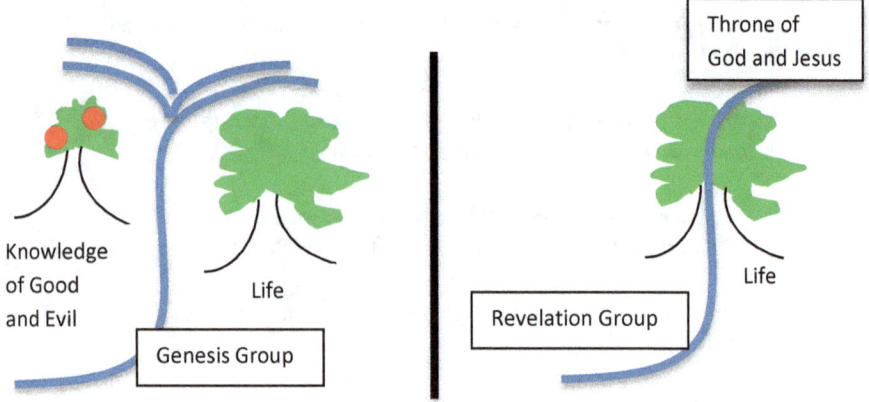

Now each group will look at the other group's drawing(s) and see if anyone can spot the similarities. They should pick out the river and Tree of Life.

Genesis Group Explains Their Reading Passage

The Genesis group then recounts the creation of Man in the Garden of Eden and how Man had "every tree that is pleasant to the sight, and good for food" so that Man did not have to toil to grow food. The Garden also had "the tree of life", which gave Man eternal life so that Man could commune with God forever. Indeed, Genesis 2:16-17 provides examples in which God and Man talk to each other directly with Man standing in the very presence of God. It is a close, intimate relationship, built on love.

Confirmand Reference Book First Edition   Page 33

<u>Revelation Group Explains Their Reading Passage</u>

This passage picks up after the great calamities of John's visions have come to an end and he sees a New Jerusalem, which is described as a huge cube, coming down from heaven. Each side was 12,000 furlongs, or about 1,500 miles. To bring that point home, if one corner of the cubic city were placed in the present-day State of Maine, the entire opposite edge could rest on the Mississippi River! More importantly, though, is what will happen within the city. There will be no need for a temple (vs. 21:22) or sun or moon (vs. 21:23) as God's Light will fill the city (vs. 22:5), and we, His servants, will "see His face" as we stand once again in His presence, and we will be marked with His name (vs. 22:4).

In other words, the close, intimate relationship with God that was enjoyed by Adam and Eve is restored with the coming of God's New Jerusalem, so that Man may again commune directly with God. To what purpose?

> Behold, the tabernacle of God is with men, and he will dwell with them, and they shall be his people, and God himself shall be with them, and be their God. And God shall wipe away all tears from their eyes; and there shall be no more death, neither sorrow, nor crying, neither shall there be any more pain: for the former things are passed away. (vs. 21:3-4)

The Tree of Life, which first appeared in the Genesis account, appears again in the New Jerusalem, whereby we will enjoy eternal life in the presence of God. This is indeed the Christian Hope!

T: How do we bridge the gap between where we were in the Garden of Eden and where we will be in the New Jerusalem? In other words, who is going to get us back to where God first intended us to be?

C: Jesus?

T: Correct.

The teacher can express this concept visually by taking one drawing by a Genesis group and one from a Revelation group and laying a cross, or Book of Common Prayer that has a cross on the cover, across the two pictures.

C. Separation of Man from God
a. Tree of Knowledge of Good and Evil

T: Why is the Tree of Knowledge of Good and Evil in the Genesis drawing but not in the Revelation drawing?

C: Evil had already been introduced into the world.

T: Right. Since the choice had been made to know evil, the Tree of Knowledge of Good and Evil no longer served a purpose.

Author's Note

In a real sense, Adam and Eve, representing Man at the Garden of Eden, opened Pandora's box[19] when they disobeyed God and let evil into the world by gaining knowledge of evil. Like Pandora who opened the box out of curiosity, there was no means to put evil back in its box, just as Adam and Eve whose curiosity led them to eat of the tree[20] could not lose the knowledge of evil once it had been acquired. Thus, there is no further need for the Tree of Knowledge of Good and Evil to reappear in Revelation.

> T: Knowing what we know about evil today, why did God place a Tree of Knowledge of Good and Evil in the Garden of Eden? Wouldn't it have been better to omit that tree so that Man would not have the opportunity to sin and separate from God?
>
> C: Yes. It would have been nicer.
>
> T: But, "would it have been better?", is what I asked. It was essential that Man had a <u>choice</u> to follow or not follow God. God created Man so He could have creatures who truly love Him, which comes through in the Creation account of Genesis 1 where God is concerned for Adam's welfare and creates, not only other creatures for Adam to subdue and rule over, but also Eve to be a companion to Adam. However, to love someone requires the option to <u>not</u> love that person: love that is forced or commanded is not love. If I say, "I command you to love me!", and, as a result, you start to act more friendly toward me, are you truly loving me?
>
> C: No.
>
> T: The Tree of Knowledge of Good and Evil provided that choice, and Man did not choose wisely! The acquisition of knowledge of evil caused Man to be separated from God. Why did God have to separate Himself from Man once Man was capable of committing evil and actually had committed evil by disobeying God?
>
> C: God could not be around evil.
>
> T: To keep it simple, let's just boil it down to a few statements from a letter from St. John: "God is light, and in him is no darkness at all" [I John 1:5], and from St. John's Gospel description of Jesus as the light entering this world, "the light shineth in darkness; and the darkness comprehended it not" [John 1:5]. God and evil, then, can no more exist together than

---

[19] From a story in Greek mythology that in some ways parallels Genesis, Pandora, the first woman on earth, was given a container (which probably was a jar but was translated centuries ago as a box) by Zeus as a wedding gift. Zeus, though, told her not to open it. However, her curiosity eventually got the better of her, and she did open the container to release terrible evils into the Earth. Pandora tried to close the container but did not succeed in stopping the flow of evil. Finally, after all the evils had left, she looked again into the container and found Hope, which was meant to follow the destructions caused by the evils of the world.

[20] Tradition had Eve picking the apple from the Tree of Knowledge of Good and Evil and then handing it to an unsuspecting Adam to eat, thus placing blame for evil on Eve. Scripture gives a different account, though. Genesis 3:6 states that Adam was with Eve when she ate the fruit (there is no specific mention of the fruit being an apple), so the two violated God's command together. Sadly, that fact did not stop Adam from attempting to shift blame when their transgression came to light. When confronted by God, Adam said "The woman whom thou gavest to be with me, she gave me of the tree, and I did eat" (Genesis 3:12).

Confirmand Reference Book First Edition   Page 35

> light and dark, and God's Light eradicates darkness.[21] If Man has darkness in his heart, then his being in the presence of Divine Light could be catastrophic. This theme appears again when we study the rituals of the Israelites later in this course.

b. Abrahamic Covenant

> T: So we know that God did not leave it there with Man separated and fending on his own; He sent Jesus. But God had a problem in that He had given Man dominion over the Earth,[22] so if God wanted to send His Son to redeem Man, he couldn't do it on His own; He had to get permission. From whom did God have to get permission?
>
> C: Man.
>
> T: The way God got permission was similar to the way we obtain permission today, by using a legal contract, and another name for a contract is a "covenant". What do we call the first covenant that precedes the arrival of Jesus on the Earth? [Look at the table of contents to the Bible if you need help with this question.]
>
> C: The Old Covenant.

D. The Way Out of This Mess

Author's Note

God will need to locate a person who is faithful to Him such that the person's faith will attribute righteousness to that person. With a righteous representative of Man, then, God can enter into a covenant. We will cover that topic in the next section, but first we need to examine a very interesting coded message God sent to foretell (or prophesy) what was to happen. Turn to:

> Genesis 3
>
> 15 And I will put enmity between thee and the woman, and between thy seed and her seed; it shall bruise thy head, and thou shalt bruise his heel.

The "thee" God was talking to is Satan, in serpent form, just after Eve identified the serpent as the one who deceived her in verse 13. Start two columns on a piece of paper titled, "Satan" and "Woman". Under each label their "seed" and add arrows to show that they are descendants:

---

[21] St. James described God as "the Father of lights, with whom is no variableness, neither shadow of turning" (James 1:17).
[22] Genesis 1:26-30.

Write the word "enmity" in the middle; "enmity" means "hatred". Now fill in the actions in the last half of the verse. The Woman's Seed will bruise the head of Satan, and Satan's seed[23] will bruise the heel of the Woman's Seed.

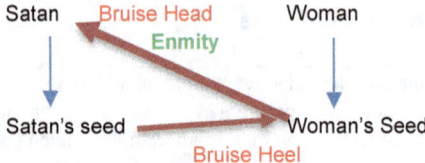

T: Which is worse, getting a bruised head or a bruised heel?

C: Head.

T: So the damage done to Woman's Seed is less than the damage Woman's Seed does to Satan. We know from the verse that Woman's Seed is a male because it references "his heel". So, to whom was God referring when He issued this prophecy regarding the Woman and the Woman's Seed?

C: Mary and Jesus.

T: So when Satan bruises Jesus' heel, what is that referring to?

C: His crucifixion.

T: Yet to Jesus, that was an injury from which He could recover because He rose from the dead. When Jesus bruises Satan's head, what does that mean?

C: Jesus does more damage to Satan.

T: Jesus triumphs over evil by rising from the dead. This coded message sets in motion the redemption of Man.

Author's Note

It is not always clear as to why this prophecy (or any prophecy) is coded such that later generations may decipher what those who first hear the prophecy do not understand. My personal opinion is that God did not need to spell out exactly what He intended for the sake of Satan, or for Adam and Eve for that matter. He simply needed to establish His Word on the matter and, by doing so, begin His plan for our salvation.

St. Paul, in writing to the Church in Rome, likely referenced the passage in Genesis 3:15 when he stated, "the God of peace shall bruise Satan under your feet shortly" (Rom. 16:20).

---

[23] The verse implies Satan, not Satan's seed, bruises the heel of the Woman's Seed. I make the assumption that Satan's seed does the bruising because Satan presumably works through his seed and, otherwise, Satan's seed would have no role in this prophecy. Feel free to draw the arrows as you wish, though. Satan's seed in this prophecy likely refers to the Israelite leadership who put Jesus to death out of fear and jealousy, but it could include anyone who practices evil.

Then, our Great Litany (at BCP p. 152) picks up on that concept when the priest and people say:

> That it may please thee to strengthen such as do stand; to comfort and help the weak-hearted; to raise up those who fall; and finally to beat down Satan under our feet,
>
> *We beseech thee to hear us, good Lord.*

III. The Old Covenant – Abraham to the Early Tabernacle

Learning Objectives

1. Confirmands will learn that Jesus had a lineage going back to Abraham, and the coming of Jesus fulfilled a promise God made to Abraham.
2. Confirmands will understand the purpose and elements of Jewish temple sacrifice as a temporary measure until Jesus resolves Man's sin problem.
3. Confirmands will understand how God viewed sin, and its magnitude, under the Old Covenant.
4. Confirmands will understand that the scapegoat used on the Day of Atonement to carry the sins of Israel was a precursor to Jesus.

A. Promise to a Righteous Man

T: Recall in the last session we discussed God's plan to get permission to send His Redeemer, who would strike Satan's head, by entering into a covenant, or legal contract, with a righteous Man. God's search for a righteous Man took Him to a person named Abram who, though he was old, as was his wife, God promised to make him the "father of many nations" and his wife the "mother of nations" (Genesis 17:4 and 16). Abram had to have faith that he and his wife could bear children, and this faith was credited to Abram as righteousness, and he changed his name to "Abraham". In other words, by exercising his faith in God and His promise, Abraham entered into a right-standing relationship with God. Out of that relationship, through the descendants of Abraham, will come the birth of the Redeemer, Jesus.

Genesis 17

1 And when Abram was ninety years old and nine, the LORD appeared to Abram, and said unto him, I am the Almighty God; walk before me, and be thou perfect.

2 And I will make my covenant between me and thee, and will multiply thee exceedingly.

3 And Abram fell on his face: and God talked with him, saying,

4 As for me, behold, my covenant is with thee, and thou shalt be a father of many nations.

5 Neither shall thy name any more be called Abram, but thy name shall be Abraham; for a father of many nations have I made thee.

6 And I will make thee exceeding fruitful, and I will make nations of thee, and kings shall come out of thee.

7 And I will establish my covenant between me and thee and thy seed after thee in their generations for an everlasting covenant, to be a God unto thee, and to thy seed after thee.

8 And I will give unto thee, and to thy seed after thee, the land wherein thou art a stranger, all the land of Canaan, for an everlasting possession; and I will be their God.

9 And God said unto Abraham, Thou shalt keep my covenant therefore, thou, and thy seed after thee in their generations.

10 This is my covenant, which ye shall keep, between me and you and thy seed after thee; Every man child among you shall be circumcised.

11 And ye shall circumcise the flesh of your foreskin; and it shall be a token of the covenant betwixt me and you.

12 And he that is eight days old shall be circumcised among you, every man child in your generations, he that is born in the house, or bought with money of any stranger, which is not of thy seed.

13 He that is born in thy house, and he that is bought with thy money, must needs be circumcised: and my covenant shall be in your flesh for an everlasting covenant.

14 And the uncircumcised man child whose flesh of his foreskin is not circumcised, that soul shall be cut off from his people; he hath broken my covenant.

15 And God said unto Abraham, As for Sarai thy wife, thou shalt not call her name Sarai, but Sarah shall her name be.

16 And I will bless her, and give thee a son also of her: yea, I will bless her, and she shall be a mother of nations; kings of people shall be of her.

17 Then Abraham fell upon his face, and laughed, and said in his heart, Shall a child be born unto him that is an hundred years old? and shall Sarah, that is ninety years old, bear?

18 And Abraham said unto God, O that Ishmael might live before thee!

19 And God said, Sarah thy wife shall bear thee a son indeed; and thou shalt call his name Isaac: and I will establish my covenant with him for an everlasting covenant, and with his seed after him.

20 And as for Ishmael, I have heard thee: Behold, I have blessed him, and will make him fruitful, and will multiply him exceedingly; twelve princes shall he beget, and I will make him a great nation.

21 But my covenant will I establish with Isaac, which Sarah shall bear unto thee at this set time in the next year.

22 And he left off talking with him, and God went up from Abraham.

23 And Abraham took Ishmael his son, and all that were born in his house, and all that were bought with his money, every male among the men of Abraham's house; and circumcised the flesh of their foreskin in the selfsame day, as God had said unto him.

T: Ishmael was the son of Abraham and the Egyptian servant of Abraham's wife.[24] Abraham's wife, Sarah, gave the servant, Hagar, to Abraham when he was 86 because Sarah had yet to conceive. Hagar then gave birth to Ishmael. What does this tell you about how Abraham and Sarah felt were their chances of having a child of their own?

C: Chances were not good; Abraham and Sarah had given up.

T: Then, when God tells Abraham that he and Sarah will have a son, what was Abraham's reaction in verse 17?

C: To fall down laughing!

T: So God's effort to find a believing, righteous man or woman was not off to a good start. However, God persisted and explained that, while He would bless Ishmael, His Covenant would be through the son of Abraham and Sarah, and that son's name would be "Isaac".[25] From verse 23, how do we know Abraham, in the end, agreed to the terms of the Covenant?

C: Abraham circumcised his household.

T: Circumcision brought Abraham and his descendants through his son, Isaac, into a Covenant with God that would last for many generations. We will see later in the course that the early Christians, who were Jews, had to determine whether circumcision was still necessary after Jesus' resurrection.

B. Abraham to Jesus

Turn to Matthew 1 and quickly scan the verses.

---

[24] See Genesis 16 for the entire background on Sarah and her servant.
[25] God has a sense of humor: the word "Isaac" means "he laughs"!

Matthew 1

1 The book of the generation of Jesus Christ, the son of David, the son of Abraham.

2 Abraham begat Isaac; and Isaac begat Jacob; and Jacob begat Judas and his brethren;

3 And Judas begat Phares and Zara of Thamar; and Phares begat Esrom; and Esrom begat Aram;

4 And Aram begat Aminadab; and Aminadab begat Naasson; and Naasson begat Salmon;

5 And Salmon begat Booz of Rachab; and Booz begat Obed of Ruth; and Obed begat Jesse;

6 And Jesse begat David the king; and David the king begat Solomon of her that had been the wife of Urias;

7 And Solomon begat Roboam; and Roboam begat Abia; and Abia begat Asa;

8 And Asa begat Josaphat; and Josaphat begat Joram; and Joram begat Ozias;

9 And Ozias begat Joatham; and Joatham begat Achaz; and Achaz begat Ezekias;

10 And Ezekias begat Manasses; and Manasses begat Amon; and Amon begat Josias;

11 And Josias begat Jechonias and his brethren, about the time they were carried away to Babylon:

12 And after they were brought to Babylon, Jechonias begat Salathiel; and Salathiel begat Zorobabel;

13 And Zorobabel begat Abiud; and Abiud begat Eliakim; and Eliakim begat Azor;

14 And Azor begat Sadoc; and Sadoc begat Achim; and Achim begat Eliud;

15 And Eliud begat Eleazar; and Eleazar begat Matthan; and Matthan begat Jacob;

16 And Jacob begat Joseph the husband of Mary, of whom was born Jesus, who is called Christ.

17 So all the generations from Abraham to David are fourteen generations; and from David until the carrying away into Babylon are fourteen generations; and from the carrying away into Babylon unto Christ are fourteen generations.

T: Here, the apostle Matthew traces the genealogy of Jesus. What is a genealogy?

C: It's a person's family tree.

It should not be necessary to read every verse. In verse 2, the Apostle Matthew began with Abraham, the one with whom God made the covenant that would lead to the coming of the Savior. Then Matthew continued to trace the lineage to King David, the one who killed Goliath with a sling, in verse 6, and on to Joseph, the husband of Mary, who gave birth to Jesus, in verse 16. Getting us to the Savior, Jesus, was essentially what the Abrahamic Covenant was all about!

T: Look at verse 2. Abraham begat, which means gave birth to, Isaac. We just read about Isaac. Who was Isaac's mother?

C: Sarah.

T: Remember, God's covenant with Abraham was to provide descendants that led to the Messiah, or Savior, Jesus. Was God's covenant with Abraham fulfilled through Isaac or though Isaac's stepbrother, Ishmael? If you are unsure, follow the lineage from verse 2 to verse 16.

C: Isaac.

Keep reading verse 2: "Isaac begat Jacob; and Jacob begat Judas [or Judah] and his brethren". So Isaac had a son named?

C: Jacob.

T: And Jacob had several sons, actually eleven brothers of Judah, and all together those sons of Jacob became the heads of the twelve tribes of Israel.

Now is the opportune time to reintroduce *The Timechart History of the World*. To gain some perspective, spread the chart out as much as possible, at least from Panels II through XI, then walk through some Biblical characters you would know:

Biblical Characters found Above the Timeline	Panel No.
Adam and Eve	II
Noah	IV
Abraham, Sarah and Isaac	VI
Jacob and his sons, who will comprise the twelve tribes of Israel	VII
Follow Jacob's son Levi to Moses and Aaron, and point out Aaron's sons, Abihu and Nadab	VII
Israel is ruled by a theocracy of Judges until Saul is anointed king	VIII
Immediately following King Saul is King David, who killed Goliath	VIII
Following King David is King Solomon	VIII

In the *Timechart* upper part of Panel VII, you will see how Jacob branches out into twelve tribes.

T: For our purposes, you just have to remember two of the twelve tribes: Judah and Levi. Judah was a large tribe that included many Israeli kings among its descendants, and today we refer to all Israelites as "Jews", a word derived from the "Judah" tribe name. But there were eleven other tribes, and among those others was the important tribe of Levi. Levi was the tribe that provided the priests to conduct worship services.

Now look at verse 17. You should know King David; he defeated Israel's enemies, including a certain giant he killed with a slingshot, and that giant's name was ...

C: Goliath.[26]

T: Right. And David and his son saw Israel prosper for many years. However, Israel later turned against God and ignored the warnings of the prophets to turn back to God.[27] Without God's protection, the Babylonians under King Nebuchadnezzar II conquered Israel in the early sixth century B.C.[28] [The *Timechart* Panel IX shows how the tribes of Judah and Benjamin come to an end in the upper section and fold into Babylon under Nebuchadnezzar.] Nebuchadnezzar forced many Israelites to relocate to Babylon,[29] hence Matthew's reference to the "carrying away into Babylon". Babylonians overran Jerusalem at least twice during 598 – 588 B.C., and during that decade the Babylonians destroyed the temple where the Israelites worshipped. Let's investigate why the "carrying away into Babylon" was so important that Matthew cited the event in his gospel.

---

[26] 1 Samuel 17.

[27] 2 Kings 22:15-17: "And [Huldah the prophetess] said unto them, Thus saith the LORD God of Israel, Tell the man that sent you to me, Thus saith the LORD, Behold, I will bring evil upon this place, and upon the inhabitants thereof, even all the words of the book which the king of Judah hath read: Because they have forsaken me, and have burned incense unto other gods, that they might provoke me to anger with all the works of their hands; therefore my wrath shall be kindled against this place, and shall not be quenched."

[28] In the bigger picture, Israel was at the crossroads where the great nations of Egypt and Babylon battled each other, and Israel had alliances or truces with both during the late seventh and early sixth centuries B.C.

[29] 1 Chronicles 9:1: "So all Israel were reckoned by genealogies; and, behold, they were written in the book of the kings of Israel and Judah, who were carried away to Babylon for their transgression."

C. The Early Tabernacle

T: To begin, let's go back to Abraham. He made a covenant with God in which he will have many descendants, eventually giving us the Savior, Jesus Christ. What about the time in between Abraham and Jesus? What were the Israelites to do about their sins until Jesus arrived? Let's turn to Chapter 40 of the book of Exodus and find out. But first let me set the stage: Moses has returned from Mount Sinai with the Ten Commandments after leading the people of Israel out of Egypt. He actually spent a long time on Mount Sinai to receive instructions on how to implement a process to remove sin from the people of Israel.[30] Since Moses was on Mount Sinai for so long, what did the people of Israel do while they were waiting for him?

C: They made a golden calf and worshiped it.[31]

T: Right. While Moses was receiving instructions on how to remove Israel's sins, Israel sinned! Can you worship a graven image like the golden calf and worship God too?

C: No.

T: The first of the Ten Commandments says, "I am the LORD thy God, which have brought thee out of the land of Egypt, out of the house of bondage. Thou shalt have no other gods before me."[32] And when Moses saw the people worshipping the golden calf, he threw the tablets of the Ten Commandments down at his feet and broke them in pieces.[33] So God replaced the tablets,[34] and they were placed in an ornate box, called the "Ark of the Covenant" or "Ark of the Testimony" as the Ten Commandments were known as the "Testimony".[35] Now let's see what other instructions God gave to Moses.

Look at the objects in the diagram below. You may find it helpful to refer to the diagram as you read Exodus 40.

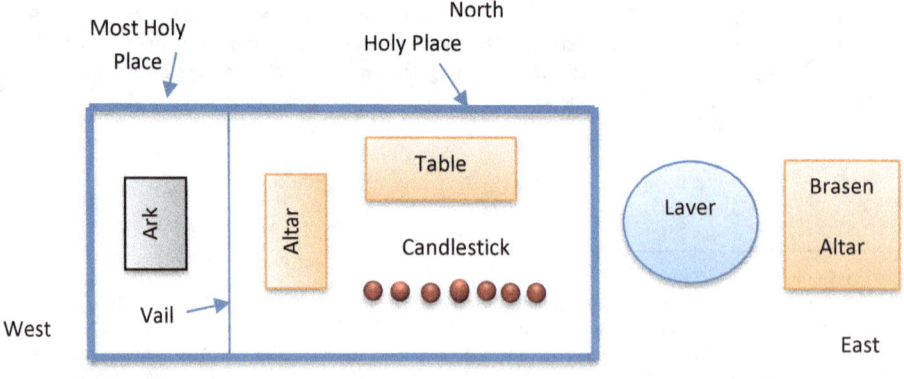

[30] Exodus 19 – 31.
[31] Exodus 32.
[32] Exodus 20:2-3.
[33] Exodus 32:19.
[34] Exodus 34:1.
[35] Exodus 40:20.

Note: The Candlestick seen from the side is shaped like this and is commonly called a "Menorah":

Source: http://www.supercoloring.com/coloring-pages/menorah. Licensed under https://creativecommons.org/licenses/by/4.0/.

One interpretation of the Ark of the Covenant:

Source: Lancastermerrin88. Licensed under https://creativecommons.org/licenses/by/4.0/.

Exodus 40

1 And the LORD spake unto Moses, saying,

2 On the first day of the first month shalt thou set up the tabernacle of the tent of the congregation.

3 And thou shalt put therein the ark of the testimony, and cover the ark with the vail.

4 And thou shalt bring in the table, and set in order the things that are to be set in order upon it; and thou shalt bring in the candlestick, and light the lamps thereof.

5 And thou shalt set the altar of gold for the incense before the ark of the testimony, and put the hanging of the door to the tabernacle.

6 And thou shalt set the altar of the burnt offering before the door of the tabernacle of the tent of the congregation.

7 And thou shalt set the laver between the tent of the congregation and the altar, and shalt put water therein.

8 And thou shalt set up the court round about, and hang up the hanging at the court gate.

9 And thou shalt take the anointing oil, and anoint the tabernacle, and all that is therein, and shalt hallow it, and all the vessels thereof: and it shall be holy.

10 And thou shalt anoint the altar of the burnt offering, and all his vessels, and sanctify the altar: and it shall be an altar most holy.

11 And thou shalt anoint the laver and his foot, and sanctify it.

12 And thou shalt bring Aaron and his sons unto the door of the tabernacle of the congregation, and wash them with water.

13 And thou shalt put upon Aaron the holy garments, and anoint him, and sanctify him; that he may minister unto me in the priest's office.

14 And thou shalt bring his sons, and clothe them with coats:

15 And thou shalt anoint them, as thou didst anoint their father, that they may minister unto me in the priest's office: for their anointing shall surely be an everlasting priesthood throughout their generations.

16 Thus did Moses: according to all that the LORD commanded him, so did he.

T: Each part of the tabernacle had a function. Within the Holy Place and outside the tabernacle, how do you think those objects were used?

C: Altar of Incense: for burning incense

        Table of Shewbread: for offerings of bread

        Golden Candlestick: for candle light

        Brasen Laver: for washing

        Brasen Altar: for burning offerings

T: Now the more important question: What did the objects in the Holy Place, the Altar of Incense, the Table of Shewbread and the Golden Candlestick, represent to God and the Israelites? Let's start with the Altar of Incense.[36] Besides making the place smell nice, when you burn incense, where does the smoke go?

C: Up towards the sky, or Heaven

T: And who lives in Heaven?

C: God.

T: So what does smoke rising up to Heaven represent?

C: It represents prayers to God going up to Heaven.[37]

T: Next, the Table of Shewbread. What does that represent?

C: Plentiful harvests?

T: Yes, and more in that the bread that was kept on the table was called "Bread of the Presence", meaning that God was present and providing for His people under His Covenant with them.[38] What "Bread of the Presence" do we have in our Church during the Holy Eucharist?

C: The Communion wafers.

T: What does the Golden Candlestick, when lit, give off?

---

[36] The Altar of Incense also had a role in the yearly atonement process. According to Exodus 30:10: "And [Chief Priest] Aaron shall make an atonement upon the horns of [the Altar of Incense] once in a year with the blood of the sin offering of atonements: once in the year shall he make atonement upon it throughout your generations: it is most holy unto the Lord." However, after events that we will discuss shortly, the atonement process was greatly expanded.

[37] Psalm 141:2: "Let my prayer be set forth before thee as incense; and the lifting up of my hands as the evening sacrifice."

[38] From Easton's 1897 Bible Dictionary: "The number of the loaves represented the twelve tribes of Israel, and also the entire spiritual Israel, 'the true Israel;' and the placing of them on the table symbolized the entire consecration of Israel to the Lord, and their acceptance of God as their God."

C: Light.

T: In a spiritual sense, what would that light represent?

C: That would be the Light of God.

T: Right. Now I will tell you that the objects outside the tabernacle, the Brasen Laver and the Brasen Altar, were used in the process of offering sacrifices to God, and we will discuss those later. So that leaves us with the Most Holy Place that stored the Ark of the Covenant containing the Ten Commandments. You see on the diagram that it is separated from the Holy Place and everything else. Why do you think that God instructed Moses to completely wall off the Most Holy Place?

C: It was special.

T: Well, more than that. If you wall off something, you don't want anyone to go in. Why would God not want anyone to go into the Most Holy Place? Let's read about what happened when some people went into the Most Holy Place when they were not supposed to.

Leviticus 9

23 And Moses and Aaron went into the tabernacle of the congregation, and came out, and blessed the people: and the glory of the LORD appeared unto all the people.

24 And there came a fire out from before the LORD, and consumed upon the altar the burnt offering and the fat: which when all the people saw, they shouted, and fell on their faces.

Leviticus 10

1 And Nadab and Abihu, the sons of Aaron, took either of them his censer, and put fire therein, and put incense thereon, and offered strange fire before the LORD, which he commanded them not.

2 And there went out fire from the LORD, and devoured them, and they died before the LORD.

3 Then Moses said unto Aaron, This is it that the LORD spake, saying, I will be sanctified in them that come nigh me, and before all the people I will be glorified. And Aaron held his peace.

4 And Moses called Mishael and Elzaphan, the sons of Uzziel the uncle of Aaron, and said unto them, Come near, carry your brethren from before the sanctuary out of the camp.

5 So they went near, and carried them in their coats out of the camp; as Moses had said.

6 And Moses said unto Aaron, and unto Eleazar and unto Ithamar, his sons, Uncover not your heads, neither rend your clothes; lest ye die, and lest wrath come upon all the people: but let your brethren, the whole house of Israel, bewail the burning which the LORD hath kindled.

7 And ye shall not go out from the door of the tabernacle of the congregation, lest ye die: for the anointing oil of the LORD is upon you. And they did according to the word of Moses.

8 And the LORD spake unto Aaron, saying,

9 Do not drink wine nor strong drink, thou, nor thy sons with thee, when ye go into the tabernacle of the congregation, lest ye die: it shall be a statute for ever throughout your generations:

10 And that ye may put difference between holy and unholy, and between unclean and clean;

11 And that ye may teach the children of Israel all the statutes which the LORD hath spoken unto them by the hand of Moses.

T: Aaron was Moses' brother; Aaron's sons, Nadab and Abihu, were Moses' nephews. All were descendants of Isaac's grandson, Levi, so they were called Levites, and Levites were the tribe of Israelites that provided the priests for worship. Look at Leviticus 9:23 and 24: what happened after Moses and Aaron came out of the tabernacle?

C: Fire came from the Lord and burned the fat of a sacrifice on the altar.

T: The fat came from an animal sacrifice. From our diagram of the tabernacle area, where do you think the fat and the altar were?

C: Probably the Brasen Altar [this is the most likely choice, though Scripture is not that specific].

T: What did the people who saw the fire do?

C: They fell on their faces.

T: So this must have been quite a sight! Now go to Leviticus 10:1-2. What did Nadab and Abihu put fire in?

C: A censer.

T: What's that? Have you seen a censer used in church?

C: Something you put incense into.

T: But why was their incense called "strange fire"? [Hint: Leviticus 10:1, last phrase.]

C: Because the Lord did not command them to do what they did.

T: So what happened next?

C: God sent fire, and the fire devoured them!

T: ... just as God had done earlier with the fat of the sacrifice. We learn from a later chapter of Leviticus that Nadab and Abihu offered their "strange fire" in the Most Holy Place, and their actions in the Most Holy Place were what upset God.[39] So Nadab and Abihu entered the Most Holy Place with their "strange fire" and wound up burned to death. Why did that happen?

C: God told them not to go there.

T: Right, but there's more. What did we say about light and darkness?

C: Light cannot coexist with darkness; light cancels out darkness.

T: So if a person with the darkness of sin enters into the Light Presence of God, what does God's Light do to that sin?

C: God's Light burns up the darkness of sin.

T: So the walls around the Most Holy Place were meant to protect the Israelites from God's presence in the Ark of the Covenant. How do we know the Israelites had sin?

C: Because they did not follow God's commandments.

T: And they carried the sin of Adam and Eve of disobeying God and eating of the Tree of Knowledge of Good and Evil.[40] That first sin has a name; what is it?

C: The Original Sin.[41]

T: So if an Israelite entered into the presence of God without purifying his or her sins, the sin in the Israelite would be consumed by God's Light. Even today, this rule is enforced among those of the Jewish Faith. We will soon study how a temple in Jerusalem was built on a hill

---

[39] There are clues in God's instructions to Aaron after the death of his sons in Leviticus 16:1-2. In those verses, God references the sons' deaths and then instructs Aaron on how properly to enter the Most Holy Place.

[40] You may ask why Adam and Eve were not harmed by God's Presence in the Garden of Eden after they sinned. However, after Adam and Eve sinned and "heard the voice of the Lord God", they "hid themselves from the presence of the Lord God amongst the trees of the garden" (Genesis 3:8). Then, God physically separated Man from Himself by removing Man from the Garden entirely (Gen. 3:23-24).

[41] St. Paul summed up the original sin saying, "Wherefore, as by one man [Adam] sin entered into the world, and death by sin; and so death passed upon all men, for that all have sinned" (Romans 5:12).

called the "Temple Mount" to house the tabernacle, and how that temple was destroyed a few years after Jesus' crucifixion, leaving only a few ruins today. However, the present-day Chief Rabbinate of Israel still instructs Jews not to walk on the ruins of the Temple Mount lest they inadvertently cross over the Most Holy Place. This is the sign posted near the Western Wall:[42]

Source: https://www.israelnationalnews.com/News/News.aspx/192778.

T: Finally, something interesting happened at the time of Jesus' crucifixion. There was an earthquake at the moment of His death, and the earthquake caused the temple veil to rip from top to bottom.[43] [You can add a break mark "=" to the veil in the tabernacle diagram.] When that rip occurred, if you were standing in the Holy Place looking in the direction of the Most Holy Place, what would you have been able to see?

C: The Ark!

T: This was God's way of sending a message. What do you think that message was?

C: That Jesus' sacrifice allows us to look at God.

T: More importantly, <u>Jesus' sacrifice broke the barrier between us and God</u>. The sacrifice that Jesus made will wash away our sins so that we can enter into the Most Holy Place. Now, let's see how God dealt with the sin problem with the Israelites. Turn to:

---

[42] There is significant debate today among Israelis to convince the Chief Rabbi to allow Jews to enter the Temple Mount out of concern that Israel's claims to the holy site may be weakened if Jews are not allowed to worship there. See, for example: https://www.israelnational-news.com/News/News.aspx/239849.

[43] Matthew 27:51, Mark 15:38 and Luke 23:45 all record this event, showing how important the ripped veil was.

Leviticus 16

1 And the LORD spake unto Moses after the death of the two sons of Aaron, when they offered before the LORD, and died;

2 And the LORD said unto Moses, Speak unto Aaron thy brother, that he come not at all times into the holy place within the vail before the mercy seat, which is upon the ark; that he die not: for I will appear in the cloud upon the mercy seat.

3 Thus shall Aaron come into the holy place: with a young bullock for a sin offering, and a ram for a burnt offering.

4 He shall put on the holy linen coat, and he shall have the linen breeches upon his flesh, and shall be girded with a linen girdle, and with the linen mitre shall he be attired: these are holy garments; therefore shall he wash his flesh in water, and so put them on.

5 And he shall take of the congregation of the children of Israel two kids of the goats for a sin offering, and one ram for a burnt offering.

6 And Aaron shall offer his bullock of the sin offering, which is for himself, and make an atonement for himself, and for his house.

7 And he shall take the two goats, and present them before the LORD at the door of the tabernacle of the congregation.

8 And Aaron shall cast lots upon the two goats; one lot for the LORD, and the other lot for the scapegoat.

9 And Aaron shall bring the goat upon which the LORD'S lot fell, and offer him for a sin offering.

10 But the goat, on which the lot fell to be the scapegoat, shall be presented alive before the LORD, to make an atonement with him, and to let him go for a scapegoat into the wilderness.

11 And Aaron shall bring the bullock of the sin offering, which is for himself, and shall make an atonement for himself, and for his house, and shall kill the bullock of the sin offering which is for himself:

12 And he shall take a censer full of burning coals of fire from off the altar before the LORD, and his hands full of sweet incense beaten small, and bring it within the vail:

13 And he shall put the incense upon the fire before the LORD, that the cloud of the incense may cover the mercy seat that is upon the testimony, that he die not:

14 And he shall take of the blood of the bullock, and sprinkle it with his finger upon the mercy seat eastward; and before the mercy seat shall he sprinkle of the blood with his finger seven times.

15 Then shall he kill the goat of the sin offering, that is for the people, and bring his blood within the vail, and do with that blood as he did with the blood of the bullock, and sprinkle it upon the mercy seat, and before the mercy seat:

16 And he shall make an atonement for the holy place, because of the uncleanness of the children of Israel, and because of their transgressions in all their sins: and so shall he do for the tabernacle of the congregation, that remaineth among them in the midst of their uncleanness.

17 And there shall be no man in the tabernacle of the congregation when he goeth in to make an atonement in the holy place, until he come out, and have made an atonement for himself, and for his household, and for all the congregation of Israel.

18 And he shall go out unto the altar that is before the LORD, and make an atonement for it; and shall take of the blood of the bullock, and of the blood of the goat, and put it upon the horns of the altar round about.

19 And he shall sprinkle of the blood upon it with his finger seven times, and cleanse it, and hallow it from the uncleanness of the children of Israel.

20 And when he hath made an end of reconciling the holy place, and the tabernacle of the congregation, and the altar, he shall bring the live goat:

21 And Aaron shall lay both his hands upon the head of the live goat, and confess over him all the iniquities of the children of Israel, and all their transgressions in all their sins, putting them upon the head of the goat, and shall send him away by the hand of a fit man into the wilderness:

22 And the goat shall bear upon him all their iniquities unto a land not inhabited: and he shall let go the goat in the wilderness.

23 And Aaron shall come into the tabernacle of the congregation, and shall put off the linen garments, which he put on when he went into the holy place, and shall leave them there:

24 And he shall wash his flesh with water in the holy place, and put on his garments, and come forth, and offer his burnt offering, and the burnt offering of the people, and make an atonement for himself, and for the people.

25 And the fat of the sin offering shall he burn upon the altar.

26 And he that let go the goat for the scapegoat shall wash his clothes, and bathe his flesh in water, and afterward come into the camp.

27 And the bullock for the sin offering, and the goat for the sin offering, whose blood was brought in to make atonement in the holy place, shall one carry forth without the camp; and they shall burn in the fire their skins, and their flesh, and their dung.

28 And he that burneth them shall wash his clothes, and bathe his flesh in water, and afterward he shall come into the camp.

T: This passage describes the procedures that Aaron, and the High Priests that followed him, were to perform on the Day of Atonement, known as "Yom Kippur", to purify the people of Israel. In a sense, the Yom Kippur purification bought one year of forgiveness of sins and then had to be repeated. The procedures Aaron was to follow would allow him to enter into the Most Holy Place once a year and see a sign of God's forgiveness. Look at verse 2: "Speak unto Aaron thy brother, that he come not at all times into the holy place within the vail before the mercy seat, which is upon the ark; that he die not: for I will appear in the cloud upon the mercy seat." Where is the Ark?

C: In the Most Holy Place.

T: And on the Ark was the "mercy seat". This was the area between the two angels carved on the Ark's cover, called "Cherubim".[44] God communicated with Aaron, and the Chief Priests who followed him, over the Ark's mercy seat,[45] and verse 2 tells us how God would appear over the mercy seat. How did He appear?

---

[44] Exodus 37:6-8: "And he made the mercy seat *of* pure gold: two cubits and a half *was* the length thereof, and one cubit and a half the breadth thereof. And he made two cherubims *of* gold, beaten out of one piece made he them, on the two ends of the mercy seat. One cherub on the end on this side, and another cherub on the *other* end on that side: out of the mercy seat made he the cherubims on the two ends thereof."

[45] Exodus 25:22: "And there I will meet with thee, and I will commune with thee from above the mercy seat, from between the two cherubims which are upon the ark of the testimony, of all things which I will give thee in commandment unto the children of Israel."

C: In a cloud.

T: But why didn't Aaron die when he came into the presence of God? Didn't he have sin within him, or do any of the verses we just read show how he purified himself?

C: Verse 6 says, "And Aaron shall offer his bullock of the sin offering, which is for himself, and make an atonement for himself, and for his house." [Verse 11 would also be a good answer.]

T: Now if Aaron or anyone else entered into the Most Holy Place at any other time of the year, what would happen to them?

C: The same thing that happened to Aaron's sons: they would die!

T: After seeing what happened to his sons, how eager do you think Aaron was to go into the Most Holy Place?

C: Not at all!

T: He had to overcome his fear and trust God. After Aaron purified himself, he entered the Most Holy Place. In verses 12 and 13, what was he doing there?

C: Burning incense to create a cloud, so that he did not die.

T: The incense cloud was a cloud that concealed[46] the Atonement Cover of the Ark from Aaron so that he might not die. But that's confusing: I thought we just said Aaron purified himself with the sacrifice of a bullock so that he could enter safely into the Most Holy Place. Why did he need the protection of the incense cloud?

C: Maybe the sacrifice of a bullock only got you so far?

T: Yes. The bullock granted the High Priest admission into the Most Holy Place once a year, but it did not allow him to look at God face-to-face. The High Priest still needed incense smoke to shield him while he performed the other tasks needed to remove sin from the people of Israel in verses 14 – 15. Summarize what happens in each verse.

C: In verse 14, Aaron was to sprinkle the bullock's blood on the Mercy Seat facing eastward.

T: And looking at the diagram, where was Aaron when he did that?

C: He would be behind the Ark facing the veil.

T: Verse 15?

C: In verse 15, Aaron was to kill a goat and sprinkle its blood on the Mercy Seat as well.

---

[46] The Hebrew text in verse 13 actually does not specifically use the word for "cloud" but refers to the smoke of the incense concealing the Atonement Cover.

T: That was actually one of two goats. Look at verses 7 – 10. One goat was to be sacrificed and the other to be kept alive. Verses 20 – 22 tell what happened to the second goat. Summarize what those verses say.

C: Aaron was to place his hands on the live goat and lay upon that goat all the sins of Israel; then the goat was led out into the wilderness to die.

T: What did that poor goat do to deserve such a fate? At least the other animals that were sacrificed were put to death quickly, but this goat was left to starve to death slowly. For all the sins put upon that goat, was that goat responsible for any of those sins?

C: No.

T: Today, what do we call someone who is blamed for something he or she did not do?

C: A scapegoat.

T: And that is the term used in verse 8 here. The scapegoat carried away the sins of Israel so that the people of Israel did not have to suffer the consequences of their sins. Now, in our Christian Faith, in the New Testament, do we have an example of a scapegoat who carried our sins, sins that the scapegoat did not commit?

C: Jesus.

T: Yes. We will see that Jesus walked upright in the sight of God and did not sin, but He carried our sins for us to the cross. The use of the scapegoat in the atonement of Israel pointed directly to the sacrifice Jesus would make when He was nailed to the cross. What other elements of the atonement process in verses 14-15 pointed to Jesus?

C: Blood, and lots of it, from the sacrifices. Jesus bled to death on the cross.

T: Correct. The sacrifice and sprinkling of blood of the first goat and other animals effectively purchased one year of forgiveness for the people of Israel, then the process had to be repeated. This was, at best, a temporary solution to provide atonement of sins until God could provide a more permanent solution. Once Jesus died, taking away our sins, do we need Him to come back every year and die for us again?

C: No.

Right. He died once for all our sins, permanently fixing the problem of our sin separating us from God. We no longer need to sacrifice anyone (or any animal) to atone for sins. What about modern-day Jews, though; do they sacrifice animals on Yom Kippur?

C: No.

T: We will shortly see why Jews stopped the ritual sacrifices. It was not by choice!

Confirmand Reference Book First Edition

IV. The Old Covenant - Temple History and The Law

A. First and Second Temples

Learning Objectives

1. Confirmands will learn the history of the temples built in Jerusalem and the role of the Second Temple during and after the Earth Ministry of Jesus.
2. Confirmands will understand the role of the Roman Empire in the destruction of the Second Temple and its impact on Judaism and the Christian Faith.
3. Confirmands will learn of the political and religious difficulties that prevent the excavation of the Second Temple today.
4. Confirmands will understand the Temple as a metaphor for entering into the presence of God.

> T: The Israelites under King Solomon (David's son) built a massive temple complex in Jerusalem to house the tabernacle, which was completed around 1000 B.C., replacing the old tent structure used to house the Holy Place and Most Holy Place.

Look to the upper left of Panel IX of the *Timechart* for a picture and brief history of the Temple.

> T: All the parts of the tabernacle were transferred to the temple, with the rituals as well. That temple was destroyed by Babylonian King Nebuchadnezzar in 588 B.C.

On Panel IX of the *Timechart*, Nebuchadnezzar appears below the timeline. After Solomon's reign, the tribes of Israel split: ten tribes formed the Kingdom of Israel and two, Judah and Benjamin, formed the Kingdom of Judah, as shown Panel VIII and continuing onto Panel IX. The Kingdom of Israel was defeated by the Assyrians in 721 B.C., and the *Timechart* shows that event on Panel IX with a line that travels down the page from the end of the Kingdom of Israel to intersect with Assyria in the Nation Stream below the timeline. The tribes of Judah and Benjamin, which constituted the remaining Kingdom of Judah, were themselves defeated by Nebuchadnezzar in 588 B.C. and brought into "Babylonian Captivity". The *Timechart* reflects that event on Panel IX by a line at the end of the Kingdom of Judah that intersects with the Chaldee-Babylonian Empire Nation Stream below.

> T: The tablets of the Ten Commandments do not appear in Scripture or in other ancient literature after that date. About 50 years later, when the Persians defeated the Babylonians, King Cyrus the Great [shown in green to the right of Nebuchadnezzar on Panel IX] authorized the re-building of a Second Temple in 538 B.C.[47] The Second Temple was used and abused by Greek and Roman conquerors over subsequent years, and then Herod the Great extensively renovated the Second Temple in 20 A.D. for political reasons to earn respect among the Israelites. [Herod appears on the far left of Panel XI, below Jesus in blue, in the Palestine Nation Stream.] This renovated temple was the "temple" referred to in the Gospels and

---

[47] Note: a new Nation Stream starts out from Cyrus which becomes "Palestine or Judea".

Book of Acts and was the scene where Jesus preached. Here is a diagram of the Temple Compound after it was expanded and rebuilt.

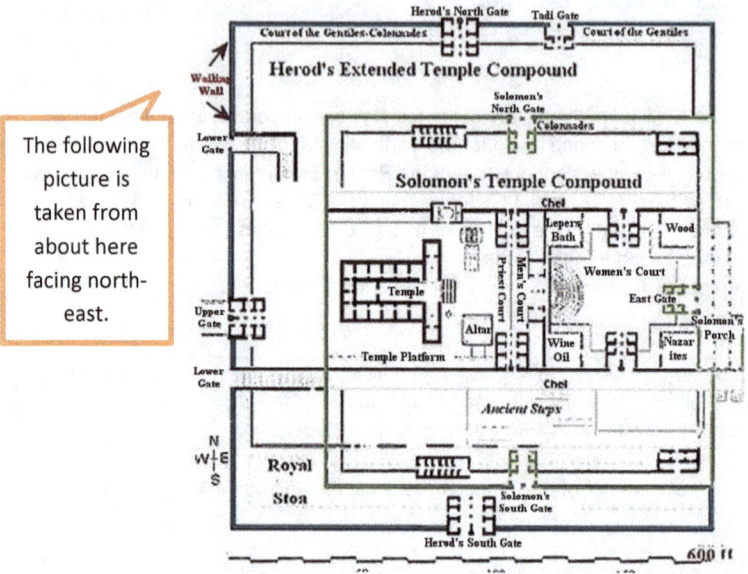

Source: http://templemountlocation.com/chapterOne.html. Used with permission.

T: But if you went to Jerusalem today, would you be able to enter the Second Temple? Here is a recent picture:[48]

---

[48] Credit: Golasso - Own work, GFDL, https://commons.wikimedia.org/w/index.php?curid=12647724. Source: Dome of the Rock and Wailing Wall by Peter Mulligan at https://commons.wikimedia.org/wiki/File:Dome_of_the_Rock_and_Wailing_wall_by_Peter_Mulligan.jpg. Creative Commons Attribution 2.0 Generic License

T: This is a picture shot from outside the Western Wall of the Second Temple, facing northeast. Where is the rest of the temple?

C: It appears to be destroyed. It must be underneath the hill behind the wall.[49]

T: Well, why hasn't someone excavated to restore the rest of the temple?

C: Politics, claims to ownership, Mideast tensions.

T: All those issues play a part, but look at the building with a gold dome to the left in the picture. What is that?

C: Umm ...

T: It is called the Dome of the Rock because it houses a large rock. What is so special about that rock?

C: It's holy?

T: Specifically, In Islam, tradition states that Muhammad ascended to heaven from the rock, and, in Judaism, tradition considers the rock to be the place where God asked Abraham to sacrifice his son as a test of his faith.[50] Abraham almost did sacrifice his son, but God stopped him at the last moment. Which son of Abraham was nearly sacrificed there, Isaac or Ishmael?

C: Isaac.

T: That's what the Old Testament states in Genesis 22:1 – 19. By arrangement with the Israeli government, the Dome of the Rock is administered today by an Islamic religious trust based in Jordan.[51] Now, knowing that, how easy do you think it would be for a team of archeologists to get permission to dig under or around the Dome?

C: Not likely.[52]

---

[49] The exact location of the Second Temple on the Temple Mount is a subject of debate. The previous diagram showing the Wailing Wall on the northwest side of the temple is one view, which places the location of the temple under the present-day Al Aqsa Mosque based on the limited archeological data available (http://templemountlocation.com/index.html). Another view, based on observations of a fifteenth century rabbi, places the temple location under the Dome of the Rock (see https://www.templeinstitute.org/birds_eye.htm) such that the Wailing Wall is in the southwest section of the temple compound. And there are other views that place the temple on other Mount locations. Even though I use a diagram illustrating the first theory, I do not take a position on any theory because the precise location on the Temple Mount is not relevant to this course.

[50] See https://www.britannica.com/topic/Dome-of-the-Rock.

[51] http://www.timesofisrael.com/israel-jordan-said-discussing-opening-dome-of-the-rock-to-non-muslims/. The Dome is under the administration of the Jordanian/Palestinian-led Islamic Waqf.

[52] Actually, the Al Aqsa Mosque, which is to the south of the Dome of the Rock (out of the picture here), is also under the administration of the Islamic Waqf and may sit directly on top of the Second Temple: see footnote 49 for a discussion of alternative theories as to the exact location of the temple. The mosque, then, would be another problematic structure should archeologists wish to excavate.

T: But what if the temple could be restored, and what if the restoration included the Most Holy Place? What if today you could fly to Israel, go to Jerusalem, and visit a restored, functioning temple? Then, when you get to the temple, you manage to sneak past the guards and actually enter the Most Holy Place. What do you think would happen? Would you be hit with a bolt of lightning?

C: It may depend on whether sin is in us.

T: Fortunately, the writer of Hebrews in the New Testament gives us some guidance.

Hebrews 10

10 By the which will we are sanctified through the offering of the body of Jesus Christ once for all.

11 And every priest standeth daily ministering and offering oftentimes the same sacrifices, which can never take away sins:

12 But this man, after he had offered one sacrifice for sins for ever, sat down on the right hand of God;

13 From henceforth expecting till his enemies be made his footstool.

14 For by one offering he hath perfected for ever them that are sanctified.

15 Whereof the Holy Ghost also is a witness to us: for after that he had said before,

16 This is the covenant that I will make with them after those days, saith the Lord, I will put my laws into their hearts, and in their minds will I write them;

17 And their sins and iniquities will I remember no more.

18 Now where remission of these is, there is no more offering for sin.

19 Having therefore, brethren, boldness to enter into the holiest [place] by the blood of Jesus,

20 By a new and living way, which he hath consecrated for us, through the veil, that is to say, his flesh;

21 And having an high priest over the house of God;

22 Let us draw near with a true heart in full assurance of faith, having our hearts sprinkled from an evil conscience, and our bodies washed with pure water.

T: So, according to verse 19, can we Christians enter into the Most Holy Place?

C: Yes.

T: But what entitles us to do so? What about sin in us?

C: The blood of Jesus washes away our sins.

T: Look back over the passage from Hebrews and point to other references to tabernacle worship.

C: Offering sacrifices in verse 11.
The Most Holy Place in verse 19.
The veil in verse 20.
The high priest in verse 21.
"Sprinkled" in verse 22.

T: As to the sacrifices described in verse 11, were they of any use after Jesus came?

C: [Pondering] No?

T: How do you know? [Hint: look at verse 10]

C: Verse 10 tells us the offering of the body of Jesus sanctified us "once for all".

T: What does sanctified mean?

C: [Reading from smartphone] "Set apart and made holy"

T: So Jesus' sacrifice once and for all satisfied the requirements to make us holy in the eyes of God. Look at verse 14: By one offering, Jesus perfected forever those of us who are sanctified. Temple sacrifices were no longer needed. Look at verse 17; what does God remember about our sins?

C: Nothing.

T: Because of Jesus' sacrifice, God no longer remembers those sins. If God Himself has no memory of those sins, it is as if those sins never existed. Now what does God forgetting our sins have to do with entering the Most Holy Place?

C: We may enter into the presence of God without fear.

T: Finish this sentence: Since God is Light, we can enter into the Most holy Place because …

C: There is no darkness in us!

T: Look at verses 19 and 22. What gets sprinkled on our hearts in verse 22? [Hint: the answer is in verse 19.]

C: The blood of Jesus.

T: Going back to the tabernacle worship process we earlier discussed, what did the High Priest do with the blood of his sacrifice when he entered the Most Holy Place?

C: He sprinkled the blood on the Mercy Seat of the Ark. [Leviticus 16:14]

T: What, then, does sprinkling blood do, in the eyes of God?

C: It washes away sins.

T: So today we cannot go into the Most Holy Place in the ruins of the Second Temple in Jerusalem because it is buried and under a Muslim holy site. But what does our being able to enter into the Most Holy Place *in theory* mean when we come face to face with God? Will His Light burn us up?

C: No.

T: Why?

C: Jesus' blood washed away our sins, so there is no darkness in us.

T: Finally, as a postscript to all our discussion of temple worship, does anyone know when the Second Temple, the temple in which Jesus preached, was destroyed? Look at the *Timechart*, Panel XI, just to the right of Herod in the large, tan area designating the Roman Empire.

C: "Taken and destroyed by Titus, Sept. 8, 70 A.D."[53]

T: Titus was a Roman military commander who re-conquered Israel after it declared independence in 68 A.D. By 70 A.D., Titus had taken Jerusalem and destroyed the Second Temple where Jewish zealots made their last stand. Does anyone know when Jesus was crucified?

C: On the *Timechart*, Jesus' life ends at 33 A.D.

T: When was the first temple built?

C: During the reign of King Solomon.

---

[53] The *Timechart* has a synopsis of the siege of Jerusalem just as the Palestine Nation Stream enters into the Roman Empire: "70 A.D. Titus approaches Jerusalem with an army of 60,000. Most horrible suffering since the world began. 1,100,000 miserably perish. Men are crucified till wood for crosses is no longer found." This account appears to come from writings of Josephus, who tended to exaggerate, but the point was that the destruction was extensive. *Handout #2* makes this clear.

T: Around 1000 B.C. So, with the exception of 48 years during the Babylonian Captivity, a temple had been in operation in Jerusalem from 1000 B.C. to 70 A.D., just over one thousand years. The last temple was destroyed by the Romans, under Titus, who were putting down a revolt by the Israelis. The revolt started in 68 A.D., and from 68 – 70 A.D., there was actually an independent nation of Israel. Their independence ended when Titus arrived with four Roman legions, roughly twenty thousand soldiers. Titus laid siege to Jerusalem where most of the rebels were defending the temple. In the process of overrunning the rebel positions, someone set fire to the temple, and it burned to the ground. Here is what the Roman historian Tacitus wrote:

Handout #2

FRAGMENTS OF THE HISTORIES, by Gaius Cornelius Tacitus, c. 56 A.D. – c. 120 A.D.

1. The Jews, being closely besieged and given no opportunity to make peace or to surrender, were finally dying of starvation, and the streets began to be filled with corpses everywhere, for they were now unequal to the duty of burying their dead; moreover, made bold to resort to every kind of horrible food, they did spare even human bodies – save those of which they had been robbed by the wasting that such food had caused.
2. It is said that Titus first called a council and deliberated whether he should destroy such a mighty temple. For some thought that a consecrated shrine, which was famous beyond all other works of men, ought not to be razed, arguing that its preservation would bear witness to the moderation of Rome, while its destruction would forever brand her cruelty. Yet others, including Titus himself, opposed, holding the destruction of this temple to be a prime necessity in order to wipe out more completely the religion of the Jews and the Christians; for they urged that these religions, although hostile to each other, nevertheless sprang from the same sources; the Christians had grown out of the Jews: if the root were destroyed, the stock would easily perish.

Source: *The Histories, Books IV-V*, Tacitus, from Loeb Classical Library, Trans. Clifford H. Moore, Harvard University Press, 2005, p. 221.

T: *The Histories* were a series of books written by Tacitus probably starting around 105 A.D., or about 35 years after the destruction of the Second Temple. Not all the books survived to this day, and the handout shows two paragraphs contained on fragments of those *Histories*. From the first paragraph, what do we know about the suffering of the Jewish defenders during the Roman siege of 70 A.D.?

C: Food was scarce and bodies were piling up!

T: Paragraph 2 gives us insight into Tacitus' war council prior to the assault that takes the temple. What were the arguments for and against destroying the temple?

Confirmand Reference Book First Edition   Page 64

> C: Against destruction: Retaining the temple "would bear witness to the moderation of Rome". For destruction: Destroying the temple would destroy the "root" of the Jewish and Christian faiths.
>
> T: The council and Titus decided in favor of destruction. It is not clear, though, whether Titus and his Roman colleagues understood the importance of the Second Temple to Christians. Would destroying the temple in 70 A.D., some 37 years after Jesus' death and resurrection, have impacted the Christian Faith?
>
> C: No. Christians did not need the temple for worship or sacrifice. It was obsolete after Jesus' sacrifice for our sins.
>
> T: We'll come back to Tacitus later. Contrary to their practice in other conquered countries, the Romans never rebuilt the temple and instead razed the city.[54] They renamed Jerusalem "Aelia Capitolina", built a temple to Jupiter on the location of the Second Temple, and told many of the Israelites to leave the area.[55] Now, why do you think God allowed the destruction of a temple, in use for over a millennium, never to see it rebuilt?
>
> C: The temple was obsolete since Jesus' sacrifice permanently took care of the sin problem.

B. The Old Testament Law

<u>Learning Objectives</u>

1. Confirmands will understand that there is an extensive, detailed set of laws, going far beyond the Ten Commandments, that govern Jewish life under the Old Testament.
2. Confirmands will understand that, for Christians, the purpose of those laws is to help us "see more clearly our sin and our need for redemption."[56] Specifically, confirmands will learn the twelve sins Jesus identified as those that "cometh out of the man, that defileth the man."[57]

> T: Moses was from the tribe of Levi, and the descendants of Levi provided the priests who would conduct worship at the tabernacle and, later, the First and Second Temples. But the Levites also provided the people of Israel with the laws they were to follow, which I will refer

---

[54] The Jewish historian Josephus, who witnessed the siege first-hand, described the destruction, with some hyperbole: "Jerusalem ... was so thoroughly razed to the ground by those that demolished it to its foundations, that nothing was left that could ever persuade visitors that it had once been a place of habitation." *(Jewish War*, 7:1:1).

[55] According to Eusibius, Jews were dispersed twice: once in 70 A.D. after the first Jewish rebellion and again in 135 A.D. after a second rebellion, the Bar Kokhba revolt ("Jerusalem in Early Christian Thought", p. 75, *Explorations in a Christian theology of pilgrimage*, ed. Craig G. Bartholomew, Fred Hughes). These dispersals impacted the early Christian Church as well because many early Christians were Jews.

[56] From the *Catechism*, BCP, p. 848.

[57] Mark 7:20.

Confirmand Reference Book First Edition

to as the "Old Testament Law".[58] What do we call the first, and most famous, set of laws that Moses gave the people?

C: The Ten Commandments

T: Where can you find the Ten Commandments?

C: The Bible

T: Yes, specifically Exodus 20 or Deuteronomy 5, and you can find the Ten Commandments in the Book of Common Prayer as well, specifically in the *Catechism*, pp. 847-848. But those were not all the commandments for the people of Israel. There were more, many more. Scholars today number the commandments under the Old Testament Law at 613!

A good summary and categorization of the 613 Mitzvot (commandments) are found in this site: http://www.jewfaq.org/613.htm. The authors at the website organized the Mitzvot into 34 categories:[59]

Mitzvot Categories

God	Family	Sabbatical & Jubilee	Idolatry	Sacrifices & Offerings
Torah	Forbidden Sex	Court	Agriculture	Ritual Purity
Signs & Symbols	Times	Injuries & Damages	Clothing	Leprosy
Prayer & Blessings	Dietary Laws	Property	The Firstborn	The King
Love & Brotherhood	Business Practices	Criminal Laws	Priests & Levites	Nazarites
The Poor	Employees	Punishment & Restitution	Tithes & Taxes	Wars

If you have access to the website, it is worthwhile bringing up the entire list and randomly reading a few of the commandments.

T: How were the Israelites supposed to learn all these commandments? Turn to:

Deuteronomy 6

4 Hear, O Israel: The LORD our God is one LORD:

---

[58] I use the term "Old Testament Law" as a shorthand for all laws found within the Old Covenant, whether originating from Moses or other sources. Christian scholars tend to divide Old Testament law into three categories: ceremonial, moral and judicial, but those distinctions are not essential to the content of this course.

[59] Judaism 101, http://www.jewfaq.org/613.htm.

5 And thou shalt love the LORD thy God with all thine heart, and with all thy soul, and with all thy might.

6 And these words, which I command thee this day, shall be in thine heart:

7 And thou shalt teach them diligently unto thy children, and shalt talk of them when thou sittest in thine house, and when thou walkest by the way, and when thou liest down, and when thou risest up.

8 And thou shalt bind them for a sign upon thine hand, and they shall be as frontlets between thine eyes.

9 And thou shalt write them upon the posts of thy house, and on thy gates.

T: So the Israelites were to discuss their commandments at almost all times of the day, with the possible exception of the time spent working in their respective professions. Now look back at verse 5. Where have you heard that verse before?

C: In a service, from the prayer book?

T: Yes, as part of the Penitential Order,[60] a series of prayers said mostly in Lent. But did you know that the Book of Common Prayer is actually quoting Jesus? Here is how St. Matthew recorded Jesus' statement:

Matthew 22

35 Then one of them, which was a lawyer, asked him a question, tempting him, and saying,

36 Master, which is the great commandment in the law?

37 Jesus said unto him, Thou shalt love the Lord thy God with all thy heart, and with all thy soul, and with all thy mind.

38 This is the first and great commandment.

39 And the second is like unto it, Thou shalt love thy neighbour as thyself.

---

[60] Penitential Oder I, p. 319; Penitential Order II, p. 351.

40 On these two commandments hang all the law and the prophets.

> T: So in response to the lawyer's question, Jesus quoted from Deuteronomy, then He went on to describe two commandments in verses 37 and 39. Go on to look at verse 40. What is Jesus talking about?
>
> C: Everything depends on these two commandments.
>
> T: Actually, the two commandments sum up all the others. Let's see how that works. In the Book of Common Prayer, turn to pages 847-848 in the *Catechism*:

The Ten Commandments

Q. What are the Ten Commandments?
A. The Ten Commandments are the laws given to Moses and the people of Israel.

Q. What do we learn from these commandments?
A. We learn two things: our duty to God, and our duty to our neighbors.

Q. What is our duty to God?
A. Our duty is to believe and trust in God;

I   To love and obey God and to bring others to know him;
II To put nothing in the place of God;
III To show God respect in thought, word, and deed;
IV And to set aside regular times for worship, prayer, and the study of God's ways.

Q. What is our duty to our neighbors?
A. Our duty to our neighbors is to love them as ourselves, and to do to other people as we wish them to do to us;

V   To love, honor, and help our parents and family; to honor those in authority, and to meet their just demands;
VI   To show respect for the life God has given us; to work and pray for peace; to bear no malice, prejudice, or hatred in our hearts; and to be kind to all the creatures of God;
VII To use all our bodily desires as God intended;
VIII To be honest and fair in our dealings; to seek justice, freedom, and the necessities of life for all people; and to use our talents and possessions

as ones who must answer for them to God;
- IX To speak the truth, and not to mislead others by our silence;
- X   To resist temptations to envy, greed, and jealousy; to rejoice in other people's gifts and graces; and to do our duty for the love of God, who has called us into fellowship with him.

Q. What is the purpose of the Ten Commandments?
A. The Ten Commandments were given to define our relationship with God and our neighbors.

Q. Since we do not fully obey them, are they useful at all?
A. Since we do not fully obey them, we see more clearly our sin and our need for redemption.

T: So which of the Ten Commandments are summed up in the Great Commandment to love God with all your heart, soul and mind?

C: The first four.

T: And how many are summed up in the command to love your neighbor as yourself?

C: The last six.

T: Look at the last Q&A. Of what use to us Christians are the Old Testament Laws, which include the Ten Commandments? Before you answer, let me add that, in the next few classes, we will see that Jesus redeemed us from the curse of the law.[61] So why should we even bother with the Old Testament Law?

C: It shows us what is sin.

T: Let's see what St. Paul says. Turn to:

Romans 3

19 Now we know that what things soever the law saith, it saith to them who are under the law: that every mouth may be stopped, and all the world may become guilty before God.

20 Therefore by the deeds of the law there shall no flesh be justified in his sight: for by the law is the knowledge of sin.

---

[61] Galatians 3:13a: "Christ hath redeemed us from the curse of the law, being made a curse for us."

T: According to verse 19, how does the world appear before God?

C: Guilty.

T: In order to determine guilt, you need some standard by which to judge human behavior. In the first part of verse 19, what is that standard?

C: The law.

T: And here St. Paul is referring to the Old Testament Law. Now look at verse 20. For each of us personally, how do we have knowledge of sin, or know what sin is?

C: The law tells us.

T: So, to Christians, the Old Testament Law is still a guide or standard by which two things happen. According to the last phrase in verse 19, what does the law do to the world?

C: The law shows the world is guilty before God.

T: According to verse 20, the law gives us what?

C: Knowledge of sin.

T: Given that the Old Testament Law has 613 commandments, how precise and explicit do you suppose the knowledge of sin to be?

C: That's pretty specific.

T: So the two things the Old Testament Law does is give Man knowledge of sin and the guilt that committing sin separates Man from God.[62] The Good News for us Christians is that the sacrifice of Jesus provides forgiveness that restores our relationship to God. More on that later! But let's look at what Jesus has to say about sin.

Mark 7

1 Then came together unto him the Pharisees, and certain of the scribes, which came from Jerusalem.

2 And when they saw some of his disciples eat bread with defiled, that is to say, with unwashen, hands, they found fault.

---

[62] Commenting on the verses cited from Romans 3, Martin Luther said, "This entire passage must be understood as being spoken in the Spirit, which means that it does not deal with men as they appear in their own eyes and before other men but as they are before God, where all are under sin, both those who are obviously evil even in the sight of men and those who appear to be good to themselves as well as to other men." *Luther: Lectures on Romans*, translated and edited by Wilhelm Pauck, The Library of Christian Classics, vol. XV (Philadelphia: Westminster, 1961), p. 86.

3 For the Pharisees, and all the Jews, except they wash their hands oft, eat not, holding the tradition of the elders.

4 And when they come from the market, except they wash, they eat not. And many other things there be, which they have received to hold, as the washing of cups, and pots, brasen vessels, and of tables.

5 Then the Pharisees and scribes asked him, Why walk not thy disciples according to the tradition of the elders, but eat bread with unwashen hands?

6 He answered and said unto them, Well hath Esaias prophesied of you hypocrites, as it is written, This people honoureth me with their lips, but their heart is far from me.

7 Howbeit in vain do they worship me, teaching for doctrines the commandments of men.

8 For laying aside the commandment of God, ye hold the tradition of men, as the washing of pots and cups: and many other such like things ye do.

9 And he said unto them, Full well ye reject the commandment of God, that ye may keep your own tradition.

10 For Moses said, Honour thy father and thy mother; and, Whoso curseth father or mother, let him die the death:

11 But ye say, If a man shall say to his father or mother, It is Corban, that is to say, a gift, by whatsoever thou mightest be profited by me; he shall be free.

12 And ye suffer him no more to do ought for his father or his mother;

13 Making the word of God of none effect through your tradition, which ye have delivered: and many such like things do ye.

14 And when he had called all the people unto him, he said unto them, Hearken unto me every one of you, and understand:

15 There is nothing from without a man, that entering into him can defile him: but the things which come out of him, those are they that defile the man.

16 If any man have ears to hear, let him hear.

17 And when he was entered into the house from the people, his disciples asked him concerning the parable.

18 And he saith unto them, Are ye so without understanding also? Do ye not perceive, that whatsoever thing from without entereth into the man, it cannot defile him;

19 Because it entereth not into his heart, but into the belly, and goeth out into the draught, purging all meats?

20 And he said, That which cometh out of the man, that defileth the man.

21 For from within, out of the heart of men, proceed evil thoughts, adulteries, fornications, murders,

22 Thefts, covetousness, wickedness, deceit, lasciviousness, an evil eye, blasphemy, pride, foolishness:

23 All these evil things come from within, and defile the man.

T: Look at verses 1 – 3 and tell me from the Mitzot table which laws did Jesus' disciples violate according to the Pharasees?

C: Not sure.

T: Washing hands was a part of the ritual of to purify one's body, so which set of commandments relate to that?

C: Ritual Purity

T: Looking at verse 4, where they talk about washing utensils, you will see some of these commandments implemented sanitation standards before anyone knew about bacteria and mold. But if you eat bread with dirty hands or off a dirty plate, should you go to Hell?

C: I hope not!

T: No, and that was Jesus' point in verse 8. The Jewish leaders had elevated the "tradition of Men", such as washing pots, to the level of commandments. In other words, they went too far. So, starting in verse 15, Jesus re-focuses us on what is really sin and what is not. What does He say?

C: "There is nothing from without a man, that entering into him can defile him: but the things which come out of him, those are they that defile the man."

T: So, putting presumably dirty bread into your body, does that "defile" you?

C: No.

T: I don't recommend it for health reasons, but in God's Eyes, that's not sin. From verse 15, what, then, is sin?

C: "the things that come out".

Confirmand Reference Book First Edition   Page 72

T: Jesus' disciples wanted more detail, so in verses 21 and 22 Jesus lists "the things that come out" which defile Man. What are they?

C: "For from within, out of the heart of men, proceed evil thoughts, adulteries, fornications, murders, Thefts, covetousness, wickedness, deceit, lasciviousness, an evil eye, blasphemy, pride, foolishness."

T: Here, Jesus has given us a list of twelve sins drawn from Old Testament law. He was able to reduce the 613 Mitzvot to these twelve by summing up related laws and discarding those that should not have ever been laws, such as Ritual Purity and quite a few others. Which is better, dealing with twelve sins or 613?

C: Twelve!

T: So let's list the twelve sins and give them modern explanations:

Handout #3

"That which cometh out of the man, that defileth the man" – Mark 7:20

Jesus' Bridge between Old Testament and New Testament Sins

Source: Mark 7:21-22

King James Term	Explanation*
Evil thoughts	Intent, often vicious, ill will, spite or hatred and degrading schemes[AMP] to accomplish such evil desires
Adulteries	Sex between a married person and someone other than that person's spouse
Fornications	Sex between two persons not married to each other
Murders	The crime of unlawfully killing a person, especially with malice previously in mind (aforethought)
Thefts	Stealing property with the intent to deprive the rightful owner of that property
Covetousness	Craving for wealth, possessions and/or power
Wickedness	Morally very bad, evil
Deceit	Causing someone to accept as true what is false
Lasciviousness	Unrestrained conduct,[AMP] being lewd and lustful
An evil eye	Envy and jealousy,[AMP] looking with intent to inflict harm
Blasphemy	Slander and profanity, showing contempt or lack of reverence for God
Pride	Arrogance,[AMP] thinking one to be superior to God
Foolishness	Poor judgment[AMP] in discerning what is good or evil

* Explanations marked with (AMP) are taken from the Amplified Bible, Copyright © 1954, 1958, 1962, 1964, 1965, 1987 by The Lockman Foundation. Used by permission. Other explanations are adapted from Webster's Dictionary (*Merriam-Webster.com*. Merriam-Webster, June 18, 2020).

Look over the list and see if there are any personal sins that come to mind. In the next section we will discuss how Jesus redeemed us from our sins, so stay tuned!

Confirmand Reference Book First Edition

V. The New Covenant – Rights, Sin and Redemption

A. Our Rights under the New Covenant

Learning Objectives

1. Confirmands will learn that there are blessings and curses under the Abrahamic Covenant but that, by dying on the cross, Jesus bore the curses so that Christians may have the right to the blessings.
2. Confirmands will understand how the blessings of the Abraham will "overtake" us when we hear what God has to say through Scripture and when we exercise our faith.

a. Blessings and Curses

T: In the previous section, we discussed a conversation Jesus had when He was challenged by a lawyer. In Matthew 22:35 – 40, how did He summarize the Old Testament Law's commandments?

C: He summarized the law in two commandments: love God and love your neighbor.

T: For the Israelites, God made clear what would happen if they followed the rules of the law and what would happen if they did not:

> Deuteronomy 11
>
> 26 Behold, I set before you this day a blessing and a curse;
>
> 27 A blessing, if ye obey the commandments of the LORD your God, which I command you this day:
>
> 28 And a curse, if ye will not obey the commandments of the LORD your God, but turn aside out of the way which I command you this day, to go after other gods, which ye have not known.

T: Now let's look at what the blessings and curses are:

> Deuteronomy 28
>
> 1 And it shall come to pass, if thou shalt hearken diligently unto the voice of the LORD thy God, to observe and to do all his commandments which I command thee this day, that the LORD thy God will set thee on high above all nations of the earth:

2 And all these blessings shall come on thee, and overtake thee, if thou shalt hearken unto the voice of the LORD thy God.

3 Blessed shalt thou be in the city, and blessed shalt thou be in the field.

4 Blessed shall be the fruit of thy body, and the fruit of thy ground, and the fruit of thy cattle, the increase of thy kine, and the flocks of thy sheep.

5 Blessed shall be thy basket and thy store.

6 Blessed shalt thou be when thou comest in, and blessed shalt thou be when thou goest out.

7 The LORD shall cause thine enemies that rise up against thee to be smitten before thy face: they shall come out against thee one way, and flee before thee seven ways.

8 The LORD shall command the blessing upon thee in thy storehouses, and in all that thou settest thine hand unto; and he shall bless thee in the land which the LORD thy God giveth thee.

9 The LORD shall establish thee an holy people unto himself, as he hath sworn unto thee, if thou shalt keep the commandments of the LORD thy God, and walk in his ways.

10 And all people of the earth shall see that thou art called by the name of the LORD; and they shall be afraid of thee.

11 And the LORD shall make thee plenteous in goods, in the fruit of thy body, and in the fruit of thy cattle, and in the fruit of thy ground, in the land which the LORD sware unto thy fathers to give thee.

12 The LORD shall open unto thee his good treasure, the heaven to give the rain unto thy land in his season, and to bless all the work of thine hand: and thou shalt lend unto many nations, and thou shalt not borrow.

13 And the LORD shall make thee the head, and not the tail; and thou shalt be above only, and thou shalt not be beneath; if that thou hearken unto the commandments of the LORD thy God, which I command thee this day, to observe and to do them:

14 And thou shalt not go aside from any of the words which I command thee this day, to the right hand, or to the left, to go after other gods to serve them.

15 But it shall come to pass, if thou wilt not hearken unto the voice of the LORD thy God, to observe to do all his commandments and his statutes which I command thee this day; that all these curses shall come upon thee, and overtake thee:

16 Cursed shalt thou be in the city, and cursed shalt thou be in the field.

17 Cursed shall be thy basket and thy store.

18 Cursed shall be the fruit of thy body, and the fruit of thy land, the increase of thy kine, and the flocks of thy sheep.

19 Cursed shalt thou be when thou comest in, and cursed shalt thou be when thou goest out.

20 The LORD shall send upon thee cursing, vexation, and rebuke, in all that thou settest thine hand unto for to do, until thou be destroyed, and until thou perish quickly; because of the wickedness of thy doings, whereby thou hast forsaken me.

21 The LORD shall make the pestilence cleave unto thee, until he have consumed thee from off the land, whither thou goest to possess it.

22 The LORD shall smite thee with a consumption, and with a fever, and with an inflammation, and with an extreme burning, and with the sword, and with blasting, and with mildew; and they shall pursue thee until thou perish.

23 And thy heaven that is over thy head shall be brass, and the earth that is under thee shall be iron.

24 The LORD shall make the rain of thy land powder and dust: from heaven shall it come down upon thee, until thou be destroyed.

25 The LORD shall cause thee to be smitten before thine enemies: thou shalt go out one way against them, and flee seven ways before them: and shalt be removed into all the kingdoms of the earth.

26 And thy carcase shall be meat unto all fowls of the air, and unto the beasts of the earth, and no man shall fray them away.

27 The LORD will smite thee with the botch of Egypt, and with the emerods, and with the scab, and with the itch, whereof thou canst not be healed.

28 The LORD shall smite thee with madness, and blindness, and astonishment of heart:

T: Compare verses 3 and 16, verses 5 and 17, verses 4 and 18, verses 6 and 19. What do you see?

C: Mirror images: one is a blessing and the other is a curse for the same thing.

T: The consequences of following or not following the Old Testament Law were stark: either very good things would happen or very bad things would happen. And how likely is it that anyone could follow all commandments all the time?

C: Not likely.

T: So if people found it harder to keep all the commandments than to disobey the commandments, which was more likely to happen to them, blessings or curses?

C: Curses.

b. Faith and Scripture as Keys to Our Rights as Christians

T: But something very important happened with Jesus' sacrifice. Save your place in Deuteronomy 28 and turn in the New Testament to St. Paul's epistle to the Galatians:

Galatians 3

6 Even as Abraham believed God, and it was accounted to him for righteousness.

7 Know ye therefore that they which are of faith, the same are the children of Abraham.

8 And the Scripture, foreseeing that God would justify the heathen through faith, preached before the gospel unto Abraham, saying, In thee shall all nations be blessed.

9 So then they which be of faith are blessed with faithful Abraham.

10 For as many as are of the works of the law are under the curse: for it is written, Cursed is every one that continueth not in all things which are written in the book of the law to do them.

11 But that no man is justified by the law in the sight of God, it is evident: for, The just shall live by faith.

12 And the law is not of faith: but, The man that doeth them shall live in them.

13 Christ hath redeemed us from the curse of the law, being made a curse for us: for it is written, Cursed is every one that hangeth on a tree:

14 That the blessing of Abraham might come on the Gentiles through Jesus Christ; that we might receive the promise of the Spirit through faith.

T: In verses 6 – 9, St. Paul talks about the faith of Abraham. What promise did God make to Abraham?

C: That through Abraham all nations would be blessed.

T: Do you remember Abraham's first reaction when he heard he was going to have a son?

C: He didn't believe God, and he laughed. [Genesis 17:17, discussed in Section III.A.]

T: Why, then, do we say Abraham had faith?

C: Eventually Abraham came around and believed God.

T: And, in verse 6, St. Paul makes clear that Abraham's faith "was accounted to him for righteousness." In verse 9, St. Paul moves from the specific to the general (called "inductive reasoning"). The specific is that faithful Abraham is blessed. What is St. Paul's general conclusion in verse 9?

C: "They which be of faith are blessed with faithful Abraham."

T: And who are "they which be of faith"?

C: We are!

T: So we Christians are to receive the blessings of Abraham. But what does that mean? Look at verse 10; where in the Old Testament have we seen warnings like that?

C: In Deuteronomy.[63]

T: Earlier, we determined that keeping all the Old Testament Laws was very difficult. St. Paul reaches the same conclusion in verses 11 and 12. He says, "no man is justified by the law in the sight of God" and "the law is not of faith". So can anyone achieve righteousness in the sight of God by following the Old Testament Law?

C: No.

---

[63] St. Paul is actually quoting from Deuteronomy 27:26, "Cursed be he that confirmeth not all the words of this law to do them."

T: From verse 11, what will the just live by?

C: "The just shall live by faith."

T: Faith in whom?

C: In Jesus.

T: And that's what St. Paul says in verses 13 – 14. But there's more. Verse 13 states, "Christ hath redeemed us from the curse of the law, being made a curse for us: for it is written, Cursed is every one that hangeth on a tree".[64] How did Jesus die?

C: He was nailed to a cross.

T: What was the cross made of?

C: Wood.

T: Where does wood come from?

C: A tree.

T: So Jesus was made a curse for us because he hanged from a cross. Since He was made a curse for us, what did St. Paul in verse 13 say He redeemed us from?

C: "The curse of the law".

T: And what are the curses of the law?

C: That long list of bad things in Deuteronomy we just read.

T: Now what about the blessings? Look at verse 14: "That the blessing of Abraham might come on the Gentiles through Jesus Christ; that we might receive the promise of the Spirit through faith." "Gentiles" refers to non-Jewish people. Are you Jews or Gentiles?

C: [Answer may be mixed if you have Jewish Christians,[65] but most will respond:] Gentiles.

T: So who receives the blessings of Abraham through Jesus Christ?

C: We do!

T: Look at the last half of verse 14. Now that Jesus has returned to Heaven to be with His Father, who brings us the blessings of Abraham?

---

[64] St. Paul here quotes from Deuteronomy 21:22-23, "And if a man have committed a sin worthy of death, and he be to be put to death, and thou hang him on a tree: His body shall not remain all night upon the tree, but thou shalt in any wise bury him that day; (for he that is hanged is accursed of God)".
[65] In case anyone asks, the Jewish Christians receive the blessings of Abraham because they are descendants of Abraham's son, Isaac, and believe in redemption from the curse of the Law through the sacrifice of Jesus.

C: The Holy Spirit.

T: The Holy Spirit brings us the blessings of Abraham through what? [Hint: it's the last word in verse 14.]

C: Faith.

T: Flip back to Deuteronomy 28, verse 2: "And all these blessings shall come on thee, and overtake thee, if thou shalt hearken unto the voice of the LORD thy God". So, in order to receive the Blessings of Abraham, faith is important, but according to verse 2, what else is important?

C: To listen to the voice of the Lord?

T: And what does that mean?

C: Umm...

T: Well, how do we hear God's voice; how does He speak to us?

C: Through Scripture, prayer, meditation, etc.

T: God gave Joshua more precise guidance. Turn to:

Joshua 1

1 Now after the death of Moses the servant of the LORD it came to pass, that the LORD spake unto Joshua the son of Nun, Moses' minister, saying,

2 Moses my servant is dead; now therefore arise, go over this Jordan, thou, and all this people, unto the land which I do give to them, even to the children of Israel.

3 Every place that the sole of your foot shall tread upon, that have I given unto you, as I said unto Moses.

4 From the wilderness and this Lebanon even unto the great river, the river Euphrates, all the land of the Hittites, and unto the great sea toward the going down of the sun, shall be your coast.

5 There shall not any man be able to stand before thee all the days of thy life: as I was with Moses, so I will be with thee: I will not fail thee, nor forsake thee.

6 Be strong and of a good courage: for unto this people shalt thou divide for an inheritance the land, which I sware unto their fathers to give them.

7 Only be thou strong and very courageous, that thou mayest observe to do according to all the law, which Moses my servant commanded thee: turn not from it to the right hand or to the left, that thou mayest prosper whithersoever thou goest.

8 This book of the law shall not depart out of thy mouth; but thou shalt meditate therein day and night, that thou mayest observe to do according to all that is written therein: for then thou shalt make thy way prosperous, and then thou shalt have good success.

9 Have not I commanded thee? Be strong and of a good courage; be not afraid, neither be thou dismayed: for the LORD thy God is with thee whithersoever thou goest.

T: The Book of Joshua picks up where Exodus leaves off. In Exodus, which translated from Greek means "going out", the book tells the story of the Israelites going out of one place and into another. What was the place the Israelites left because they were being treated as slaves? (Hint: Anyone who has seen any version of the movie *The Ten Commandments* or the animation *The Prince of Egypt* will know this.)

C: Egypt.

T: And after they left Egypt and crossed the Red Sea, to where were they headed?

C: The Promised Land.

T: Approximately where modern-day Israel is today. The Book of Joshua begins just as the Israelites were about to enter their Promised Land as they stood on the banks of the Jordan River. But there was a problem: Other people were living on that land, and the Israelites were going to have to conquer them to take it, and their leader, Moses who brought them miraculously out of Egypt and across the Red Sea, just died. To make matters worse, the Israelites had been wandering in the desert for 40 years, so their military preparedness was probably not at 100%, and, if you read further on, the first enemy standing in their way were the people of the fortified city of Jericho. Now focus on verses 7 and 8. With the context I've just given you, you can understand why God is saying "Be thou strong and very courageous". But tell me from verse 8, how is Joshua going to have "good success"?

C: He was to meditate on the book of the law.

T: How often was Joshua to meditate?

C: Day and night!

T: Is that the same as coming to church once a week and listening to a few Scriptures read?

> C: Not quite. It has to be daily, and probably several times a day!

> T: At the time that Joshua was crossing the Jordan River, the only books of the Bible he had to meditate on were to become the first five books, called "The Torah" by our Jewish friends.[66] Indeed, Joshua did have "good success"; he went on to lead the conquest of much of what is modern-day Israel.[67] Today, we have how many books of the Bible?

> C: [Counting from the table of contents] 39 books of the Old Testament and 27 books of the New Testament.

> T: So we have more Scripture to meditate upon! Now, what did St. Paul say in our readings from Galatians that we needed to obtain the Blessings of Abraham? [Hint: we just discussed how It came through the Holy Spirit.]

> C: Faith.

> T: So what are the two things we need for "good success"?

> C: Faith and constant meditation on Scripture.

> T: We will explore these further later in the course.

B. Sin and Jesus' Role in Redemption

Learning Objectives

1. Confirmands will understand the consequences of sin.
2. Confirmands will understand that contrition, combined with faith in Jesus, leads to forgiveness of our sins.
3. Confirmands will learn that, when we sin and ask for forgiveness, Jesus intercedes for us before God as our Great High Priest.

a. The Nature of Sin

> T: To review quickly, when the tabernacle or the temple was in operation, tell me who was at all times present within the Most Holy Place?

> C: God.

> T: And what would happen if an Israelite entered the Most Holy Place burdened by sin?

---

[66] Written versions of the first five books of the Bible, organized as they are today, probably did not appear for at least a millennium after Joshua's time. Joshua likely had access to some written scrolls and oral histories that comprised what are the first five books today.

[67] Joshua 12 sums up the Israelites' conquests, which included portions of modern-day Jordan as well as large sections of present-day Israel.

C: He would be burned to death!

T: Why?

C: The sin within him could not remain in the presence of God: God's light will overcome darkness.

T: For us Christians, though, what did Jesus' sacrifice of His blood do about our sin problem?

C: His blood washed away our sins. [Sec. IV.A.; Hebrews 10:19]

T: But to take advantage of what Jesus purchased for us, after we realize we have sinned, we must do something. What is that something?

C: Ask God to forgive us.

T: And the act of asking God to forgive us is called "repentance". If you refuse to repent, what happens?

C: Something not good!

T: Let's see what St. Paul said about sin and repentance:

Romans 2

5 But after thy hardness and impenitent heart treasurest up unto thyself wrath against the day of wrath and revelation of the righteous judgment of God;

6 Who will render to every man according to his deeds:

7 To them who by patient continuance in well doing seek for glory and honour and immortality, eternal life:

8 But unto them that are contentious, and do not obey the truth, but obey unrighteousness, indignation and wrath,

9 Tribulation and anguish, upon every soul of man that doeth evil, of the Jew first, and also of the Gentile;

10 But glory, honour, and peace, to every man that worketh good, to the Jew first, and also to the Gentile:

11 For there is no respect of persons with God.

12 For as many as have sinned without law shall also perish without law: and as many as have sinned in the law shall be judged by the law;

13 (For not the hearers of the law are just before God, but the doers of the law shall be justified.

14 For when the Gentiles, which have not the law, do by nature the things contained in the law, these, having not the law, are a law unto themselves:

15 Which shew the work of the law written in their hearts, their conscience also bearing witness, and their thoughts the mean while accusing or else excusing one another;)

16 In the day when God shall judge the secrets of men by Jesus Christ according to my gospel.

T: So there will be a judgment day when God judges the "secrets of men". Verses 6 – 8 show what happens "to every man according to his deeds". If you patiently continue to pursue "well doing", what do you receive?

C: Eternal life.

T: If you "do not obey the truth, but obey unrighteousness", what do you receive?

C: Indignation and wrath.

T: Look back at verse 5. What does St. Paul say about the person who "treasurest up unto thyself wrath against the day of wrath"? What does the first part of the verse tell us about why God is displeased with that person?

C: He has "hardness and [an] impenitent heart".

T: What does that mean?

C: He is stubborn and does not repent of his sins.

T: That's what gets you in trouble with God: hardness of heart and refusing to repent when you know you are wrong. Now jump to verse 12: "For as many as have sinned without law shall also perish without law: and as many as have sinned in the law shall be judged by the law." To what "law" is St. Paul referring?

C: The Old Testament Law.

T: Right, this is the law he studied as a Jew. If you broke one of the 613 commandments, you would be judged by that law, and what was that judgment? Remember the curses?

C: Yes – not good!

T: St. Paul is saying you can perish with or without the Old Testament Law. With the law, according to St. Paul, if you sin, the law will condemn you. If you sin without knowing the law, what does St. Paul say will happen?

C: The same thing: you will perish.

What follows is an optional section which expresses my view on salvation theology. I believe that Jesus is "the way, the truth, and the life: no man cometh unto the Father, but by" Him (John 14:6), but I also believe that Jesus can manifest Himself in people who, while never having heard of Jesus, show "the work of the law written in their hearts" with "their conscience also bearing witness" (Romans 2:15). C.S. Lewis put it this way: "We do know that no man can be saved except through Christ; we do not know that only those who know Him can be saved through Him."[68] Nevertheless, if this position does not comport with your views, feel free to ignore this part.

T: This is a question that often comes up: What about those people who never hear about the law, or Jesus for that matter, but live a life of good works? Are they condemned? Look at verses 13 – 15, and focus on verse 14: "For when the Gentiles, which have not the law, do by nature the things contained in the law, these, having not the law, are a law unto themselves". Who are the Gentiles?

C: We are.

T: Anyone who is not a descendant of Isaac, which for shorthand we say "non-Jews". So substitute "non-Jews" for "Gentiles" and let me paraphrase: "For when non-Jews who do not know about the law do by nature the things contained in the law, even though they do not know the law, they are a law unto themselves." Verse 15 goes on to say, and I paraphrase, such people "show the work of the law written in their hearts, their conscience also bearing witness, and their thoughts both accusing or else excusing one another." In other words, these are not just people who do good deeds but have not heard about Jesus; the law unto themselves in their conscience both accuses them when they sin and excuses them when they recognize their sin. Later in this course, we will see what C.S. Lewis says about your conscience, but for now, think about those few people today who have not heard about the law or Jesus. Will they perish?

C: Maybe not.

T: The issue of what happens to those who never heard of Jesus seems to trouble many non-Christians and cause them to doubt that our God is a loving God. However, C.S. Lewis had an interesting observation about anyone who asked the question: "What happens to those who never heard the Gospel of Christ?" Lewis said that:

---

[68] *Mere Christianity*, by C.S. Lewis copyright © C.S. Lewis Pte. Ltd. 1942, 1943, 1944, 1952, p. 64. Extract reprinted by permission.

Confirmand Reference Book First Edition

> ..., if you are worried about the people outside [the Body of Christ], the most unreasonable thing you can do is remain outside yourself. Christians are Christ's body, the organism through which he works. Every addition to that body enables Him to do more. If you want to help those outside you must add your own little cell to the body of Christ who alone can help them.[69]

So what should we do if we are concerned about those who have never heard the Good News of Jesus Christ?

C: Become missionaries?

T: Not necessarily, though some of you may be called to do so! The bottom line, however, is to join with those willing to spread the Good News of salvation through Jesus!

---

b. Confession and Forgiveness

T: We have talked a little about confessing sins and God's forgiveness. Let's look at an account of when Jesus encountered a sinner who, in her own unique way, confessed her sins.

Luke 7

36 And one of the Pharisees desired him that he would eat with him. And he went into the Pharisee's house, and sat down to meat.

37 And, behold, a woman in the city, which was a sinner, when she knew that Jesus sat at meat in the Pharisee's house, brought an alabaster box of ointment,

38 And stood at his feet behind him weeping, and began to wash his feet with tears, and did wipe them with the hairs of her head, and kissed his feet, and anointed them with the ointment.

39 Now when the Pharisee which had bidden him saw it, he spake within himself, saying, This man, if he were a prophet, would have known who and what manner of woman this is that toucheth him: for she is a sinner.

40 And Jesus answering said unto him, Simon, I have somewhat to say unto thee. And he saith, Master, say on.

---

[69] *Mere Christianity*, by C.S. Lewis copyright © C.S. Lewis Pte. Ltd. 1942, 1943, 1944, 1952, p. 64. Extract reprinted by permission.

41 There was a certain creditor which had two debtors: the one owed five hundred pence, and the other fifty.

42 And when they had nothing to pay, he frankly forgave them both. Tell me therefore, which of them will love him most?

43 Simon answered and said, I suppose that he, to whom he forgave most. And he said unto him, Thou hast rightly judged.

44 And he turned to the woman, and said unto Simon, Seest thou this woman? I entered into thine house, thou gavest me no water for my feet: but she hath washed my feet with tears, and wiped them with the hairs of her head.

45 Thou gavest me no kiss: but this woman since the time I came in hath not ceased to kiss my feet.

46 My head with oil thou didst not anoint: but this woman hath anointed my feet with ointment.

47 Wherefore I say unto thee, Her sins, which are many, are forgiven; for she loved much: but to whom little is forgiven, the same loveth little.

48 And he said unto her, Thy sins are forgiven.

49 And they that sat at meat with him began to say within themselves, Who is this that forgiveth sins also?

50   And he said to the woman, Thy faith hath saved thee; go in peace.

T: Look back at verses 37 – 39. What was the woman known for?

C: She was a sinner.

T: Whatever her sin was, it was notorious and known by all the locals. That probably meant she was a prostitute, though Luke does not so state.   What does she do when she sees Jesus?

C: She wets His feet with her tears, wipes them with her hair and then pours perfume on them.

T: The custom at the time was to recline on cushions when eating a meal. So, to wipe His feet, physically speaking, where is the woman in relation to Jesus?

C: She must be bowed down at His feet.

T: What, then, does Jesus do?

C: He forgives her.

T: Not so fast! Jesus actually turns to His host, Simon the Pharisee,[70] to respond to the comment he made in verse 40. What was that comment?

C: If Jesus were a prophet, He would have known the woman was a sinner.

T: Did the host make the comment audibly, to where others could hear it?

C: No, "he spake within himself".

T: So after he said to himself, "if Jesus were a prophet, ...", Jesus responds with an allegory. What is an "allegory"?

C: [From Dictionary.com] "A representation of an abstract or spiritual meaning through concrete or material forms".

T: It's essentially a story with a deeper meaning, and a short allegory is called a "parable". What was the parable Jesus told Simon?

C: If you owe a great debt that is forgiven, you will be more thankful than someone who owed a smaller debt that was forgiven.

T: And between the woman and Simon, who owed the greater debt?

C: The woman.

T: So, do you think Simon ever figured out whether Jesus was a prophet? In other words, did Simon catch on that Jesus knew of the bad reputation of the woman crying at his feet?

C: Probably.

T: By verse 47, it's pretty clear Jesus knows the woman had many sins. So, now, what does Jesus do?

C: He forgives her sins.

T: Her **many** sins. But, according to verse 50, what saved the woman?

C: Her faith.

T: In whom?

C: Jesus.

---

[70] A Pharisee was a member of a Jewish sect that awaited the coming of the Messiah and acknowledged the afterlife. In contrast, another Jewish sect popular during this period was the Sadducees, who did not believe in an afterlife.

T: So when it comes to asking forgiveness of your many sins, do you have to go find Jesus and pour perfume on His feet?

C: No, hopefully!

T: No, the woman poured perfume as a sign of her respect. Why did she cry, though?

C: She was truly sorry for her sins.

T: That's the important part to remember. It's called "contrition". Contrition combined with faith in Jesus are the keys to forgiveness of your sins. In most every church service, we say a prayer that deals with sin and contrition. Turn in the Book of Common Prayer to page 360:

Minister and People

Most merciful God,
we confess that we have sinned against you
in thought, word, and deed,
by what we have done,
and by what we have left undone.
We have not loved you with our whole heart;
we have not loved our neighbors as ourselves.
We are truly sorry and we humbly repent.
For the sake of your Son Jesus Christ,
have mercy on us and forgive us;
that we may delight in your will,
and walk in your ways,
to the glory of your Name. Amen.

The Bishop when present, or the Priest, stands and says

Almighty God have mercy on you, forgive you all your sins through our Lord Jesus Christ, strengthen you in all goodness, and by the power of the Holy Spirit keep you in eternal life. *Amen.*

T: Remember how Jesus summarized the Old Testament Law in two commandments; what were the two commandments Jesus gave?

C: Love God and love your neighbor.

T: Where do those commandments show up in the prayer we just read?

C: In the middle: "We have not loved you with our whole heart; we have not loved our neighbors as ourselves."

T: Then what do we say?

C: "We are truly sorry and we humbly repent."

T: My challenge to you is that the next time you say that prayer in church, you think about the woman with many sins crying at the feet of Jesus, and ask yourself if you "are truly sorry" and "humbly repent." And if you have trouble coming up with any recent sins you may have committed, where could you go to look for suggestions?

C: The Ten Commandments?

T: That's a good start, but there is a list of sins we've seen that gets even more specific than the Ten Commandments. Where is that list?

C: *Handout #3.*

T: Right. If you scan that handout before you leave for church, I guarantee it will give you some thoughts to reflect upon! Also, these are the sins Jesus tells us to pay attention to because they are those that "cometh out of the man, that defileth the man."[71] What happens after we say the prayer on page 360?

C: The Bishop or Priest says that God forgives us of our sins.

T: This statement is sometimes referred to as the "Absolution" in that the Bishop or Priest speaks for God to absolve us, that is to say, to free us from blame for our sins.[72] We will study Church structure later in this course, but tell me who ranks higher, a Bishop or a Priest?

C: Bishop.

T: And how often do you see the Bishop at your church?

C: Not much![73]

T: A Bishop visit is usually a special occasion, yet if the Bishop is present, the Book of Common Prayer instructs that the Bishop say this statement declaring forgiveness of our sins. Why do you think the Book of Common Prayer gives this task to our highest-ranking clergy?

C: Because forgiveness of sins is important.

T: Well, who on the Day of Atonement was allowed into the Most Holy Place to ask for forgiveness of Israel's sins?

C: The High Priest.

T: Was forgiveness of sins important to God when the Israelites worshiped at the tabernacle and the temple?

---

[71] Mark 7:20.
[72] For more information, see the definition of "absolution" from the Episcopal Church's Glossary at http://www.episcopalchurch.org/library/glossary/absolution.
[73] Frequency of Bishop visitations can be a sore subject in some dioceses!

C: Yes.

T: Is forgiveness of sins important to God today?

C: Yes.

T: And having the Bishop, when available, pronounce our forgiveness brings home that point. We will study this topic more when we get to the Sacraments.

c. Jesus as Great High Priest

T: So what do we know about forgiveness of sins so far?

C: [Several answers could be appropriate. One such answer is:] If we "humbly repent" of our sins, we are forgiven.

T: And what does Jesus' sacrifice on the cross have to do with forgiveness?

C: The sacrifice of His Blood washed away our sins.[74]

T: Ok. Now let's explore how this actually happens, and by that I mean what happens in Heaven. First, where is Jesus right now?

C: In Heaven.

T: Yeah, but where in Heaven? Floating around on a cloud somewhere?

C: No. He is at God's right hand.[75]

T: Scripture[76] and our Creeds tell us Jesus is seated at God's right hand. But is He just sitting there playing videogames? Did His ministry end when He ascended into Heaven and handed things over to the Holy Spirit? Let's look at:

> Hebrews 7
>
> 23 And they truly were many priests, because they were not suffered to continue by reason of death:
>
> 24 But this man, [Jesus,] because he continueth ever, hath an unchangeable priesthood.

---

[74] Hebrews 10:19.

[75] Surprisingly, I have found at least one confirmand in every class knows this from reciting the Nicene or Apostles Creeds in Sunday services: Jesus "... is seated at the right hand of the Father".

[76] There are numerous scriptural references, for example Colossians 3:1: "If ye then be risen with Christ, seek those things which are above, where Christ sitteth on the right hand of God."

25 Wherefore he is able also to save them to the uttermost that come unto God by him, seeing he ever liveth to make intercession for them.

26 For such an high priest became us, who is holy, harmless, undefiled, separate from sinners, and made higher than the heavens;

27 Who needeth not daily, as those high priests, to offer up sacrifice, first for his own sins, and then for the people's: for this he did once, when he offered up himself.

28 For the law maketh men high priests which have infirmity; but the word of the oath, which was since the law, maketh the Son, who is consecrated for evermore.

Hebrews 8

1 Now of the things which we have spoken this is the sum: We have such an high priest, who is set on the right hand of the throne of the Majesty in the heavens;

2 A minister of the sanctuary, and of the true tabernacle, which the Lord pitched, and not man.

3 For every high priest is ordained to offer gifts and sacrifices: wherefore it is of necessity that this man have somewhat also to offer.

4 For if he were on earth, he should not be a priest, seeing that there are priests that offer gifts according to the law:

5 Who serve unto the example and shadow of heavenly things, as Moses was admonished of God when he was about to make the tabernacle: for, See, saith he, that thou make all things according to the pattern shewed to thee in the mount.

6 But now hath he obtained a more excellent ministry, by how much also he is the mediator of a better covenant, which was established upon better promises.

T: Even though we are reading from the New Testament, what does this passage remind you of from our studies of the Old Testament?

C: Worship in the tabernacle and temples.

Confirmand Reference Book First Edition

T: The Epistle to the Hebrews does not name an author, but it has many passages similar to St. Paul's letters, so it was certainly influenced by St. Paul if not written by him. In the passages we just read, the author of Hebrews is talking to his fellow Jews. We pick up the discussion in verse 23 where the author is talking about priests, and these are priests who are mortal, that is they eventually suffer death. If these were priests working at the tabernacle or temple, what would they be doing?

C: Offering sacrifices.

T: What were the names of the first priests we read about when we started discussing worship at the tabernacle?

C: Moses and Aaron, and Aaron's sons.

T: Does anyone remember which of the twelve tribes of Israel Moses and Aaron belonged to?

C: Levi.

T: In verse 24, though, we have something odd. Who continues forever in an unchangeable priesthood?

C: Jesus.

T: But how can Jesus be a priest? Save your place in the Bible in Hebrews and flip back to Matthew, Chapter 1. Look down the list of Jesus' ancestors and see if He is a descendant of Levi. Anyone see "Levi" listed as one of Jesus' ancestors?

C: No.

T: Yeah. Look at verse 2, Levi was one of Jacob's twelve sons, but instead of seeing the words "and Jacob begat Levi", what do we see?

C: "… and Jacob begat Judas and his brethren."

T: Judas, who we also call "Judah", was one of Levi's brothers. Judah's descendants were many; so many that we now refer to <u>all</u> Israelites to this day as …

C: Jews.

T: Right. So Jesus was a descendant of Judah, not Levi. But how could Jesus be a priest if all priests came from the tribe of Levi?

C: [silence]

T: Store that question away, and we will come back to it. OK, now look back at Hebrews 7, verse 25, and substitute the word "Jesus" for the words "he" and "him": "Wherefore [Jesus] is able also to save them to the uttermost that come unto God by [Jesus], seeing [Jesus] ever liveth to make intercession for them." So who does Jesus save?

C: "... them to the uttermost that come unto God by [Jesus]".

T: That's the Good News: we are saved by faith in Jesus. But the last half of that verse tells us what Jesus is doing now. What is that?

C: "[Jesus] ever liveth to make intercession for them."

T: If I intercede for someone, what does that mean?

C: You get involved.

T: Yes, but more. To "intercede" means to speak up for someone in trouble. If you have sinned, are you in trouble?

C: Yes.

T: So Jesus' job TODAY is to intercede for you when you sin. He is seated where?

C: At God's right hand.

T: So when you confess your sins, Jesus intercedes for you with God. The author of Hebrews does not tell us exactly what Jesus says, but I suspect He reminds God of His sacrifice that paid for your sins and asks for forgiveness on your behalf. So, did Jesus' ministry end when He ascended into Heaven?

C: No, He still intercedes for us.

T: In verse 1 of Chapter 8, you see Jesus referred to as "High Priest". And where is He?

C: "... who is set on the right hand of the throne of the Majesty in the heavens".

T: Which means He is at the right hand of ...

C: God.

T: In verse 2, you see the "true tabernacle". The original tabernacle was a tent pitched by the Israelites. Who pitched the "true tabernacle"?

C: The Lord, that is to say God.

T: Now jump to verse 6 and substitute "Jesus" for "he": "But now hath [Jesus] obtained a more excellent ministry, by how much also [Jesus] is the mediator of a better covenant, which was established upon better promises." What is the "better covenant" "established upon better promises"?

C: [Any number of responses are possible:] Jesus saved us from our sins once and for all. Jesus sacrificed Himself so that we did not need other sacrifices.

Confirmand Reference Book First Edition   Page 95

> T: Do we need to slaughter animals once a year and sprinkle blood on an altar?
>
> C: No.
>
> T: Right. Jesus brought us a "better covenant". Now let's return to the question we have yet to answer: how did Jesus, who descended from Judah and not Levi, become a High Priest for us? Let's go back to the time of Abraham, also known as "Abram", just after Abram won a great battle against his enemies:

> Genesis 14
>
> 18 And Melchizedek king of Salem[77] brought forth bread and wine: and he was the priest of the most high God.
>
> 19 And he blessed him, and said, Blessed be Abram of the most high God, possessor of heaven and earth:
>
> 20 And blessed be the most high God, which hath delivered thine enemies into thy hand. And [Abram] gave him tithes of all.

> T: The "tithe" means ten percent, so Abram gave Melchizedek ten percent of his winnings from defeating his enemies. In verse 18, Melchizedek had two titles; what were they?
>
> C: King of Salem and "the priest of the most high God".
>
> T: Melchizedek was "the priest", meaning he was the High Priest. Now why did I have you read three verses from the first book of the Bible to explain why Jesus was a High Priest? Flip back to Hebrews.

> Hebrews 6
>
> 19 Which hope we have as an anchor of the soul, both sure and stedfast, and which entereth into that within the veil;
>
> 20 Whither the forerunner is for us entered, even Jesus, made an high priest for ever after the order of Melchisedec.

> T: What is the "veil" in reference to?
>
> C: The divider in the tabernacle or temple that blocks out the Most Holy Place.
>
> T: And, from verse 20, who was the forerunner who entered the veil before us?
>
> C: Jesus.

---

[77] A term of reference for Jerusalem.

T: Before Jesus, who was the only person allowed to enter into the Most Holy Place?

C: The High Priest.

T: And that's why Jesus was referred to as a High Priest as well. He wasn't from the tribe of Levi, though. The last part of verse 20 tells you the order from which Jesus received his priesthood. Which order was that?

C: Melchizedek.

T: But look at when Melchizedek served as High Priest. He served around the time Abram and Sarah give birth to Isaac, which according to the *Timechart,* Panel VI, was around 1900 B.C. Moses and Aaron do not appear until around 1500 B.C. in Panel VII, and Aaron was the first "High Priest" of the tabernacle, being a descendant of Levi. So at the time of Melchizedek, was Levi even born?

C: No.

T: So Melchizedek was a High Priest before there were even high priests! From *Chronicles of Narnia, The Lion the Witch and the Wardrobe*, do you remember what Aslan says brought him back to life after he sacrificed himself?

C: Magic.

T: "Deeper Magic", magic that went back further and farther than that used by others to capture him. You can think of the priesthood of Melchizedek as the "Deeper Magic", the ancient priesthood that pre-dated the oldest priest, Aaron. Jesus was a High Priest after the order of Melchizedek, the order of the "Deeper Magic", and so we call Jesus "The Great High Priest".[78]

Author's Note

A short synopsis of *The Chronicles of Narnia*

The Chronicles of Narnia consisted of seven novels by C.S. Lewis. In *The Lion, the Witch and the Wardrobe,* four sibling children, Lucy, Edmund, Susan and Peter, evacuated from London to the English countryside during World War II, enter the world of Narnia through a magical wardrobe in their new home. Narnia consists of talking beasts and other creatures, but their world becomes trapped in winter by the evil White Witch, Jadis. The Witch wins cooperation from Edmund by offering him candy and other goodies, but Edmund incurs the Witch's anger when he fails to bring his siblings to the Witch as she desires and escapes to Aslan the Lion and the others. For that act, Edmund is branded a "traitor" and the Witch demands that Aslan hand Edmund over to be killed because the "Deep Magic" demands "blood" from traitors or else the Law says all Narnia will perish (Ch. 13). Instead, Aslan negotiates

---

[78] There is no evidence that C.S. Lewis had the priesthood of Melchizedek in mind when he wrote *The Lion, the Witch and the Wardrobe*, but the allegory fits well, so I use it as a pedagogical tool here!

his surrender to the Witch to die in place of Edmund. Upon his surrender, the Witch's henchmen bind and muzzle Aslan, and they shear him to mock him. Then the henchmen place Aslan on a great Stone Table, and the Witch kills him (Ch. 14). Lucy and Susan witness this scene over the course of a night, but in the morning they discover Aslan gone and the Table broken in two from end to end. When the girls find Aslan, he explains that beyond the Deep Magic, "there is a magic deeper still" going back to "the stillness and darkness before Time dawned;" that Deeper Magic brings Aslan back to life and satisfies that "blood" requirement of the Deep Magic (Ch. 15). With Aslan's aid, the creatures, led by Peter, defeat the Witch in a final battle.

There are numerous parallels to Jesus' crucifixion: the Deep Magic is the Old Testament Law; the Deeper Magic is God's Plan of Redemption that fulfills the requirements of the Deep Magic/ Old Testament Law; Aslan/Jesus sacrifice themselves for others and are mocked for doing so; the Stone table and the temple veil are both broken from end to end; girls/women are the first to discover the resurrected Aslan/Jesus in the morning. As for the final battle for Narnia, there will be a final battle in this world, too, which is described in Revelation 20:7-10.

VI. The Trinity

Learning Objectives

1. Confirmands will learn that God the Father, God the Son and God the Holy Spirit are One, are co-equal, and have been so since the Beginning.
2. Confirmands will understand that God the Father is not just Creator but is also One who desires to show mercy because He loves us.
3. Confirmands will understand that there were numerous prophecies of Jesus' birth and death by many different prophets, rendered centuries before Jesus walked the Earth, that Jesus fulfilled.
4. Confirmands will understand Jesus' New Commandment and why He went to the cross for us.
5. Confirmands will understand that the Holy Spirit will help us accomplish great works in Jesus' Name.
6. Confirmands will learn that the Holy Spirit used the gift of unknown tongues to signal to the disciples that the Christian Faith was not for Jews only.
7. Confirmands will understand how the Gifts of the Spirit work together to help them and others.

A Note about the Material

This is difficult material, so this section on the Trinity only covers God the Father and God the Son; we cover God the Holy Spirit in the following section. That said, don't feel you have to achieve near-perfect understanding. Every priest I've known has groaned when confronting a Trinity Sunday sermon because the subject matter is abstract. I've tried to use anecdotes to illustrate abstract concepts, so hopefully they get the point across.

A. The Third Creed

> T: Now we will turn to a concept that is at the core of our Faith: the Trinity. The word "trinity" means a group of three. When we Christians say "The Trinity", we are referring to three persons who are part of, or comprise, God: God the Father, God the Son and God the Holy Spirit. But while we say there are three persons, there is just one God. Let's see how early Christians explained this concept. Turn to page 865 of the Book of Common Prayer, and we will start reading from the middle of The Creed of St. Athanasius:[79]

> So the Father is God, the Son is God, and the Holy Ghost is God.
>
> And yet they are not three Gods, but one God.
>
> So likewise the Father is Lord, the Son Lord, and the Holy Ghost Lord.
>
> And yet not three Lords, but one Lord.

---

[79] St. Athanasius (d. 373 A.D.) likely did not write this creed; the creed was likely authored in the ninth century but named after Athanasius in recognition of his views on the Trinity. See *Creeds of Christendom*, Philip Schaff, Vol. 1 §10. The Athanasian Creed.

For like as we are compelled by the Christian verity to acknowledge every Person by himself to be both God and Lord,

So are we forbidden by the Catholic Religion, to say, There be three Gods, or three Lords.

The Father is made of none, neither created, nor begotten.

The Son is of the Father alone, not made, nor created, but begotten.

The Holy Ghost is of the Father and of the Son, neither made, nor created, nor begotten, but proceeding.

So there is one Father, not three Fathers; one Son, not three Sons; one Holy Ghost, not three Holy Ghosts.

And in this Trinity none is afore, or after other; none is greater, or less than another;

But the whole three Persons are co-eternal together and co-equal.

So that in all things, as is aforesaid, the Unity in Trinity and the Trinity in Unity is to be worshipped.

He therefore that will be saved must thus think of the Trinity.

T: We have two commonly used creeds in our services. Can someone name one?

C: Nicene Creed.

T: And the other is the Apostles Creed, which is used less often. But the Creed of St. Athanasius is a third creed in our Faith. How many of you have ever seen this one before?

C: [no hands raised]

T: And if you want to have some fun, go home tonight and talk about the Creed of St. Athanasius with your parents; I bet they haven't heard of it either! Just from the passage we read, what topic was discussed in the Athanasian Creed?

C: The Trinity.

T: So God the Father, God the Son and God the Holy Spirit, are they three Gods?

C: No, they are one God.

T: Is God the Father greater than God the Son, and God the Son greater than God the Holy Spirit?

C: No, they are "co-equal".

T: Did God the Father come before God the Son and God the Holy Spirit?

C: Maybe?

T: That's a trickier question. The Athanasian Creed says "no", and that "in this Trinity none is afore, or after other", but what support is there? Just because the creed is attributed to a saint doesn't mean we blindly accept everything it says.[80] Let's start with how the world was created in Genesis:

> Genesis 1
>
> 1 In the beginning God created the heaven and the earth.
>
> 2 And the earth was without form, and void; and darkness was upon the face of the deep. And the Spirit of God moved upon the face of the waters.

T: So in the first two verses of the Bible, who shows up?

C: God and the Spirit of God.

T: And the reference to "God" here is to "God the Father", the Creator of Heaven and Earth. The "Spirit of God" is who?

C: The Holy Spirit.

T: Now what about Jesus? Turn to the Gospel of John:

> John 1
>
> 1 In the beginning was the Word, and the Word was with God, and the Word was God.
>
> 2 The same was in the beginning with God.
>
> 3 All things were made by him; and without him was not any thing made that was made.
>
> 4 In him was life; and the life was the light of men.
>
> 5 And the light shineth in darkness; and the darkness comprehended it not.

---

[80] What follows is a short exercise in exegesis, in this case, a critical examination of a phrase in the Athanasian Creed. We will employ the three cornerstones of the Episcopal faith, Scripture, tradition and reason. Here, you will see that we apply reason to test the tradition of the creed's statement using Scripture.

6 There was a man sent from God, whose name was John.

7 The same came for a witness, to bear witness of the Light, that all men through him might believe.

8 He was not that Light, but was sent to bear witness of that Light.

9 That was the true Light, which lighteth every man that cometh into the world.

10 He was in the world, and the world was made by him, and the world knew him not.

11 He came unto his own, and his own received him not.

12 But as many as received him, to them gave he power to become the sons of God, even to them that believe on his name:

13 Which were born, not of blood, nor of the will of the flesh, nor of the will of man, but of God.

14 And the Word was made flesh, and dwelt among us, (and we beheld his glory, the glory as of the only begotten of the Father,) full of grace and truth.

T: In that last verse, the "Word" is a person who "was made flesh, and dwelt among us"; who was that person?

C: Jesus.

T: According to verse 1, "In the beginning was the Word, and the Word was with God, and the Word was God". So when God the Father created the Heavens and the Earth, where was Jesus?

C: He was with God the Father.

T: Now then, who was present when the world was created?

C: From Genesis: God the Father, God the Holy Spirit, and from John: God the Son.

T: Was the Athanasian Creed right, then, to say "in this Trinity none is afore, or after other"?[81]

---

[81] In stating that the Trinity had no member "afore, or after", the Athanasian Creed could well have been referring to relative importance or precedence of one member of the Godhead to another and not

> C: Yes.

B. God the Father

> T: God the Father is Creator, I get that, but does He have a personality, or is He just some far off Being? Let's listen to God[82] talking and see. Turn to this passage and you will hear God's Words:

Hosea 6

> 4 O Ephraim, what shall I do unto thee? O Judah, what shall I do unto thee? for your goodness is as a morning cloud, and as the early dew it goeth away.
>
> 5 Therefore have I hewed them by the prophets; I have slain them by the words of my mouth: and thy[83] judgments are as the light that goeth forth.
>
> 6 For I desired mercy, and not sacrifice; and the knowledge of God more than burnt offerings.

> T: This passage is God speaking to the Israelites through the prophet Hosea in about 700 B.C., and God is not happy with them. To find out why, look at the last half of verse 4. God compares Israel's goodness to what?
>
> C: A morning cloud.
>
> T: And what happens to the morning cloud after the sun rises?
>
> C: It goes away.
>
> T: So Israel starts with goodness, but over time what happens?
>
> C: The goodness goes away.
>
> T: Like someone who set off intending to do good but gets off course. So, in verse 5, who does God send to the people of Israel?

---

simply making a temporal reference as I have done here. Nevertheless, I believe a temporal reference is valid in this context, and I wanted to put the confirmands through an exercise in exegesis made manageable by keeping the scope narrow.

[82] I am going back to using the shorthand name "God" for "God the Father" so that the discussion does not bog down.

[83] More recent translations interpret the Hebrew to say, "<u>my</u> judgments are like the light that goes forth." (Hosea 6:5 taken from the Amplified Bible, Copyright © 1954, 1958, 1962, 1964, 1965, 1987 by The Lockman Foundation. Used by permission. Emphasis added.)

C: Prophets.

T: Further in that verse, God says, "I have slain them by the words of my mouth". I don't think God means His Words literally cut their bodies; assuming I'm right, what are God's Words cutting? If someone says, "that just slays me", what is getting slayed?

C: Their hearts?

T: Probably. God is sending prophets to keep Israel on the right path. The prophets will likely say things that are difficult to hear, like having one of your best friends tell you that you are doing something wrong and you should stop. Has someone ever had to do that for you or have you had to intervene to stop your friends from doing something wrong or dumb?

C: Yes.

T: Then that's what God was doing to the people of Israel. In the last phrase of verse 5, God says His "judgments are as the light that goeth forth". Where else have we discussed God's light?

C: Worship in the tabernacle and the temple.

T: Right. Remember the statements from a letter from St. John: "God is light, and in him is no darkness at all" [I John 1:5], and from St. John's Gospel description of Jesus as the light entering this world, "the light shineth in darkness; and the darkness comprehended it not" [John 1:5]. Now we see God's judgments are light as well. Then let's go to verse 6: God says He desires mercy, not sacrifice, and knowledge of Him more than burnt offerings. When did we last discuss sacrifices and burnt offerings?

C: Again, worship in the tabernacle and the temple.

T: That verse turned out to provide a very important insight into who God is, so important that Jesus quoted this Scripture. Keep your place in Hosea and turn to:

> Matthew 9
>
> 9 And as Jesus passed forth from thence, he saw a man, named Matthew, sitting at the receipt of custom: and he saith unto him, Follow me. And he arose, and followed him.
>
> 10 And it came to pass, as Jesus sat at meat in the house, behold, many publicans and sinners came and sat down with him and his disciples.
>
> 11 And when the Pharisees saw it, they said unto his disciples, Why eateth your Master with publicans and sinners?
>
> 12 But when Jesus heard that, he said unto them, They that be whole need not a physician, but they that are sick.

13 But go ye and learn what that meaneth, I will have mercy, and not sacrifice: for I am not come to call the righteous, but sinners to repentance.

T: In which verse did Jesus quote Hosea?

C: Verse 13.

T: In verses 9 and 10, we see Jesus and his disciples were eating a meal with tax collectors and other notorious sinners. Tax collectors were hated because they collected taxes for the Roman Emperor, Tiberius at the time. In verse 11, a sect of Jewish leaders, called Pharisees, criticizes Jesus for eating with such sinners. How does Jesus respond in verse 12?

C: Only the sick need a physician.

T: In Jesus' response, who is the "physician" and who are the "sick"?

C: Jesus is the "physician", so the "sick" must be the sinners.

T: Then, to really drive home His point, in verse 13 Jesus quotes from Hosea and then adds His own ending: "I will have mercy, and not sacrifice: for I am not come to call the righteous, but sinners to repentance." For the Jewish leaders who thought it wrong to associate with sinners, do you think they practiced "mercy"?

C: No.

T: For Jewish leaders during the time of the Second Temple, which was still in operation at the time Jesus walked the Earth, would they have practiced "sacrifice"?

C: Yes.

T: So, for the Jewish leaders, did they follow God's Words, first recited by Hosea and then quoted by Jesus, "I will have mercy, and not sacrifice"?

C: No.

T: Then Jesus reveals His purpose in the last words of verse 13. What is His purpose?

C: To call sinners to repentance.

T: And what does God do for sinners who repent?

C: He forgives them.

T: So we've seen God's Words in Hosea and then Jesus repeating God's Words in Matthew. What do those Words tell us about what God will do when sinners repent?

C: He will show them mercy.

T: Now you have just uncovered a very important part of God's personality: He wants to show mercy. God the Father said it; seven hundred years later God the Son repeated it; so you can take that promise to the very gates of Heaven! But there's more to God than being a Creator who shows mercy. Let's look at Jesus speaking in a passage with which you are probably familiar:

John 3

16 For God so loved the world, that he gave his only begotten Son, that whosoever believeth in him should not perish, but have everlasting life.

17 For God sent not his Son into the world to condemn the world; but that the world through him might be saved.

18 He that believeth on him is not condemned: but he that believeth not is condemned already, because he hath not believed in the name of the only begotten Son of God.

19 And this is the condemnation, that light is come into the world, and men loved darkness rather than light, because their deeds were evil.

20 For every one that doeth evil hateth the light, neither cometh to the light, lest his deeds should be reproved.

21 But he that doeth truth cometh to the light, that his deeds may be made manifest, that they are wrought in God.

T: This is Jesus talking about His Father. Look at John 3:16; what does that verse tell us about who God is?

C: God loves the world.

T: Or more simply, God loves us! Indeed, St. John,[84] in addition to this gospel, also wrote a letter, called an "epistle", and in that letter he stated plainly: "God is love".[85] So we see another aspect of God. What are the characteristics of God the Father we have found so far?

C: Creator, Merciful, and Loving.

T: Creator, Merciful, and Loving. And there are many more traits of God described in the Scriptures. When a disciple asked Jesus to show him God the Father, Jesus' answer was

---

[84] See the first footnote in Section XIII for a discussion on authorship of epistles written by St. John.
[85] I John 4:16: "And we have known and believed the love that God hath to us. God is love; and he that dwelleth in love dwelleth in God, and God in him."

straightforward: "he that hath seen me hath seen the Father".[86] So, if we really want to know God the Father better, to whom should we look?

C: Jesus.

C: Now, in verse 19, who is the light that "is come into the world"? The answer is in verses 17 and 18.

C: Jesus.

T: Previously, we talked about God the Father being Light. When was that?

C: In Hosea [verse 6:5].

T: That was when we discussed worship in the tabernacle and temple, and in God's statement in Hosea that His "judgments are as the light that goeth forth." Now we see that God the Son is the light that "is come into the world". In verse 19, who is condemned?

C: "Men [who] loved darkness rather than light, because their deeds were evil."

T: In verse 21, what does a person who lives in truth do?

C: He comes to the light.

T: And the light is …

C: Jesus.

T: Let's take a closer look at Jesus, then, to find out why He is the light that came into the world.

C. God the Son

a. Prophecies

Author's Note

The prophecies concerning Jesus' birth, death and resurrection are many. I have identified a few that show different persons, or prophets, in different times gave prophetic statements foretelling these key events in Jesus' life. Also, the fulfillment of these prophecies is the first evidence presented in this course that specifically addresses Christian Apologetics, the proof of the Faith. We will study the original Old Testament prophecy and the time it was given, then we will locate the New Testament source for its fulfillment. Hopefully, as you read this discussion, you will appreciate the movement of the Holy Spirit among the prophets to reveal these key events centuries, and sometimes millennia, before they occurred.

---

[86] John 14:8-9.

Instructions for the Prophecy and Fulfillment Table

In the table below, I list the prophecy and its respective fulfillment. Select a few that are of interest and look up both the prophecy and its fulfillment. Then, if available, turn to *The Timechart History of the World*. Spread the chart out so that at least Panels VIII to XI are showing; this should reveal events from 1400 B.C. to 400 A.D. After you make a match between a given prophecy and its fulfillment, go to the *Timechart* and identify the Old Testament prophet who gave the prophecy and then count the centuries until Jesus' time on Earth shown on Panel XI. Old Testament prophets are listed in the upper row, above the timeline. Then, at the end of the process, average the number of centuries for the prophecies you selected. This exercise drives home how far in advance God set in motion the prophecies that would lead to our salvation. Also, you should appreciate that the Holy Spirit must have been speaking through the prophets because the prophecies were specific yet given by people who had little in the way of visible clues or indicators of the events to come. Indeed, I consider that, for prophecies identified with a specific prophet, simply going on record by stating the prophecy was an act of faith on the part of that prophet. Finally, you should recognize that, in order to fulfill so many specific prophecies, Jesus had to be the One of whom the prophets spoke![87]

Prophecy and Fulfillment Table[88]

Prophecy	Old Testament	New Testament
Born in Bethlehem	Micah 5:2	Matthew 2:1
Born of a virgin	Isaiah 7:14	Matthew 1:18
Journey to Egypt	Hosea 11:1	Matthew 2:14-15
Slaughter of the innocents	Jeremiah 31:15	Matthew 2:16-18
Rejected by His own people	Isaiah 53:3	John 1:11
Riding on a donkey	Zechariah 9:9	John 12:13-14
Betrayal by a trusted one	Psalm 41:9	Matthew 26:20-25
Thirty pieces of silver	Zechariah 11:12	Matthew 26:15
Money returned to the potter	Zechariah 11:13	Matthew 27:6-7
Silent when accused	Isaiah 53:7	Matthew 26:62-63
Spit on and struck	Isaiah 50:6	Mark 14:65
Suffered for us	Isaiah 53:4-5	Romans 4:25
Crucified	Psalm 22:16	John 19:17
Hurling insults	Psalm 22:6-8	Matthew 27:39-40
Given gall[89] and vinegar	Psalm 69:21	John 19:29
Side pierced	Zechariah 12:10	John 19:34

---

[87] You may wonder why God took so long before sending Jesus after the Fall of Man. While any answer to this question is speculative, keep in mind that God took the time between Abraham and Jesus to send prophets who would prophesy about the coming of the Messiah, and, when those prophecies were fulfilled, the centuries that separated prophecy and fulfillment were further evidence that Jesus was the Messiah.
Since I like to speculate, though, I would say that if God were looking for a period in Earth history when a single power could provide military protection over a large area and a communications network that would allow the Early Church to spread and grow, and if He required that such a power include Judea since the Messiah was to come from the descendants of Isaac (see Sec. III.A.), the Roman Empire met those requirements and nothing before did!

[88] Derived from *The Thompson Chain-Reference Bible*, New International Version, Zondervan/Kirkbride, 1983, pp. 1567-1570.

[89] Something bitter.

Cast lots for clothes	Psalm 22:18	Mark 15:24
No broken bones	Psalm 34:20	John 19:33
Buried with the rich	Isaiah 53:9	Mark 27:57-60
Resurrection	Psalm 16:10	Luke 24:36-48
Ascension	Psalm 68:18	Luke 24:50-51

For each prophecy, locate the Old Testament book on the *Timechart*. The books appear above the timeline as yellow and red scrolls. Most books appear on Panel IX; the Psalms were written over a long period of time, but some are attributed to David, who appears on Panel VIII. After identifying the Old Testament book on the *Timechart*, read the dates to the right and left of each book scroll that indicate the B.C. dates. Those dates tell you over how many years that particular book was written before Jesus' birth. Then fold out the *Timechart* to show Jesus' birth on Panel XI to get an idea of over how many centuries these prophets foresaw these events. These prophecies, given by multiple prophets centuries before Jesus walked on Earth and fulfilled in His lifetime, are a remarkable testimony to the Holy Spirit's influence on the prophets, who were receptive to His guidance. The fulfilled prophecies, then, are a testament to the divine inspiration of Scripture.

b. Love goes to the cross

T: There is no more defining act in Jesus' life than when He went to the cross for our salvation. To better understand that act, let's see what a prophet named Isaiah prophesied about Jesus. First, find Isaiah on Panel IX of the *Timechart*. Who came first, Isaiah or Nebuchadnezzar?

C: Isaiah.

T: So even before the destruction of the First Temple by Nebuchadnezzar, sometime just before 700 B.C., Isaiah prophesied about the coming Messiah:

> Isaiah 53[90]
>
> 3 He is despised and rejected of men; a man of sorrows, and acquainted with grief: and we hid as it were our faces from him; he was despised, and we esteemed him not.
>
> 4 Surely he hath borne our griefs, and carried our sorrows: yet we did esteem him stricken, smitten of God, and afflicted.
>
> 5 But he was wounded for our transgressions, he was bruised for our iniquities: the chastisement of our peace was upon him; and with his stripes we are healed.

---

[90] The discussion that follows this Scripture reading omits verses 8, 11 and 12, but I include them in this reading to give the confirmands more context.

6 All we like sheep have gone astray; we have turned every one to his own way; and the LORD hath laid on him the iniquity of us all.

7 He was oppressed, and he was afflicted, yet he opened not his mouth: he is brought as a lamb to the slaughter, and as a sheep before her shearers is dumb, so he openeth not his mouth.

8 He was taken from prison and from judgment: and who shall declare his generation? for he was cut off out of the land of the living: for the transgression of my people was he stricken.

9 And he made his grave with the wicked, and with the rich in his death; because he had done no violence, neither was any deceit in his mouth.

10 Yet it pleased the LORD[91] to bruise him; he hath put him to grief: when thou shalt make his soul an offering for sin, he shall see his seed, he shall prolong his days, and the pleasure of the LORD shall prosper in his hand.

11 He shall see of the travail of his soul, and shall be satisfied: by his knowledge shall my righteous servant justify many; for he shall bear their iniquities.

12 Therefore will I divide him a portion with the great, and he shall divide the spoil with the strong; because he hath poured out his soul unto death: and he was numbered with the transgressors; and he bare the sin of many, and made intercession for the transgressors.

T: Verse 3 talks of the Messiah being "despised". After Jesus had been handed over to the Romans for crucifixion, the Romans forced Him to carry His cross through the streets of Jerusalem to the place of His execution. Did anyone come to rescue Jesus while He waked through the city?

C: No.

T: Even while Jesus was crucified on the cross, people in the crowd watching ridiculed him.[92] Verses 4 and 5 talk about our "griefs", sorrows, transgressions and iniquities. What is a single word that sums up all those bad things we do?

---

[91] The *NIV Interlinear Hebrew-English Old Testament* (Zondervan, 1987) translates this phrase "Yet it was the Lord's will", implying that God allowed the Messiah to be bruised, not that God directly bruised the Messiah.
[92] From Matthew 27:39-43: "And they that passed by reviled him, wagging their heads, And saying, Thou that destroyest the temple, and buildest *it* in three days, save thyself. If thou be the Son of God, come down from the cross. Likewise also the chief priests mocking *him*, with the scribes and elders, said, He saved others; himself he cannot save. If he be the King of Israel, let him now come down from

C: Sins.

T: Right. Isaiah was describing our sins and the consequences of our sins. Then he went on to say at the end of verse 5, "with his stripes we are healed". What "stripes" did Jesus receive at the time of His crucifixion?

C: He was whipped before He was sent to the cross.[93]

T: So what did His "stripes" heal?

C: Our sins?

T: I think Isaiah had a little more in mind. We discussed the issue of sin before; when God removes our sin from us, can we enter into God's Presence, that is, see Him Face to face?

C: Yes.

T: So, Jesus heals what?

C: Our ability to be with God: our relationship with God.

T: Verse 6 says God "laid on him the iniquity of us all". Substitute the word "sins" for "iniquity", what did Isaiah mean?

C: God laid on Jesus the sins of us all.

T: Did Jesus sin?

C: No.

T: So Jesus, who had never sinned, had to pay for all our sins on the cross. From our study of worship in the tabernacle and temples, what did the High Priest do on the Day of Atonement that resembles what God did to Jesus?

C: The High Priest put the sins of Israel on the scapegoat.

T: Therefore, Jesus was the final scapegoat. In verse 8, Isaiah said Jesus "was cut off out of the land of the living". What happened to the scapegoat after the High Priest put the sins of Israel on it?

C: Someone led the scapegoat out into the desert to die.

T: So the scapegoat, just like Jesus, was cut off from the land of the living. Why was it necessary for Jesus to be cut off?

---

the cross, and we will believe him. He trusted in God; let him deliver him now, if he will have him: for he said, I am the Son of God."

[93] See, for example, Matthew 27:26.

C: To pay for our sins.

T: In verse 7, Isaiah correctly described Jesus' trial before Pontius Pilate, the Roman proconsul in charge of Judea, because Jesus refused to defend Himself against charges brought by the Jewish leaders.[94] Jump to verse 9 and you see Isaiah correctly foretold that Jesus would die with criminals – one was crucified on His right and the other was crucified on His left[95] – and that Jesus would be buried "with the rich" because the tomb where He was buried was provided by a prominent member of the Jewish ruling council.[96] Again, Isaiah saw these events 700 years before they actually occurred. Then, in verse 10, we see that God allowed the Messiah to be "bruised" to "make his soul an offering for sin". Where have we seen a reference to Jesus being "bruised" before?

C: In the first prophecy we discussed; the prophecy God delivered soon after Adam and Eve ate from the Tree of Knowledge of Good and Evil.[97]

T: We've covered a lot about what Jesus' sacrifice meant by redeeming us from our sins, but we still have not answered why He did it. Let's take a look at a portion of a discussion Jesus had with His disciples.

John 15

12 This is my commandment, That ye love one another, as I have loved you.

13 Greater love hath no man than this, that a man lay down his life for his friends.

14 Ye are my friends, if ye do whatsoever I command you.

T: So why did Jesus lay down His life for us?

C: His love for us as His friends.

T: If you are Jesus' friend, what does He command you to do?

C: Love one another, as He has loved us.

T: This commandment was one Jesus himself developed, so we call it the "New Commandment".

---

[94] Mark 15:3-5: "And the chief priests accused him of many things: but he answered nothing. And Pilate asked him again, saying, Answerest thou nothing? behold how many things they witness against thee. But Jesus yet answered nothing; so that Pilate marvelled."
[95] Mark 15:27.
[96] Mark 15:43 describes Joseph of Arimathea as "a prominent and respected member of the Council (Sanhedrin, Jewish High Court)" [Amplified Bible, Copyright © 1954, 1958, 1962, 1964, 1965, 1987 by The Lockman Foundation. Used by permission.].
[97] Genesis 3:15, discussed in Section II.D. above. Isaiah also made reference in verse 10 to the Messiah as God's "seed", which was another similarity to the Genesis prophecy.

VII. The Gifts of the Holy Spirit

Learning Objectives

1. Confirmands will learn that the Holy Spirit is God dwelling within us.
2. Confirmands will understand that we are to accomplish more than Jesus did while here on Earth through the Holy Spirit working in us.
3. Confirmands will understand that physical manifestations of the Holy Spirit were a sign to the Jewish Disciples that the Good News of salvation was available to Gentiles as well.
4. Confirmands will learn the Gifts of the Spirit.
5. Confirmands will understand that we access the Gifts of the Spirit through prayer, meditation and fasting.

A. God dwelling in us

T: The Holy Spirit is perhaps the least-known element of the Triune God, but He is most important to us because He is the One to be with us every day, day-to-day. Let's see what Jesus said about the Holy Spirit:

John 14

8 Philip saith unto him, Lord, shew us the Father, and it sufficeth us.

9 Jesus saith unto him, Have I been so long time with you, and yet hast thou not known me, Philip? he that hath seen me hath seen the Father; and how sayest thou then, Shew us the Father?

10 Believest thou not that I am in the Father, and the Father in me? the words that I speak unto you I speak not of myself: but the Father that dwelleth in me, he doeth the works.

11 Believe me that I am in the Father, and the Father in me: or else believe me for the very works' sake.

12 Verily, verily, I say unto you, He that believeth on me, the works that I do shall he do also; and greater works than these shall he do; because I go unto my Father.

13 And whatsoever ye shall ask in my name, that will I do, that the Father may be glorified in the Son.

14 If ye shall ask any thing in my name, I will do it.

15 If ye love me, keep my commandments.

16 And I will pray the Father, and he shall give you another Comforter, that he may abide with you for ever;

17 Even the Spirit of truth; whom the world cannot receive, because it seeth him not, neither knoweth him: but ye know him; for he dwelleth with you, and shall be in you.

T: St. Philip was one of Jesus' disciples. What did he ask that started this discussion?

C: Show us the Father.

T: In verse 9, how does Jesus respond?

C: Jesus said, "he that hath seen me hath seen the Father".

T: So, if you understand who Jesus is, you understand His Father. Now, Jesus performed many miracles when He walked the Earth. What do verses 10 and 11 tell us about how Jesus was able to perform these miracles?

C: The Father that dwells in Jesus does the works, and that Jesus is in Father and the Father is in Him.

T: Can we do the same miracles Jesus did? Look at verse 12, and tell me what you see.

C: Yes. Jesus said, "He that believeth on me, the works that I do shall he do also; and greater works than these shall he do."

T: Alright, but how are we going to do works greater than those done by Jesus? The answer starts in the last phrase of verse 12.

C: Because Jesus is going to His Father.

T: Jesus said these words just before His crucifixion. He would later rise from the dead on Easter and then ascend into Heaven after seeing His disciples one last time. Skip to verses 16 and 17. Who is the "Comforter" Jesus will send after He goes to His Father?

C: The Holy Spirit.

T: Where is Jesus right now?

C: With God in Heaven, seated at God's right hand.

T: According to verse 17, where is the Holy Spirit right now?

C: Within us.

T: So, by who's power do we do greater works than Jesus did?

C: The Holy Spirit.

T: Now return to verses 13 and 14. What does Jesus say you should do to get your prayers answered?

C: Ask anything in His Name, and He will do it.

T: How can Jesus make such a broad statement? Does that mean that if you are tired of your pesky little brother you can ask in Jesus' Name to move him to a far-away planet?

C: Not likely.

T: The key is in verse 15. What is the requirement to be able to ask Jesus, in His Name, and He will give it to you?

C: To love Him and keep His commandments.

T: So would you be keeping His commandment to love your neighbor as yourself if you ask Jesus to relocate your pesky brother to Mars?

C: No.

T: So, your prayer has to agree with Jesus' commandments. Then, when you pray in Jesus' Name, He asks God the Father to send you the Comforter, the Holy Spirit, who fulfills your request. Therefore, what is the key to having God answer your prayers?

C: To love Jesus and keep His commandments.

T: To love Jesus means to act the way He acts. Where can we look to see how Jesus acts?

C: The Bible.

T: We will explore prayer a little more when we cover the Gifts of the Spirit [VII.C.]. Flip open the Book of Common Prayer, pages 228-229. A Collect is the short prayer said by a priest in each Sunday service just before we hear readings from the Bible. There are different Collects for different church seasons, each labeled "Proper" with a number. In this case, a "Proper" is a prayer that occurs at a particular point in time. What you are looking at are Propers 1 - 5 for the season of Pentecost. You will notice that, while each Collect is different, each has one phrase that is the same. What is that phrase that repeats?

C: "... through Jesus Christ our Lord, who lives and reigns with you and the Holy Spirit, one God, for ever and ever. Amen."

T: Flip the page and look at pages 230 – 231, Propers 6 -12. With slight variations, do you see the same language?

C: Yes.

T: I will represent that there are many more prayers in our prayer book that end the same way. Based on what you have seen, can you tell me if we pray in Jesus' Name in our Church?

C: Yes.

B. Early Church: for Jews only?

T: Before they were Christians, to what religion did Jesus' disciples belong? C: Judaism. T: When those disciples went out from Jerusalem to proclaim the Good News of salvation through Jesus Christ, who do you think they were most comfortable talking to? C: Jews. T: Right. And the Church may have remained a Jews-only organization had God not intervened to tell the disciples that they should take the Good News to the Gentiles – Gentiles means people who are not Jews. Let's see how God got the message to St. Peter, who was the leader of the Early Church after Jesus rose to be with His Father in Heaven. We are going to read from the Book of Acts, which chronicles the events of the early Church after Jesus' resurrection and ascension to Heaven. The Book of Acts was written by St. Luke, the same writer of one of the four Gospels.

Acts 10

1 There was a certain man in Caesarea called Cornelius, a centurion of the band called the Italian band,

T: What empire ruled Israel during the time of Jesus? C: Rome T: In the Roman Army, what was a centurion? C: An officer. T: A centurion commanded a "century" of about 80 soldiers, except the centurion of a legion's First Cohort, who commanded a century of about 160 men.[98] The First Cohort consisted of the most experienced soldiers, known for their valor. It was unusual for a centurion

---

[98] At the time of the early Church, during the reign of Tiberius, the standard cohort consisted of six centuries of 80 men each, or 480 men. There were ten cohorts in a legion, and, when added to the cavalry and support troops, brought the legion's strength to about 5,000. Each century was commanded by a centurion, and, within a cohort, each centurion was ranked by experience; the highest-ranking centurion, the *pilus prior*, commanded the entire cohort. During this time and continuing into the Late Roman era, some legions adopted the concept of the First Cohort consisting of five centuries of 160 men each, mostly proven veterans, for a total of 800 men. The most senior centurion of the First Cohort, the *primus pilus*, "enjoyed immense prestige, ... living in substantial houses rather than barrack rooms in a permanent camp." (*The Complete Roman Army*, Goldsworthy, Adrian, 2003, Thames &

to be allowed to bring his family with him while on duty, and that privilege was reserved only for those of the First Cohort. You will come to see that this centurion, Cornelius,[99] lives with his family in the Roman settlement of Caesarea. For that reason, Cornelius may be a centurion of the First Cohort.

2 A devout man, and one that feared God with all his house, which gave much alms to the people, and prayed to God alway.

3 He saw in a vision evidently about the ninth hour of the day an angel of God coming in to him, and saying unto him, Cornelius.

4 And when he looked on him, he was afraid, and said, What is it, Lord? And he said unto him, Thy prayers and thine alms are come up for a memorial before God.

5 And now send men to Joppa, and call for one Simon, whose surname is Peter:

6 He lodgeth with one Simon a tanner, whose house is by the sea side: he shall tell thee what thou oughtest to do.

7 And when the angel which spake unto Cornelius was departed, he called two of his household servants, and a devout soldier of them that waited on him continually;

8 And when he had declared all these things unto them, he sent them to Joppa.

T: Joppa is about 30 miles due south of Caesarea; both towns are on the Mediterranean coast of present-day Israel.

9 On the morrow, as they went on their journey, and drew nigh unto the city, Peter went up upon the housetop to pray about the sixth hour:

10 And he became very hungry, and would have eaten: but while they made ready, he fell into a trance,

---

Hudson, Ltd., p. 55). Based on the descriptions of Cornelius and his family in Acts 10, it is highly likely that Cornelius was a *primus pilus* or other high-ranking centurion in a prestigious position.
[99] For those who watched the miniseries, *Jesus of Nazareth*, the centurion in command of the crucifixion detail, played quite well by Ernest Borgnine, was named "Cornelius", but I have not found any record of that centurion's name in the crucifixion accounts, nor is there any indication that the Cornelius of Acts 10 was the centurion mentioned in Matthew 27:54, Mark 15:39 and Luke 23:47 who, upon seeing Jesus die, said "Truly this man was the Son of God."

11 And saw heaven opened, and a certain vessel descending unto him, as it had been a great sheet knit at the four corners, and let down to the earth:

12 Wherein were all manner of fourfooted beasts of the earth, and wild beasts, and creeping things, and fowls of the air.

13 And there came a voice to him, Rise, Peter; kill, and eat.

14 But Peter said, Not so, Lord; for I have never eaten any thing that is common or unclean.

> T: The animals in the vision were presumably prohibited to eat under Jewish law.

15 And the voice spake unto him again the second time, What God hath cleansed, that call not thou common.

16 This was done thrice: and the vessel was received up again into heaven.

17 Now while Peter doubted in himself what this vision which he had seen should mean, behold, the men which were sent from Cornelius had made enquiry for Simon's house, and stood before the gate,

18 And called, and asked whether Simon, which was surnamed Peter, were lodged there.

19 While Peter thought on the vision, the Spirit said unto him, Behold, three men seek thee.

20 Arise therefore, and get thee down, and go with them, doubting nothing: for I have sent them.

21 Then Peter went down to the men which were sent unto him from Cornelius; and said, Behold, I am he whom ye seek: what is the cause wherefore ye are come?

22 And they said, Cornelius the centurion, a just man, and one that feareth God, and of good report among all the nation of the Jews, was warned from God by an holy angel to send for thee into his house, and to hear words of thee.

23 Then called he them in, and lodged them. And on the morrow Peter went away with them, and certain brethren from Joppa accompanied him.

24 And the morrow after they entered into Caesarea. And Cornelius waited for them, and had called together his kinsmen and near friends.

25 And as Peter was coming in, Cornelius met him, and fell down at his feet, and worshipped him.

26 But Peter took him up, saying, Stand up; I myself also am a man.

27 And as he talked with him, he went in, and found many that were come together.

28 And he said unto them, Ye know how that it is an unlawful thing for a man that is a Jew to keep company, or come unto one of another nation; but God hath shewed me that I should not call any man common or unclean.

T: Stop here. For a Jew to enter into the house of a Gentile caused that Jew to become unclean, and, after doing so, the Jew had to undergo a purification process. But Peter knew to ignore that rule because God showed him that he "should not call any man common or unclean". What did God show Peter that told him he "should not call any man common or unclean"?

C: The vision Peter had of the animals.

---

29 Therefore came I unto you without gainsaying, as soon as I was sent for: I ask therefore for what intent ye have sent for me?

30 And Cornelius said, Four days ago I was fasting until this hour; and at the ninth hour I prayed in my house, and, behold, a man stood before me in bright clothing,

31 And said, Cornelius, thy prayer is heard, and thine alms are had in remembrance in the sight of God.

32 Send therefore to Joppa, and call hither Simon, whose surname is Peter; he is lodged in the house of one Simon a tanner by the sea side: who, when he cometh, shall speak unto thee.

33 Immediately therefore I sent to thee; and thou hast well done that thou art come. Now therefore are we all here present before God, to hear all things that are commanded thee of God.

34 Then Peter opened his mouth, and said, Of a truth I perceive that God is no respecter of persons:

35 But in every nation he that feareth him, and worketh righteousness, is accepted with him.

36 The word which God sent unto the children of Israel, preaching peace by Jesus Christ: (he is Lord of all:)

37 That word, I say, ye know, which was published throughout all Judaea, and began from Galilee, after the baptism which John preached;

38 How God anointed Jesus of Nazareth with the Holy Ghost and with power: who went about doing good, and healing all that were oppressed of the devil; for God was with him.

39 And we are witnesses of all things which he did both in the land of the Jews, and in Jerusalem; whom they slew and hanged on a tree:

T: Where did we see the reference to Jesus being "hanged on a tree"?

C: When we talked about St. Paul saying Jesus hanged on a tree to carry the curse of the Law. [Section V.A.b.]

---

40 Him God raised up the third day, and shewed him openly;

41 Not to all the people, but unto witnesses chosen before of God, even to us, who did eat and drink with him after he rose from the dead.

42 And he commanded us to preach unto the people, and to testify that it is he which was ordained of God to be the Judge of quick and dead.

43 To him give all the prophets witness, that through his name whosoever believeth in him shall receive remission of sins.

44 While Peter yet spake these words, the Holy Ghost fell on all them which heard the word.

45 And they of the circumcision which believed were astonished, as many as came with Peter, because that on the Gentiles also was poured out the gift of the Holy Ghost.

46 For they heard them speak with tongues, and magnify God.

T: Hold up here. In verse 45, who are "they of the circumcision"?

C: Those who are circumcised. The Jews.

T: A group of Jewish Christians accompanied Peter – see verse 23. This group saw something, described in verse 45, that astonished them. What was it?

C: The Gentiles received the "gift of the Holy Ghost".

T: Verse 46 tells you what that gift was …

C: "they heard them speak with tongues"

T: We will cover Gifts of the Spirit in the next section, but, for now, you should know that the gift of speaking with tongues was something the disciples knew well. They experienced that gift shortly before this encounter with Cornelius during the Jewish festival of Pentecost when Jews from many nations came to Jerusalem. There, the disciples spoke to them in their native languages – all without having studied or learned those languages![100]

Then answered Peter,

47 Can any man forbid water, that these should not be baptized, which have received the Holy Ghost as well as we?

48 And he commanded them to be baptized in the name of the Lord. Then prayed they him to tarry certain days.

T: So Peter and his Jewish Christian colleagues hear Cornelius and "his kinsmen and near friends" (described in verse 24), all Gentiles, speaking in languages the Gentiles do not understand, magnifying God. Peter recognizes that he is seeing an outpouring of the Holy Spirit, so what does he decide to do?

C: Baptize them.

---

[100] Acts 2.

T: Baptize the Gentiles, to be more precise. Up until this time, Christians were likely either Jews or Jewish converts. What do you think would have happened if Cornelius had not done as the angel instructed, or if Peter had refused to go to Cornelius' home because Cornelius was a Gentile?

C: The Christian Faith would be limited to Jews!

T: How many of you in this class are Jews?

C: [usually none, or very few]

T: Then, if Cornelius or Peter had failed to follow God's instructions, how many of you could become Christians, without first converting to Judaism?

C: None.[101]

T: Even though this series of events with Cornelius and Peter was amazing, the debate over whether Christians needed to be circumcised into the Jewish Faith continued, but the Christian Faith spread rapidly among all levels of Roman society, so those who "were of the circumcision" [Acts 11:2] were quickly overwhelmed, both by numbers and by arguments of St. Peter and, later, St. Paul.

C. Gifts of the Spirit

Authors Note

The Gifts of the Spirit discussion in this sub-section brings the class deeper into the topic of prayer, which we covered at a high level earlier in sub-section A. Time and other constraints do not allow a confirmation course to adequately address this important topic, but the Catechism does discuss prayer and emphasizes the role of the Holy Spirit, so I found it best to integrate aspects of prayer into the Gifts of the Spirit topic.

Specifically, the Catechism (BCP, p. 856) casts prayer as a "response to God":

Q. What is prayer?
A. Prayer is responding to God, by thought and by deeds, with or without words.

Q. What is Christian Prayer?
A. Christian prayer is response to God the Father, through Jesus Christ, in the power of the Holy Spirit

---

[101] This answer presumes God did not have a backup plan had Cornelius or Peter caved. I believe He would have found someone else, but I leave you to ponder this question to emphasize the importance of listening to and obeying the Holy Spirit.

The Catechism earlier (BCP, p. 853) states that "We recognize truths to be taught by the Holy Spirit when they are in accord with the Scriptures." Therefore, to respond to God, through Jesus, "in the power of the Holy Spirit", prayer must be grounded in Scripture.

The Catechism (BCP, p. 856) lists seven principal kinds of prayer: adoration, praise, thanksgiving, penitence, oblation, intercession, and petition. The Gifts of the Spirit may be employed in all areas of prayer, but the Gifts are best suited for the latter two principal kinds, which the Catechism (BCP, p. 857) defines accordingly: "Intercession brings before God the needs of others; in petition, we present our own needs, that God's will may be done." So the objective of using the Gifts in the context of intercession or petition prayer is to implement God's Will, and we discern (discernment is one of the Gifts) God's Will from Scripture.

This sub-section will show how the Gifts of the Spirit are used with intercession or petition prayer. Most importantly, though, this discussion ends with the need to build a picture of God's Will so that you are "responding to God", and Scripture teaches us that such a picture comes through the consistent application of prayer, meditation and fasting.

> T: Now let's look more closely at the gifts of the Holy Spirit with this passage from one of St. Paul's letters.

I Corinthians 12

1 Now concerning spiritual gifts, brethren, I would not have you ignorant.

2 Ye know that ye were Gentiles, carried away unto these dumb idols, even as ye were led.

3 Wherefore I give you to understand, that no man speaking by the Spirit of God calleth Jesus accursed: and that no man can say that Jesus is the Lord, but by the Holy Ghost.

4 Now there are diversities of gifts, but the same Spirit.

5 And there are differences of administrations, but the same Lord.

6 And there are diversities of operations, but it is the same God which worketh all in all.

7 But the manifestation of the Spirit is given to every man to profit withal.

8 For to one is given by the Spirit the word of wisdom; to another the word of knowledge by the same Spirit;

9 To another faith by the same Spirit; to another the gifts of healing by the same Spirit;

10 To another the working of miracles; to another prophecy; to another discerning of spirits; to another divers kinds of tongues; to another the interpretation of tongues:

11 But all these worketh that one and the selfsame Spirit, dividing to every man severally as he will.

12 For as the body is one, and hath many members, and all the members of that one body, being many, are one body: so also is Christ.

13 For by one Spirit are we all baptized into one body, whether we be Jews or Gentiles, whether we be bond or free; and have been all made to drink into one Spirit.

Verses 8-10 set out the following gifts of the Spirit:

1. Wisdom
2. Knowledge
3. Faith
4. Healing
5. Miracles
6. Prophecy
7. Discernment
8. Tongues
9. Interpretation

T: Which of these gifts of the Holy Spirit appeared at the home of Cornelius when St. Peter was talking?

C: Tongues [Acts 10:46]

T: For the early Church, speaking in unknown tongues was a clear sign of God's presence. We read this earlier, but for reference, here is how St. Luke described the scene at Cornelius' house:

Acts 10

44 While Peter yet spake these words, the Holy Ghost fell on all them which heard the word.

45 And they of the circumcision which believed were astonished, as many as came with Peter, because that on the Gentiles also was poured out the gift of the Holy Ghost.

46 For they heard them speak with tongues, and magnify God.

T: As we read verse 44 before, remember that St. Peter had just told Cornelius and his household about Jesus rising from the dead on the third day, that is, Easter. How did St. Luke, the author of the book of Acts, describe in verse 44 what happened to the non-Jewish Christians when Peter spoke about the resurrection?

C: "the Holy Ghost fell on all them which heard the word."

T: Look at verse 45: why were the Jewish Christians "astonished"?

C: Because "on the Gentiles also was poured out the gift of the Holy Ghost".

T: So the Holy Spirit either "fell upon" the Gentile Christians or the Holy Spirit "was poured out" on the Gentile Christians. How could the Jewish Christians tell that the Holy Spirit fell upon or was poured out on the Gentile Christians? What in verse 46 tells us what the Jewish Christians experienced?

C: They heard the Gentile Christians speaking with tongues and magnifying God.

T: So, what purpose does the gift of speaking in Tongues serve?

C: It is a sign of the presence of the Holy Spirit.

T: Does the person speaking in unknown tongues know what he is saying?

C: No.

T: Right – the language is unknown to the speaker. But here's the problem with speaking in tongues: if the speaker does not know what the speaker is saying, and if no one happens to know the language the speaker is using, then what purpose does it serve?

C: Well, it is still a sign from the Holy Spirit.

T: Yes, but is there a way to translate the message from a speaker in unknown tongues? Hint: look at the list of gifts of the Spirit.

C: Interpretation of tongues.

T: Right. Let's look at the rest of the list, but a little out of order. What do you think is the gift of Knowledge?

C: Knowing stuff.

T: Knowing stuff at the moment you need to know stuff. Like studying for a test at school and then taking the test. Does it do you any good if you study and then forget everything on the day of the test?

C: No.

T: So timing is important. The Holy Spirit can help you recall important information, when you need that information. Now move up to Wisdom on the list. What is Wisdom?

C: Knowing lots of stuff?

T: It's more than that. It's closer to knowing how to <u>apply</u> the knowledge that you have. Drawing on Knowledge, Wisdom tells you what to do, what to say, and when you need to do or say it. Have you ever felt down in the dumps and had a friend tell you something that changes your mood?

C: [Nods].

T: Well, when that friend knew what to say and when to say it, the friend was using Wisdom. I find Wisdom and Knowledge work hand-in-hand. The gift of Wisdom can help you discern what to study for a test; the gift of Knowledge helps you recall what you studied when you take the test. Do you remember the curses and the blessings under the Old Testament Law?[102]

C: Sort of – there were lots of them.

T: I'm thinking of one blessing in particular:

> Deuteronomy 28
>
> 13 And the LORD shall make thee the head, and not the tail; and thou shalt be above only, and thou shalt not be beneath; if that thou hearken unto the commandments of the LORD thy God, which I command thee this day, to observe and to do them:
>
> 14 And thou shalt not go aside from any of the words which I command thee this day, to the right hand, or to the left, to go after other gods to serve them.

T: So, "hearken unto the commandments of the LORD thy God", God has promised to make you "the head, and not the tail" and "above only", not beneath. In school, where do you think this applies?

C: Class rankings.

T: Yes, though it can apply more generally. As you pursue your own goals, whether they are academic, athletic, artistic, or whatever your goals are, you should be "the head" and "above only", not necessarily ahead of everyone else, but ahead in pursuit of your personal goals. In sports, do you know what "personal best" means?

C: The fastest time or best personal score that an athlete achieves in competition.

T: So, if an athlete is operating under the blessings of the Law and is "above only", what is happening to his or her personal best time or score?

---

[102] Section V.A.a.

C: It's constantly improving.

T: Right. Now here is a memory test: what entitles you, a Christian, to the blessings of the Old Testament Law?

C: Umm ....

T: I'll help you out. Turn to:[103]

> Galatians 3
>
> 13 Christ hath redeemed us from the curse of the law, being made a curse for us: for it is written, Cursed is every one that hangeth on a tree:
>
> 14 That the blessing of Abraham might come on the Gentiles through Jesus Christ; that we might receive the promise of the Spirit through faith.

T: What tree did Jesus hang on?

C: The cross.

T: So when Jesus went to the cross, what does verse 14 say we should receive?

C: "the blessing of Abraham".

T: From the passage in Deuteronomy 28 that we just read, what was the blessing that applies to your work in school and on the athletic field?

C: That we will be "the head, and not the tail".

T: And back to Galatians 3:14, the last half of the verse says that "we might receive the promise of the Spirit through faith". Now think back to what we just talked about regarding the gifts of the Spirit. What gifts of the Spirit could help you become "the head, and not the tail"?

C: The gifts of Wisdom and Knowledge.

T: And what are the last two words of Galatians 3:14?

C: "through faith."

T: So let's look at the gift of Faith.

---

[103] Discussed in Section V.A.b.

Luke 17 [104]

5 And the apostles said unto the Lord, Increase our faith.

6 And the Lord said, If ye had faith as a grain of mustard seed, ye might say unto this sycamine tree, Be thou plucked up by the root, and be thou planted in the sea; and it should obey you.

T: How big is a mustard seed? [105]

Draw on whiteboard: •

C: Not large!

T: So the quantity of faith needed for prayer is small. But how do we build that small amount of faith needed? Let's take a look at St. Paul describing why God sent preachers to the Israelites:

Romans 10

17 So then faith cometh by hearing, and hearing by the word of God.

T: What is the source of faith?

C: The word of God.

T: Remember back to what we read about God's instruction to Joshua? [106]

Joshua 1

1 Now after the death of Moses the servant of the LORD it came to pass, that the LORD spake unto Joshua the son of Nun, Moses' minister, saying,

2 Moses my servant is dead; now therefore arise, go over this Jordan, thou, and all this people, unto the land which I do give to them, even to the children of Israel.

3 Every place that the sole of your foot shall tread upon, that have I given unto you, as I said unto Moses.

---

[104] A similar account of this parable is found in Matthew 17:20, where Jesus refers to moving a mountain by faith the size of a mustard seed.
[105] If you can get to a store or order ahead from an internet retailer, you can pass out some mustard seeds. They are usually found in the spice section of the store.
[106] Covered in Section V.A.b.

4 From the wilderness and this Lebanon even unto the great river, the river Euphrates, all the land of the Hittites, and unto the great sea toward the going down of the sun, shall be your coast.

5 There shall not any man be able to stand before thee all the days of thy life: as I was with Moses, so I will be with thee: I will not fail thee, nor forsake thee.

6 Be strong and of a good courage: for unto this people shalt thou divide for an inheritance the land, which I sware unto their fathers to give them.

7 Only be thou strong and very courageous, that thou mayest observe to do according to all the law, which Moses my servant commanded thee: turn not from it to the right hand or to the left, that thou mayest prosper whithersoever thou goest.

8 This book of the law shall not depart out of thy mouth; but thou shalt meditate therein day and night, that thou mayest observe to do according to all that is written therein: for then thou shalt make thy way prosperous, and then thou shalt have good success.

9 Have not I commanded thee? Be strong and of a good courage; be not afraid, neither be thou dismayed: for the LORD thy God is with thee whithersoever thou goest.

T: So based on what God told Joshua, what should you do to have "good success"?

C: Meditate, day and night. [Verse 8]

T: Meditate on what?

C: The "book of the law".

T: For Christians, what is our "book of the law"?

C: The Bible.

T: Both Old and New Testaments.[107] So combine Romans 10 with Joshua 1: Faith comes by hearing God's Word, and you "hear", or learn, God's Word by doing what?

---

[107] The "book of the law" for Christians is found in the New Testament. John 13:34 states: "A new commandment [law] I give unto you, That ye love one another; as I have loved you, that ye also love one another." However, there are parts of the Old Testament that still apply to us: Galatians 3:13-14: "Christ hath redeemed us from the curse of the law, being made a curse for us: for it is written, Cursed is every one that hangeth on a tree: That the blessing of Abraham might come on the Gentiles through Jesus Christ; that we might receive the promise of the Spirit through faith." Also, the Old Testament

C: Meditating in God's Word day and night.

T: It is through the process of meditating on God's Word that you receive the gift of Faith. Think about what we just read, if you meditate on God's Word a lot, what will happen?

C: You'll get to know it very well.

T: And, if you know God's Word well, you can incorporate that Word into your prayers. I'll give you a hint: if you know God's Word very well, you can construct prayers that are almost entirely built from the Word! Quite a few prayers in our Book of Common Prayer are constructed that way. Using this approach, though, can you ever pray a prayer that does not agree with God's Word?

C: No.

T: So, you are only asking for things that are found in Scripture. We will now look at the two remaining gifts of the Holy Spirit: Healing and Miracles. Is healing found in Scripture?

C: I think so.

T: Actually, in the Gospels alone, numerous healings are recorded. Most of the Gospel healings were done by Jesus, though the disciples reported many healings done by themselves as well.[108] But to learn what to do to pray effectively for healing, let's learn from what happened when things went wrong and prayer wasn't answered.[109]

Mark 9

15 And straightway all the people, when they beheld [Jesus], were greatly amazed, and running to him saluted him.

16 And he asked the scribes, What question ye with them?

17 And one of the multitude answered and said, Master, I have brought unto thee my son, which hath a dumb spirit;[110]

---

law both shows us the nature of sin and our inability to escape judgment without faith in Jesus. Romans 3:19-20 is instructive here: "Now we know that what things soever the law saith, it saith to them who are under the law: that every mouth may be stopped, and all the world may become guilty before God. Therefore by the deeds of the law there shall no flesh be justified in his sight: for by the law is the knowledge of sin."

[108] See Luke 10:1-20 for an account of Jesus sending disciples out to preach and to heal and, upon their return, hearing them say, "even the devils are subject unto us through thy name."

[109] A wise lawyer told me that, while it is good to learn from your mistakes, it is even better to learn from other people's mistakes!

[110] The son was described as a "lunatic" in a parallel account found in Matthew 17:14-21.

18 And wheresoever he taketh him, he teareth him: and he foameth, and gnasheth with his teeth, and pineth away: and I spake to thy disciples that they should cast him out; and they could not.

19 He answereth him, and saith, O faithless generation, how long shall I be with you? how long shall I suffer you? bring him unto me.

20 And they brought him unto him: and when he saw him, straightway the spirit tare him; and he fell on the ground, and wallowed foaming.

21 And he asked his father, How long is it ago since this came unto him? And he said, Of a child.

22 And ofttimes it hath cast him into the fire, and into the waters, to destroy him: but if thou canst do any thing, have compassion on us, and help us.

23 Jesus said unto him, If thou canst believe, all things are possible to him that believeth.

24 And straightway the father of the child cried out, and said with tears, Lord, I believe; help thou mine unbelief.

25 When Jesus saw that the people came running together, he rebuked the foul spirit, saying unto him, Thou dumb and deaf spirit, I charge thee, come out of him, and enter no more into him.

26 And the spirit cried, and rent him sore, and came out of him: and he was as one dead; insomuch that many said, He is dead.

27 But Jesus took him by the hand, and lifted him up; and he arose.

28 And when he was come into the house, his disciples asked him privately, Why could not we cast him out?

29 And he said unto them, This kind can come forth by nothing, but by prayer and fasting.

T: So, a father came to the disciples with his son, who was deaf and dumb and, apparently, suicidal in that the son attempted to injure himself with fire and water. The term for such mental illness at the time was "demonic possession". Were the disciples able to cast the evil spirit out of the son and cure the illness?

C: No.

T: What did the father do next?

C: He brought his son to Jesus.

T: Jesus asked the father how long had the evil spirit been in the son. From verse 21, when did the possession start?

C: When the son was a child.

T: From the context of the account, we can assume the son was an adult when he was brought to Jesus, so the evil spirit had been in the son for a long time. This healing was not going to be easy![111] Did Jesus succeed?

C: Yes.

T: Then the disciples did what any of us would have done when they prayed for healing and did not get the result they wanted, what was that?

C: They asked Jesus why.

T: And what was Jesus' answer in verse 29?

C: "This kind can come forth by nothing, but by prayer and fasting."

T: To the disciples who heard this, the phrase "prayer and fasting" meant a period of conversation with God, over days or even weeks, while abstaining from normal duties and pleasures.[112] In other words, Jesus built His faith through a routine of time spent with talking to God and listening for His response, while not letting everyday life and problems get in the way. Now remember from our readings in Joshua, what else should we do, day and night, to build our faith?

C: Meditate in God's Word.

T: So meditation, prayer and fasting are the faith-building tools we use to tackle tough problems. Now look at what else Jesus talked about in this passage; in verse 23, he said this to the father of the man needing healing: "If thou canst believe, all things are possible to him that believeth." What was Jesus talking about?

C: Believe and then all things are possible.

---

[111] The context of this encounter with Jesus, in verse 16, is that scribes, or religious lawyers, were questioning the disciples while the disciples were attempting to heal the father's son. I will leave it to you to determine whether the role of legalistic theologians was hindering the application of faith!

[112] The prophet Daniel prayed for an end to the Babylonian Captivity and forgiveness of Israel's sins, saying "... I set my face unto the Lord God, to seek by prayer and supplications, with fasting, and sackcloth, and ashes" (Daniel 9:3). The answer he received went well beyond return to Jerusalem and restoration of the Second Temple; the angel Gabriel set out the timeline for the coming of the Messiah! Likewise, the disciples would have known that other Old Testament prophets employed prayer and fasting.

T: Believe how? Here, Jesus is asking the father to believe that something will happen. What?

C: That his son will be healed.

T: So Jesus is asking the father to lock on to a picture that is different than the current one. The current picture is the son that "foameth, and gnasheth with his teeth, and pineth away" (in verse 18). What is the picture Jesus wanted the father to see?

C: A healed son.

T: That's what Jesus was asking the father to believe. And the father got the picture and, in verse 24, "said with tears, Lord, I believe; help thou mine unbelief". <u>Meditating, praying and fasting until you get the picture of God's solution to a problem is not just a demonstration of the spiritual gift of Healing, it is also the key to all other answered prayer, including the gift of Miracles.</u> The gifts of Healing and Miracles, then, are closely linked and have their root in the same practice of spiritual discipline.

VIII. Christian Apologetics within and without Scripture

A. Authority of the Scriptures

Learning Objectives

1. Confirmands will understand that Scripture is inspired by God.
2. Confirmands will understand that the New Testament canon developed over a period of three centuries after the Resurrection under the guidance of the Holy Spirit.

a. God-breathed Scriptures

T: We have talked a lot about meditating on Scripture, but what is Scripture's purpose? Let's look at how St. Paul described Scripture to his young assistant, St. Timothy:

> II Timothy 3
>
> 14 But continue thou in the things which thou hast learned and hast been assured of, knowing of whom thou hast learned them;
>
> 15 And that from a child thou hast known the holy Scriptures, which are able to make thee wise unto salvation through faith which is in Christ Jesus.
>
> 16 All Scripture is given by inspiration of God, and is profitable for doctrine, for reproof, for correction, for instruction in righteousness:
>
> 17 That the man of God may be perfect, throughly furnished unto all good works.

T: Look at verse 16. Where does Scripture come from?

C: Inspiration of God.

T: The Amplified Bible translates the first part of that verse as "Every Scripture is God-breathed".[113] Who does God breath on to create Scripture?

C: Disciples?

T: For the New Testament, yes. Many were people who met and followed Jesus during His time on Earth, with one notable exception, St. Paul, who converted later after first persecuting

---

[113] II Timothy 3:16 taken from the Amplified Bible, Copyright © 1954, 1958, 1962, 1964, 1965, 1987 by The Lockman Foundation. Used by permission.

Christians.[114] So God breathed on these writers, or inspired these writers as the King James translation states.[115] If someone inspires you to write something, did that person tell you precisely what to write or just give you an idea about what to write?

C: Gave just the idea.

T: Does that mean that as the writers wrote out their gospels and epistles, God was whispering in their ears so that they could take down each word precisely as God spoke?

C: No.

T: That's why we say Scripture was "God-breathed"; it is not dictation but is inspired by God. For this reason, you can find multiple accounts of the same event, such as the crucifixion of Jesus for example, but while one writer may quote Jesus' last words as "It is finished", referring to His role as fulfilling the requirements of Old Testament Law,[116] another writer quotes Jesus as last saying from the cross "Father, into thy hands I commend my spirit",[117] quoting from a Psalm of David to show His trust in His Father.[118] Which is right?

C: Both? Neither?

T: Both are simply different perspectives from two different writers, St. John and St. Luke. Jesus likely made both statements, but which words were precisely His last is up for debate. This example is an illustration of the types of discussions we Christians get into because Scripture is the inspired Word of God, not the dictated Word of God. Indeed, the other two Gospels record Jesus last saying "Eli, Eli, lama sabachthani? that is to say, My God, my God, why hast thou forsaken me?",[119] so we have at least three versions of the final words of Jesus before His death on the cross. How could that have happened?

C: Some people may have heard Jesus say one thing but not heard another.

T: The crucifixion had to be a tumultuous scene with the Roman centurion commanding a unit of soldiers,[120] priests yelling at Jesus,[121] while all Jesus' acquaintances "stood afar off".[122] In the final analysis, though, does it matter to you which were Jesus' precise last words?

C: Probably not.

T: Right. The differences are simply different accounts of the same event from the perspectives of different writers, and each has something to offer us.

---

[114] See Acts 9:1-22.
[115] The Catechism at BCP p. 853 states:
    Q. Why do we call the Holy Scriptures the Word of God?
    A. We call them the Word of God because God inspired their human authors
    and because God still speaks to us through the Bible.
[116] John 19:30.
[117] Luke 23:46.
[118] Psalm 31:5.
[119] Matthew 27:46 and Mark 15:34. Here, Jesus is quoting from another Davidic Psalm, 22:1.
[120] Matthew 27:54.
[121] Matthew 27:41-43.
[122] Luke 23:49.

b. Development of the Canon

> T: How many books of the New Testament are there?
>
> C: [Flipping to the table of contents and counting] 27.
>
> T: Correct. The 27 books of the New Testament are considered "canon", or the authorized list of books. But how did we get the current canonical books of the New Testament? And why aren't there other books? Did a group of early Christians sit around a table, pass around copies of the Gospels, the Epistles and any other writings that existed at the time and then vote on what got in the Bible and what didn't?
>
> C: That seems reasonable.
>
> T: Well, that's not quite what happened! The books that comprise the New Testament we use today were adopted by early Christians in the first few centuries of the early Church, then those Gospels and Epistles [123] in wide-spread use were simply ratified at various Church councils held in the fourth century. To see this, let's look at the *Timechart*.

The canonical books of the New Testament number 27. That number started as a smaller set in use by the earliest of Christians and then grew slowly over the next three centuries. To illustrate this growth, label self-stick flags with the following numbers: 8, 10, 13, 23, 23, 20 and 27. Each flag represents the number of books of the New Testament in use at a given point in time. Go to Panel XI of the *Timechart* and locate the following early Church fathers in the area above the timeline and place the appropriate flag near each name:

Church Father	Number of Books Acknowledged	Background Notes
Clement of Rome	8	In an epistle titled *I Clement* written to Christians in Corinth around 95 A.D., he references passages in the three Synoptic Gospels (Matthew, Mark and Luke) as well as several of St. Paul's letters. Interestingly, Clement references the Pauline epistles as though they were as readily available in Corinth as in Rome, implying their widespread use and acceptance before the end of the first century A.D.[124]
Ignatius	10[125]	Ignatius was martyred in Rome in 110 A.D., after passing through provinces in modern-day Turkey on his way (the *Timechart* shows the date as 107, so there is some uncertainty). He wrote

---

[123] For shorthand, my reference to "Gospels and Epistles" does not specifically mention the Book of the Acts of the Apostles, which many consider a class of New Testament Scripture unto itself. I do not disagree, but for convenience, I will include Acts with the Epistles since it is indeed a letter from Luke to Theophilus.

[124] Metzger, Bruce, *The Canon of the New Testament*, Oxford, 1987, © Bruce M. Metzger, 1987, pp.40-43. Reproduced with permission of the Licensor through PLSclear.

[125] *Id.*, p. 49.

		several letters while on this trip, which reference passages from numerous Gospels and epistles. He met with Polycarp while in Smyrna (present-day Izmir).[126] Ignatius probably traveled further north through Bithynia. Bithynia was governed at the time by Pliny the Younger, who in 112 A.D. wrote a letter to Emperor Trajan complaining about how widely the Christian Faith had spread. We will read correspondence between Pliny and Trajan in the next subsection.
Polycarp	13	Polycarp, bishop of Smyrna, was inspired by the martyrdom of Ignatius to write to Christians in Philippi, where Ignatius had traveled on his way to Rome. His letters cited many Pauline epistles as well as Hebrews and I John.[127]
Irenæus	23	Irenæus lived at a time of great persecution of the Christian Church in Lyons around 177 A.D. During this time, he created one opus citing 1,075 passages from most of the current New Testament books.[128]
Tertullian	23[129]	Tertullian was a highly educated lawyer who converted to Christianity late in the second century A.D. He developed the concept of the "Rule of Faith", by which he meant the fundamental belief of the Church passed down through generations in the form of the baptismal covenant expressed as the Apostles Creed.[130] He wrote extensively.
Cyprian	20	Cyprian, Bishop of Carthage, produced a large body of written work and, in the process, quoted about one-ninth of present-day New Testament Scripture. He did not quote from Hebrews and a few other books, however. Cyprian likely knew of Hebrews by reading Tertullian's writings but did not consider it canonical. The other six omitted books (Philemon, James, II Peter, II and III John and Jude) may not have had application to his subject matter and thus were likely skipped,

---

[126] *Id.*, p. 59.
[127] *Id.*, p. 62.
[128] *Id.*, p. 154.
[129] *Id.*, p. 160.
[130] *Id.*, p. 158.

		and we can draw no inference on his view of their canonicity.[131]
Athanasius	27	Athanasius, then Bishop of Alexandria, drew upon the astronomical scholars resident in his city to develop a process to determine the date for Easter. In his 39th annual Easter letter of 367, he listed the canonical books of the Old and New Testaments, and the books cited are those we have today.[132] The canon was later confirmed by Jerome[133] and Augustine of Hippo.[134]

Then, when the above names are flagged, note the progression over time. The progression is not chronologically accretive, which demonstrates that there was some disagreement on the composition of the New Testament. That discussion, though, reached a conclusion during the time of St. Athanasius and was confirmed at the Synods of Hippo in 393 A.D. and of Carthage in 397 and 419 A.D.

T: Where have we seen St. Athanasius before?

C: Was he the author of that long creed?

T: Close. We are not sure who wrote the creed, but the third creed was named after St. Athanasius and is found on pages 864-865 of the Book of Common Prayer. He also provided a list of what would become the canonical books of the New Testament. This list was finally approved as canon at a council of Church Fathers at the Synod of Hippo in 393 A.D.[135] But over how many years had the early Church been using books of the New Testament before the meeting in Carthage? Look at the first person on the timeline to provide a list of books: St. Clement. When did he die? [Hint: look at Panel XI, near the feet of the picture of Jesus.]

C: 101 A.D., though there is a "?" near the date.

T: It's an approximate date. A few years before his death, he wrote a long letter in 95 A.D. that cited 8 Gospels and Epistles, which we just talked about. From St. Clement's letter of 95 A.D. to the Synod of Hippo in 393 A.D. is how many years?

C: Nearly 300 years; 298 years.

T: So the authoritative canonical list of books of the New Testament developed over about three centuries of use by the early Church. When we finally get to the Synod of Hippo in 393 A.D., all that was left to do was ratify what had already been in use. No single group of all-wise theologians gathered around a table deciding which books were in or out of the New Testament, just a long line of early Christians over time gravitating toward using certain

---

[131] *Id.*, p. 161-162.
[132] *Id.*, p. 211-212.
[133] *Id.*, p. 236.
[134] *Id.*, p. 237.
[135] As noted earlier, there were three synods that confirmed the canonicity of Scripture. For simplification, I chose to discuss the first synod only. Unfortunately, this council does not appear on the Timechart. Note that St. Athanasius died twenty years earlier, in 373 A.D.

books and not using others.[136] But who guided these early Christians when looking at what would be considered Holy Scripture? Was it an accident that the set of books cited by St. Clement in 95 A.D. wound up in the same list cited by St. Athanasius three hundred years later?

C: Probably not!

T: Who guided St. Clement and St. Athanasius and all the others over that time as to which books they would choose to rely upon?

C: God.

T: Through His Holy Spirit. Why would God be so interested in what becomes considered Holy Scripture?

C: It's His book!

T: As we have already seen, God takes His Word very seriously. St. John tells us that Jesus is the expression of God's Word.[137] The Holy Spirit came to guide us "into all truth."[138] Therefore, the Holy Spirit guided these early Christians into the truth of the canon they, and we, will use to understand our Lord.

B. Extra-Biblical Texts and the Resurrection

Author's Note

Over the years, this section of the course has proven to be the most popular with confirmands. There are likely several reasons why that is the case. The reason I can most clearly identify, though, springs from popular culture's treatment of all religions as silly superstitions without factual basis. When, in this subsection, however, I lay out historical evidence of the

---

[136] From the writings of St. Augustine, we can infer that the process of developing the canon of Scripture appeared to be a combination of how popular a particular book was and how much authoritative weight was given to the church using that book:
> [The Christian reader] will hold fast therefore to this measure in the canonical Scriptures, that he will prefer those that are received by all Catholic Churches to those which some of them do not receive. Among those, again, which are received by all, let him prefer those which the more numerous and the weightier churches receive to those which fewer and less authoritative churches hold. But if, however, he finds some held by the more numerous, and some held by the churches of more authority (though this is not very likely to happen), I think that in such a case they ought to be regarded as of equal authority (*de Doctrina Christiana*, bk. ii. 12).

[137] John 1:1: "In the beginning was the Word, and the Word was with God, and the Word was God." John 1:14: "And the Word was made flesh, and dwelt among us, (and we beheld his glory, the glory as of the only begotten of the Father,) full of grace and truth."

[138] John 16:13: "Howbeit when he, the Spirit of truth, is come, he will guide you into all truth: for he shall not speak of himself; but whatsoever he shall hear, that shall he speak: and he will shew you things to come."

Resurrection from people who never were Christians, the confirmands' eyes light up because they now find there is evidence outside the Bible and Christian writings.

No doubt, many confirmands have come or will come to know Jesus as a personal savior through faith, exhibited in an experiential individual encounter with the Risen Lord. I know from my attempts as a teenager to share my faith, though, that it is very difficult to convey that experience to non-believers, and I find today's teenagers face the same issue. This section and the next arm confirmands with additional arguments found in the realm of reason. The first set of arguments, presented in this subsection, relates to extra-biblical texts. To see how these arguments are made in an academic setting, I recommend that you view the following Veritas Forum talk by Paul Maier: https://www.youtube.com/watch?v=XAN3kQHT-KWI#action=share. In the following section, we will explore a second set of arguments derived from C.S. Lewis which look inward to simple, rational conclusions based on what a person knows from his or her own experience.

Learning Objectives

1. Confirmands will learn that Extra-Biblical historical evidence, particularly evidence from historians who were never Christians, provides the following findings:
    a. A person calling himself "Christ" preached in Judea, when Pontius Pilate was Prefect, and attracted a significant number of believers.
    b. During Pilate's tenure as Prefect, and during the reign of Roman Emperor Tiberius, Pilate ordered the crucifixion of Christ.
    c. Roman authorities subsequently outlawed the Christian Faith and attempted to eradicate the religion through vicious persecution during the first decades after Jesus was crucified.
    d. By the early second century A.D., however, the Christian Faith had spread so quickly throughout Roman society that Emperor Trajan had to adopt a "don't ask; don't tell" policy that tolerated Christians as long as the Christ-followers kept their beliefs secret.
2. Confirmands will understand that many early Christians, some of whom claimed they saw the Risen Jesus, others who may have come one or two lifespans later, endured horrific torture and death, especially under Roman Emperor Nero, yet did not recant their faith, and that the martyrs' steadfast determination had to be grounded in something worth dying for: their unwavering belief in Jesus' Resurrection.
3. Confirmands will understand that the testimony of the Christian martyrs provides us today with strong evidence that Jesus did indeed rise from the dead!

T: Most every document we have read from so far in this course has come from or was adopted by a Christian source. Our New Testament readings were written by early Christians in the late first century A.D. Even our readings from the Old Testament were translated from the original Hebrew into Greek,[139] Latin,[140] and, later, the Shakespearian English we encounter in the King James Version of the Bible.[141] But what did non-Christians who lived around the time of Christ have to say about our Faith?

C: Not nice things?

T: Mostly, but what they did say speaks volumes about what was happening. First, let's focus on non-Christians who never converted to Christianity. These writers would certainly be impartial, if not down-right antagonistic, towards our Faith. Second, let's focus on the resurrection and the time immediately thereafter. For the most part, these non-Christian writers denied that Jesus rose from the dead, and they thought the early Christians who believed in the resurrection to be fools. But these non-Christians described persecutions of the early Christians that would point to something unique and special that caused the early Christians to endure these persecutions. To start, what was the official religion of Rome at the time of Jesus in the first century A.D.?[142]

C: Worshipping lots of gods.

T: Remember your ancient history? Some of the Roman gods were:

- **Jupiter**: The mighty king of the gods. Husband of Juno.
- **Neptune**: One of the brothers of Jupiter, one of the prime gods and ruler of the seas.
- **Juno**: Queen of the Gods and wife of Jupiter. Goddess of Marriage and Women. Protector and Counsellor of Rome.
- **Mars**: God of War, Spring and Justice. Patron of the Roman Legions and divine father of Romulus and Remus.

---

[139] The most significant Greek translation of the Old Testament was begun under a Greek king of Egypt, Ptolemy II (the son of one of Alexander the Great's generals) in the third century B.C. and was completed in 132 B.C. Over seventy Jewish scholars worked on the translation, which acquired the name "Septuagint", from the Latin title, *versio septuaginta interpretum*, "translation of the seventy interpreters". Many New Testament quotations of the Old Testament quote directly from the Septuagint, including Jesus' Old Testament references, implying the Septuagint was widely used and accepted during the first century A.D.

[140] In the fourth century A.D., St. Jerome translated the Old Testament into Latin, mostly using the Hebrew texts. St. Jerome's translation became known as the *versio vulgata* (the "version commonly used"), or the "Vulgate".

[141] King James I of England commissioned a translation of the Bible into English in 1604, and the work was completed by 1611, using the Septuagint and the Vulgate as sources, among others. King Henry VIII, though, had earlier commissioned an English translation in 1539, called the "Great Bible". The Church of England first used the Great Bible in early services and then moved to incorporate readings from the King James Bible into subsequent versions of the Book of Common Prayer. Those confirmands who have read Shakespearian plays in school will recognize the similarities of reading the King James Version with the Elizabethan English of William Shakespeare, who lived from 1564 to 1616.

[142] Based upon archeological discoveries of the number of temple ruins and artifacts found in ancient cities of the Roman Empire, there were a surprising number of worshipers of Egyptian and other, non-Roman gods, in addition to the Roman gods, during the first century A.D. For an excellent summary and analysis of those findings, see *Cities of God* by Rodney Stark, HarperCollins, 2006. I refer to worship of Roman gods as "the" official religion in this discussion as a simplification.

> - **Venus**: Goddess of Love and consort of Mars. Divine mother of Aeneas, ancestor of the Romans.

> Each god had a role to play in the workings of the Universe, and, for the most part, the gods treated humans as toys to be played with at their pleasure. Humans, then, were constantly trying to placate the gods with offerings and obeisance. Was Jesus or God the Father on that list of official gods?
>
> C: No.
>
> T: So Christianity was not the official religion and was outlawed.[143] Keeping that in mind, let's begin with the Roman historian Tacitus, from whom we read previously about the destruction of the Second Temple in *Handout #2*. In *Handout #4*, Tacitus is describing actions taken by the Roman Emperor Nero in 64 A.D. to deflect criticism that Nero "fiddled while Rome burned" in a fire that destroyed much of the city. This is about 30 years after the crucifixion of Jesus, and Christianity had spread to Rome with the Good News of Jesus having risen from the dead. Nero's plan was to blame the new religious sect with setting the massive fire, though he had no proof that Christians did so, and rumors spread that Nero was responsible.

Handout #4

THE ANNALS, Book XV, by Gaius Cornelius Tacitus, c. 56 A.D. – c. 120 A.D.

1. Consequently, to get rid of the report [that Nero purposely set fire to Rome], Nero fastened the guilt and inflicted the most exquisite tortures on a class hated for their abominations, called Christians by the populace.
2. Christus, from whom the name had its origin, suffered the extreme penalty during the reign of Tiberius at the hands of one of our procurators, Pontius Pilatus, and a most mischievous superstition, thus checked for the moment, again broke out not only in Judaea, the first source of the evil, but even in Rome, where all things hideous and shameful from every part of the world find their center and become popular.
3. Accordingly, an arrest was first made of all who pleaded guilty; then, upon their information, an immense multitude was convicted, not so much of the crime of firing the city, as of hatred against mankind.
4. Mockery of every sort was added to their deaths. Covered with the skins of beasts, they were torn by dogs and perished, or were

---

[143] Romans also accepted foreign religions of peoples they conquered, hence the presence of non-Roman gods discussed in the previous footnote. For example, Roman authorities allowed the Jews to continue to worship their one God after Judea was conquered, as long as the local population was relatively peaceful. (This arrangement came to an abrupt end after the defeat of the Jewish rebellion of 68 – 70 A.D and the destruction of the Second Temple.) Roman authorities, though, had difficulty with anyone wishing to convert to an unrecognized faith such as Christianity, which they considered "superstition", as we will see later in this section when discussing writings of Roman historians.

nailed to crosses, or were doomed to the flames and burnt, to serve as a nightly illumination, when daylight had expired.
5. Nero offered his gardens for the spectacle, and was exhibiting a show in the circus, while he mingled with the people in the dress of a charioteer or stood aloft on a car.
6. Hence, even for criminals who deserved extreme and exemplary punishment, there arose a feeling of compassion; for it was not, as it seemed, for the public good, but to glut one man's cruelty, that they were being destroyed.

Source: Tacitus, *Annales*, Book 15, paragraph 44. Numbers preceding each paragraph were not in the original but added to make references easier.

T: Look first at paragraph 2. What did Tacitus say about Jesus' crucifixion?

C: It was the "extreme penalty".

T: And who inflicted that penalty?

C: Pontius Pilatus.

T: Know to us as ...

C: Pontius Pilate.

T: And Tacitus places the time of Jesus' crucifixion during the reign of what Roman Emperor?

C: Tiberius.

Look at the *Timechart* Panel XI. Place a ruler on the date of Jesus' crucifixion at 33 A.D. (just below the timeline on the chart) and look down the ruler to the line of Roman rulers near the bottom of the chart. Read the name of the Roman ruler at the time of Jesus' death: Tiberius. You can locate Nero, a little to the right.

T: So Tacitus fixed the crucifixion of Jesus to the reign of Tiberius at the hands of the Roman procurator[144] Pontius Pilate. Now, just from reading paragraph 2, do you think there is any doubt in Tacitus' mind that Pilate actually ordered the crucifixion of Jesus?

C: No.

---

[144] Pilate's title was either "procurator" or "prefect", or both. Accounts differ. Part of the confusion rests in changes made in the first century A.D. when military prefects were gradually replaced by civilian procurators as governors of Roman provinces.

T: More importantly, is there any doubt in Tacitus' mind that a person claiming to be "Christus" existed, in the flesh, in human form, and began a religion that Tacitus referred to as "a most mischievous superstition"?

C: No doubt.

T: Right. Thanks to this historian, who thinks our Faith is a "hideous and shameful" religion, he has confirmed that a person named Christ existed and was put to death by Procurator Pilate during the reign of Tiberius Caesar. How do we know when Pilate was procurator, or prefect, of Judea? Look at *Handout 4A.*

Handout 4A

Credit: The Israel Museum, Jerusalem/Bridgeman Images.

This picture, taken at the Israel Museum in Jerusalem, shows a stone that was part of a dedication plaque set into a building used as a temple to worship the then-current emperor of Rome, Tiberius. That temple was referred to as a "Tiberieum", which you can make out in the first line of the inscription above. The complete inscription is:

> To the Divine Augusti [this] Tiberieum
> ...Pontius Pilate
> ...prefect of Judea
> ...has dedicated [this]

The inscription acknowledges the prior emperor and his wife, the "Augusti", as divine because all emperors and their wives, beginning with Augustus, were elevated to the position of gods. The next phrase is more important, though. It establishes that Pontius Pilate was the Roman "prefect of Judea" at the time of the temple's dedication. "When was the dedication?" is the next question.

The Jewish historian Josephus (37 A.D. - c. 100 A.D.) described the events relating to Pontius Pilate in detail in his work, *The Antiquities of the Jews*, written late in the first century A.D. Josephus tells us when Pilate was recalled to Rome, ending his time in Judea:

The Antiquities of the Jews

translated by William Whiston

18.89 So Vitellius [the legate in charge of the province of Syria] sent Marcellus, a friend of his, to take care of the affairs of Judea, and ordered Pilate to go to Rome, to answer before the emperor to the accusations of the Jews [relating to certain attacks on Samaritans]. So Pilate, when he had tarried ten years in Judea, made haste to Rome, and this in obedience to the orders of Vitellius, which he durst not contradict; but before he could get to Rome Tiberius was dead.

Tiberius died on March 26, 37 A.D., so Pilate's ten years likely covered the period 26 A.D. – 36 A.D. The Tiberieum temple, then, was dedicated during that same period. The period also corresponds to the date of Jesus' crucifixion in 33 A.D.

T: Forget for the moment what you know from the Christian gospels and creeds. If you knew only what we just read in *Handouts 4 and 4A*, can you say that Pontius Pilate was a real person?

C: Yes.

T: Did Pilate hold the Roman office of prefect?

C: Yes.

T: When Pilate was prefect, was he prefect of Judea?

C: Yes.

T: What evidence do you have that Pilate was prefect of Judea?

C: The stone inscription and the writings of Tacitus.

T: What in the stone inscription tells us that Pilate was prefect of Judea?

C: "...Pontius Pilate, ...prefect of Judea"

T: What did Tacitus write that tells us Pilate was prefect of Judea?

C: "Christus, from whom the name had its origin, suffered the extreme penalty during the reign of Tiberius at the hands of one of our procurators, Pontius Pilatus, and a most mischievous superstition, thus checked for the moment, again broke out not only in Judaea, the first source of the evil, but even in Rome, where all things hideous and shameful from every part of the world find their center and become popular."

T: When was Pilate prefect of Judea?

C: [Referencing *Handout 4A*] 26 – 36 AD.

T: And what did Josephus write that indicates those years?

C: "So Pilate, when he had tarried ten years in Judea, made haste to Rome, and this in obedience to the orders of Vitellius, which he durst not contradict; but before he could get to Rome Tiberius was dead."

T: That passage tells us Pilate served ten years in Judea. How did we figure out that the ten years ran from 26 – 36 AD?

C: Tiberius died while Pilate was travelling to Rome.

T: Look at the *Timechart*, Panel XI, and give me the date of Tiberius' death.

C: Tiberius was suffocated[145] on March 26 of 37 AD [The year of death is in small numbers just below the blue box for Tiberius Caesar. The notation of "22½" in the blue box is the length in years of Tiberius' reign.]

T: Tiberius ruled as emperor for 22½ years and died in early 37 AD. So, based on the date of Tiberius' death, when did Pilate serve as prefect of Judea?

C: So the ten-year period had to come before that date: 26 – 36 AD.

T: Look at the *Timechart* again. In what year was Jesus crucified?

---

[145] In a series of events that could become a script for a Mel Brooks movie, Tiberius was thought to have died, then came back to life, and then was killed because his successor had been named and undoing the process seemed to be unthinkable! While at a ceremonial game in 37 A.D., Tiberius became severely ill and was declared dead by his physicians. The palace guard, the Praetorians, who held considerable control over the selection of emperors, declared their allegiance for Tiberius' successor, Caligula. Then Tiberius awoke and surprised the ruling elite. To avoid embarrassment and confusion, the Praetorian commander used blankets to smother Tiberius so as not to disrupt the transfer of power.

Confirmand Reference Book First Edition

C: 33 AD.

T: So, let's test some Bible passages against these non-Christian historical sources. Turn to:

> Luke 3
>
> 1 Now in the fifteenth year of the reign of Tiberius Caesar, Pontius Pilate being governor of Judaea, and Herod being tetrarch of Galilee, and his brother Philip tetrarch of Ituraea and of the region of Trachonitis, and Lysanias the tetrarch of Abilene,
>
> 2 Annas and Caiaphas being the high priests, the word of God came unto John the son of Zacharias in the wilderness.

T: Here Luke is setting the stage for the beginning of John the Baptist's ministry. John started preaching fifteen years into Tiberius' reign; Tiberius ruled for 22½ years, so how much of Tiberius' reign was left before he would die?

C: 22½ - 15 = 7½ years.

T: Let's round that number to eight years to keep the math simple. If Tiberius died in 37 AD, in what year did John start preaching?

C: 37 AD – 8 years = 29 AD.

T: Now here's the test: If John the Baptist started preaching in 29 AD, Luke says that Pontius Pilate is "governor", or prefect, of Judea. Does the extra-Biblical evidence we just looked at confirm that Pilate was prefect of Judea in 29 AD? Over what period was Pilate prefect of Judea?

C: 26 – 36 AD. So, yes, Pilate was prefect in 29 AD.

T: Does the extra-Biblical evidence agree with Luke's statement about Pontius Pilate being governor of Judea in the fifteenth year of the reign of Tiberius Caesar?

C: Yes.

T: Now let's test the most important claims in all of Scripture: that Jesus was crucified, died and rose again. We will take this in steps, though. Let's look first Jesus' crucifixion, picking up just after Jesus' arrest in the Garden of Gethsemane on the Mount of Olives.

> Luke 23
>
> 1 And the whole multitude of them arose, and led [Jesus] unto Pilate.
>
> 2 And they began to accuse him, saying, We found this fellow perverting the nation, and forbidding to give tribute to Caesar, saying that he himself is Christ a King.

Confirmand Reference Book First Edition

3 And Pilate asked him, saying, Art thou the King of the Jews? And he answered him and said, Thou sayest it.

4 Then said Pilate to the chief priests and to the people, I find no fault in this man.

5 And they were the more fierce, saying, He stirreth up the people, teaching throughout all Jewry, beginning from Galilee to this place.

6 When Pilate heard of Galilee, he asked whether the man were a Galilaean.

7 And as soon as he knew that he belonged unto Herod's jurisdiction, he sent him to Herod, who himself also was at Jerusalem at that time.

8 And when Herod saw Jesus, he was exceeding glad: for he was desirous to see him of a long season, because he had heard many things of him; and he hoped to have seen some miracle done by him.

9 Then he questioned with him in many words; but he answered him nothing.

10 And the chief priests and scribes stood and vehemently accused him.

11 And Herod with his men of war set him at nought, and mocked him, and arrayed him in a gorgeous robe, and sent him again to Pilate.

12 And the same day Pilate and Herod were made friends together: for before they were at enmity between themselves.

13 And Pilate, when he had called together the chief priests and the rulers and the people,

14 Said unto them, Ye have brought this man unto me, as one that perverteth the people: and, behold, I, having examined him before you, have found no fault in this man touching those things whereof ye accuse him:

15 No, nor yet Herod: for I sent you to him; and, lo, nothing worthy of death is done unto him.

16 I will therefore chastise him, and release him.

17 (For of necessity he must release one unto them at the feast.)

18 And they cried out all at once, saying, Away with this man, and release unto us Barabbas:

19 (Who for a certain sedition made in the city, and for murder, was cast into prison.)

20 Pilate therefore, willing to release Jesus, spake again to them.

21 But they cried, saying, Crucify him, crucify him.

22 And he said unto them the third time, Why, what evil hath he done? I have found no cause of death in him: I will therefore chastise him, and let him go.

23 And they were instant with loud voices, requiring that he might be crucified. And the voices of them and of the chief priests prevailed.

24 And Pilate gave sentence that it should be as they required.

25 And he released unto them him that for sedition and murder was cast into prison, whom they had desired; but he delivered Jesus to their will.

26 And as they led him away, they laid hold upon one Simon, a Cyrenian, coming out of the country, and on him they laid the cross, that he might bear it after Jesus.

27 And there followed him a great company of people, and of women, which also bewailed and lamented him.

28 But Jesus turning unto them said, Daughters of Jerusalem, weep not for me, but weep for yourselves, and for your children.

29 For, behold, the days are coming, in the which they shall say, Blessed are the barren, and the wombs that never bare, and the paps which never gave suck.

30 Then shall they begin to say to the mountains, Fall on us; and to the hills, Cover us.

31 For if they do these things in a green tree, what shall be done in the dry?[146]

32 And there were also two other, malefactors, led with him to be put to death.

---

[146] If you have time, you may want to explore why Jesus, in the middle of being crucified, warns the "Daughters of Jerusalem". *Handout #2* describes the destruction of Jerusalem by Titus to put down the Jewish rebellion, and Jesus may have been referring to that event.

33 And when they were come to the place, which is called Calvary, there they crucified him, and the malefactors, one on the right hand, and the other on the left.

T: While this Bible passage has a lot of detail, I would like to focus on a key element we can test: Pilate ordered the crucifixion of Christ, after being pressured by the mob. From what you read in *Handout #4*, what did Tacitus say that tells us Pilate ordered the crucifixion of Jesus?

C: In paragraph 2, he refers to "Christus".

T: And what happened to Christus?

C: He "suffered the extreme penalty during the reign of Tiberius at the hands of one of our procurators, Pontius Pilatus".

T: So, here, we have Tacitus verifying the account of Pilate sentencing Jesus in Luke 23:24, and from Tacitus' account, what was the result of Jesus having "suffered the extreme penalty"?[147]

C: Jesus died.

T: Now, look at the third paragraph of *Handout #4*. Tacitus describes an investigative technique used to this day: police rounded up people who confessed to their crimes and were willing to turn on others, "then, upon their information, an immense multitude was convicted". But their conviction was "not so much of the crime of firing the city, as of hatred against mankind". Really? The Christian message of God sending His Son to save mankind was considered "hatred against mankind"? Why do you think the Romans considered the Christian message "hatred against mankind"?

C: [Many answers are possible, but most likely the cause was Roman moral standards during the time.]

T: The Christian message of love for your neighbor conflicted with the Roman sense of superiority above all others, especially those Rome had conquered. Read on to the fourth paragraph. What happened to the Christians captured by the Roman authorities?

C: They were dressed as animals and then torn apart by dogs; they were nailed to crosses or were burned.

T: Paragraph 5 tells us where some of these executions happened. Where was that?

C: Nero's gardens?

T: Maybe, but see the reference to the "circus"?

---

[147] The "extreme penalty" was crucifixion. See, for example, https://www.catholicworldreport.com/2015/04/03/the-violence-of-the-crucifixion-2/ citing to Julius Paulus, a jurist living a century after Tacitus.

C: Yeh.

T: That was a specific structure called the Circus Maximus, which was a huge oval race track – think of the movie *Ben Hur* where chariot races took place. It is likely that Nero's garden overlooked the Circus Maximus.[148] Here is a model depicting the Circus around the fourth century A.D. by architect and historian Paul Bigot:

Source: Pascal Radigue - Own work, CC BY-SA 3.0, https://commons.wikimedia.org/w/index.php?curid=4054747

Note: The Coliseum, which had yet to be constructed during the time of Nero, can be seen to the right.

T: What was Nero doing in his gardens?

C: Mingling with his guests, dressed as a charioteer.

T: Or he "stood aloft in a car". Charioteers rode in "cars" that were pulled by teams of horses, so Nero must have had a chariot car brought in for him to stand on while watching Christians being torn apart in the Circus Maximus. What would he do, though, if the sun set and he needed light to keep the party going?

---

[148] Nero's palace was on the nearby Palatine Hill.

C: Find torches?

T: The answer is in paragraph 4: Christians "were doomed to the flames and burnt, to serve as a nightly illumination, when daylight had expired." So when Nero needed a "torch", what did he use?

C: Christians [yuk!]

T: So now you should have the picture: Nero is having Christians dressed as animals being torn apart by dogs in the Circus Maximus while he is in his garden, standing in a chariot car and dressed as a charioteer, talking with his guests, while Christians are being burned alive to provide light for his party. Here is a portrayal of Nero's garden party by 19th century painter Henryk Hektor Siemiradzki called *The Torches of Nero*:[149]

T: Now let's move forward about 50 years. Christianity had spread to large areas of the Roman Empire by the early second century. By about 112 A.D., a newly appointed governor of the Roman province of Bythnia (present-day northwestern Turkey), named Pliny the Younger, was trying to deal with the growing problem of illegal Christian worship. Pliny decided to write to Emperor Trajan in Rome for advice. Here is their exchange of letters.

Handout #5

LETTERS, Book X, XCVI and XCVII, by Gaius Plinius Caecilius Secundus (Pliny the Younger), 61 A.D. – c. 113 A.D.

Pliny to the Emperor Trajan:

---

[149] Art Heritage/Alamy Stock Photo.

1.	It is a rule, Sir, which I inviolably observe, to refer myself to you in all my doubts; for who is more capable of guiding my uncertainty or informing my ignorance? Having never been present at any trials of the Christians, I am unacquainted with the method and limits to be observed either in examining or punishing them. Whether any difference is to be allowed between the youngest and the adult; whether repentance admits to a pardon, or if a man has been once a Christian it avails him nothing to recant; whether the mere profession of Christianity, albeit without crimes, or only the crimes associated therewith are punishable -- in all these points I am greatly doubtful.

2.	In the meanwhile, the method I have observed towards those who have denounced to me as Christians is this: I interrogated them whether they were Christians; if they confessed it I repeated the question twice again, adding the threat of capital punishment; if they still persevered, I ordered them to be executed. For whatever the nature of their creed might be, I could at least feel no doubt that contumacy [rebelliousness] and inflexible obstinacy deserved chastisement. There were others also possessed with the same infatuation, but being citizens of Rome, I directed them to be carried thither.

3.	These accusations spread (as is usually the case) from the mere fact of the matter being investigated and several forms of the mischief came to light. A placard was put up, without any signature, accusing a large number of persons by name. Those who denied they were, or had ever been, Christians, who repeated after me an invocation to the gods, and offered adoration, with wine and frankincense, to your image, which I had ordered to be brought for that purpose, together with those of the gods, and who finally cursed Christ -- none of which acts, it is into performing -- these I thought it proper to discharge. Others who were named by that informer at first confessed themselves Christians, and then denied it; true, they had been of that persuasion but they had quitted it, some three years, others many years, and a few as much as twenty-five years ago. They all worshipped your statue and the images of the gods, and cursed Christ.

4.	[The Christians] affirmed, however, the whole of their guilt, or their error, was, that they were in the habit of meeting on a certain fixed day before it was light, when they sang in alternate verses a hymn to Christ, as to a god, and bound themselves by a solemn oath, not to any wicked deeds, but never to commit any fraud, theft, or adultery, never to falsify their word, nor deny a trust when they should be called upon to deliver it up; after which it was their custom to separate, and then reassemble to partake of food -- but food of an ordinary and innocent kind. Even this practice, however, they had abandoned after the publication of my edict, by which, according to your orders, I had forbidden political associations. I judged it so much the more necessary to extract the real truth, with the assistance of torture, from two female slaves, who were styled deaconesses: but I could discover nothing more than depraved and excessive superstition.

5. I therefore adjourned the proceedings, and betook myself at once to your counsel. For the matter seemed to me well worth referring to you, especially considering the numbers endangered. Persons of all ranks and ages, and of both sexes are, and will be, involved in the prosecution. For this contagious superstition is not confined to the cities only, but has spread through the villages and rural districts; it seems possible, however, to check and cure it.

Source: Plinius Secundus, *Epistles*, X.96. Paragraph numbers were not in the original but were added as a reference tool.

Trajan to Pliny:

You have followed the right course of procedure, my dear Pliny, in your examination of the cases of persons charged with being Christians, for it is impossible to lay down a general rule to a fixed formula. These people must not be hunted out; if they are brought before you and the charge against them is proved, they must be punished, but in the case of anyone who denies that he is a Christian, and makes it clear that he is not by offering prayers to the gods, he is to be pardoned as a result of his repentance however suspect his past conduct may be. But pamphlets circulated anonymously must play no part in any accusation. They create the worst sort of precedent and are quite out of keeping with the spirit of our age.

Source: Plinius Secundus, *Epistles*, X.97.

T: In paragraphs 1 and 2, Pliny explains that he is writing the Emperor for advice in handling the problem of how to deal with Christians and those accused of being Christians. From paragraph 2, what would happen if you were brought before Pliny and confessed to being a Christian?

C: Pliny would ask two more times if you were a Christian, and if you said yes, you would be executed.

T: Confessing to be a Christian was a capital offense, punishable by death. The only ones who escaped immediate death were Roman citizens, as you see in the last sentence of paragraph 2, who would be sent to Rome for trial, which was a right of any Roman citizen. But what does Pliny's last sentence in paragraph 2 tell you about who became believers of Jesus?

C: Roman citizens.

T: As well as non-citizens. In paragraph 3, what would someone have to do if they were accused of being a Christian but wanted to prove they no longer were?

C: Repeat an invocation to the gods, and offer adoration, with wine and frankincense, to the image of Trajan.

T: All Roman emperors, after the first emperor, Augustus, considered themselves gods, along with Jupiter, Mars, and the others, so an offering to the emperor was seen not just as recognition of his authority but also acknowledgement of his deity. Now look at the first sentence of paragraph 4. What is Pliny describing? He said the Christians met on a certain day of the week, before dawn, to sing hymns to Christ and take "oaths" to "never to commit any fraud, theft, or adultery, never to falsify their word, nor deny a trust". What is Pliny describing?

C: A Christian worship service.

T: And then read on: the Christians would "reassemble to partake of food -- but food of an ordinary and innocent kind". What is Pliny likely describing here?

C: Communion.

T: Most likely. Without understanding what he was told, Pliny has described what we today would call the "Holy Eucharist". Pliny issued a ban on "political associations", which probably drove the church meetings underground. Then, in the last sentence of paragraph 4, we see Pliny ordered the torture of two women deaconesses "to extract the real truth", but what happened when he tortured them?

C: He did not discover anything.

T: Apparently the women held to their faith in Jesus, and Pliny could discover nothing more than what he called "depraved and excessive superstition." What do you suppose Pliny heard from the deaconesses that he thought was "depraved and excessive superstition"?

C: [Could include several answers, such as Jesus healing people, Jesus walking on water or feeding 5,000, but the best answer is] Jesus has risen from the dead.

T: Probably. And for that statement, the women likely died as a result of the torture. Now paragraph 5 is very interesting. The first three sentences explain why Pliny is seeking Trajan's advice. What is the problem Pliny is facing?

C: People of all ranks, ages and sexes will be involved.

T: In other words, if Pliny went forward, his court would be clogged with people accused of being Christians. Now look at the last sentence: "For this contagious superstition is not confined to the cities only, but has spread through the villages and rural districts". From paragraph 2, we know that Christianity had spread among Roman and non-Roman citizens. Here, Pliny admits it has spread to both cities and rural areas. If I told you that Pliny likely wrote this letter in 112 A.D., how many years after Jesus' crucifixion and resurrection was the letter written? [Confirmands could use the Timechart to calculate the years from 33 A.D. to 112 A.D.]

C: 79 years.

T: If I told you that life expectancy for a Roman during this time was about 47.5 years,[150] how many lifespans passed from 33 A.D. to 112 A.D.?

C: Less than two. [112 − 33 = 79; 79 / 47.5 = 1⅔ lifespans]

T: So within two lifespans of Jesus' resurrection, Christianity had spread through the Roman Empire to include people of all ranks and ages living in both cities and rural areas. What do you think you would say if you were Trajan and had received Pliny's letter? Would you try to lock up and try all those Christians?

C: Not likely.

T: Regarding Christians, Trajan told Pliny, "These people must not be hunted out; if they are brought before you and the charge against them is proved, they must be punished". What was Trajan saying?

C: Don't go looking for Christians, but if you find them, punish them.

T: That's a remarkable statement from the Roman emperor. He is saying that the Christian movement had so thoroughly permeated Roman society by 112 A.D. that Roman authorities should no longer hunt them out! By about 200 years later in 313 A.D., Christianity had spread so far and fast that another Roman Emperor, named Constantine, lifted the ban on Christian worship and allowed the Faith to come out into the open.

Locate Constantine on the *Timechart* and the date he came to power in 312 A.D. the following describes a pivotal battle Constantine fought that brought him to power:

T: By the early fourth century, Rome had multiple emperors for both the eastern and western parts of the Empire.[151] Constantine's father held one of the imperial positions, but upon his death, others asserted claims to succeed him. Constantine rallied his father's troops and fielded an army of modest size. His principal adversary, Maxentius, fielded an army twice the size and positioned it between Constantine and Rome in front of the Tiber River. Maxentius had a pontoon bridge built so that his army could cross the river to confront Constantine. The bridge is today referred to as the Milvian Bridge, which gave the battle its name. But before the battle, something interesting happened to Constantine.

A Christian[152] bishop at the time, named Eusebius, described what happened to Constantine while marching toward Maxentius. Constantine, who was sympathetic to Christians after the

---

[150] Cokayne, Karen (2013-01-11). *Experiencing Old Age in Ancient Rome*. Routledge. p. 3. ISBN 9781136000065. Assuming the Roman lived past childhood and reached age 10, he/she could expect to live another 37.5 years to attain the age of 47.5. Due to illness and other causes, one-half of children died by age 10 during this time, and, for that reason, measures of life expectancy for adults are stated on the condition that persons out-live childhood.

[151] The system of government established by Diocletian in 293 A.D., known as the "Tetrarchy", crested a senior emperor (an "Augustus") for each of the eastern and western parts of the Roman Empire, with a junior emperor (a "Caesar") reporting to each senior emperor.

[152] Some sources for the Battle of Milvian Bridge are Christian, which I identify in the text. All others are secular.

persecutions of 302-303 A.D.,[153] "saw with his own eyes in the heavens a trophy of the cross arising from the light of the sun, carrying the message, *In Hoc Signo Vinces*", meaning "with this sign, you will conquer".   Then after seeing the cross, Constantine had a dream the following night, in which Christ appeared with the same heavenly sign, and told him to make a standard, the labarum,[154] for his army in that form. Eusebius describes the sign as Chi (X) traversed by Rho (P): ☧, a symbol representing the first two letters of the Greek spelling of the word Christos or Christ.[155]

Handout #6: Battle of Milvian Bridge, October 28, 312 A.D.

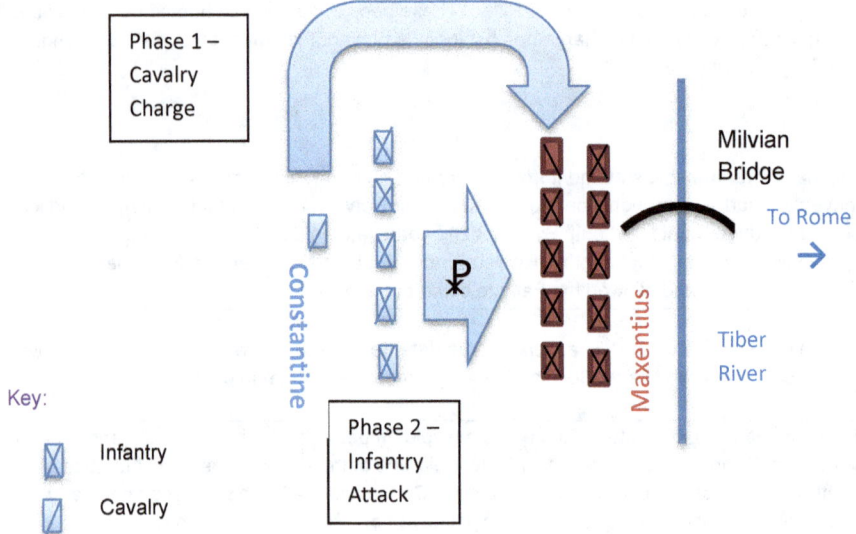

Note: The key symbols are modern NATO military symbols, not symbols used in ancient times!

T: To implement the command, "with this sign, you will conquer", Constantine ordered that his soldiers paint the symbol, ☧, on their shields. He arrived at the battlefield to see Maxen-

---

[153] The persecutions of Diocletian from 302 A.D. – 303A.D. were among the most severe in the history of the Roman Empire and became known as the "Great Persecution". Essentially, the persecutions sprang from Rome's last-ditch efforts to enforce worship of its pagan gods through more vigorous enforcement of laws that prohibited Christian worship and stripped Christians of positions of importance in government and society. Notably, Constantine's father, Constantius, did not enforce the anti-Christian edicts in regions under his control.

[154] From Merriam-Webster: an imperial standard of the later Roman emperors resembling the vexillum; *especially*: the standard bearing the Chi-Rho adopted by Constantine after he converted to Christianity.

[155] For a concise account of the battle, see Cavandish, Richard, "The Battle of the Milvian Bridge", *History Today*, October 10, 2012, at http://www.historytoday.com/richard-cavendish/battle-milvian-bridge.

tius' forces deployed close to the Tiber River in front of the Milvian Bridge, so close to the Tiber that Maxentius had little room to maneuver his forces. Constantine's battle plan was a simple, two-phase attack. In Phase 1, he launched his cavalry to disrupt Maxentius' cavalry and charge the infantry who were packed in close to the river. That cavalry charge caused panic among Maxentius' forces, and seeing that, Constantine implemented Phase 2, an attack with his infantry whose shields were painted with the ☧ symbol. Constantine and his troops pushed Maxentius and his army into the Tiber where many drowned. Constantine marched on to Rome and declared himself emperor of the Western Empire.[156] Now, typically, Roman generals would stage a parade in Rome and offer sacrifices to the Roman gods in the Temple of Jupiter after a great victory. Do you think Constantine would offer sacrifices to Jupiter upon entering Rome?

C: No.

T: Why? Did Jupiter have anything to do with Constantine's victory?

C: No, Jesus did!

T: Instead of going to the Temple of Jupiter, Constantine went to the Roman Senate and offered to restore their privileges, which had been taken away by previous emperors. But since he attributed his victory to obeying the words of Jesus, what do you think he did about the official state religion?

C: He changed the religion to Christianity?

T: Not quite. Christianity did not become the official religion of the Roman Empire for another 67 years.[157] In 313 A.D., Constantine, ruler of the Western Empire, and Licinius, ruler of the Eastern Empire, agreed to issue the Edict of Milan that gave Christians legal status, placing Christians on par with those who still worshipped the Roman gods. Think about the spread of Christianity, though. In less than three centuries, the Christian Faith, though heavily persecuted and despised by those in power in its early years, grew from the band of Jesus' followers at the time of His resurrection in 33 A.D. to legal acceptance throughout the entire Roman Empire in 313 A.D.[158] Now think about those who spread the Good News of a Risen Lord during the time of those persecutions. From *Handout #4*, what persecutions did Christians have to endure under Nero?

C: Being set on fire to provide entertainment and light for his garden parties.

T: And, from *Handout #5*, what did Roman governors such as Pliny the Younger do to Christians?

---

[156] Constantine would share rule of the empire with Licinius, who ruled the Eastern Empire, until 324 A.D. when Constantine defeated Licinius at the Battle of Chrysopolis.
[157] Christianity became the official religion of the Roman Empire under Emperor Theodosius in 380 A.D.
[158] Legal acceptance of Christianity provided some measure of tolerance but not universal acceptance. Pagan religions continued through the fall of the Roman Empire, even after Christianity became its official religion.

C: He put them on trial and executed them if they confessed to being Christians.

T: From paragraph 4, who did Pliny torture to get information on the Christian sect?

C: Deaconesses.

T: What did the deaconesses tell Pliny when they were tortured?

C: About the resurrection.

T: Most likely, because all Pliny heard was something that sounded like "depraved and excessive superstition" to him. And what usually happened to people that the Romans tortured?

C: They died from their injuries.

T: This resurrection story, then, cost the deaconesses their lives, after having to endure torture. If the torture of the deaconesses occurred in 112 A.D., do you think these deaconesses were old enough to have seen Jesus rise from the dead in 33 A.D.?

C: Not likely.

T: So the deaconesses had to have heard the story of Jesus rising from the dead from someone else. Let's try to see who could have told the deaconesses. After Jesus rose from the dead, who first saw Him in His resurrected body?

C: Women coming to the tomb.

T: Mary Magdalene, to be precise. "Mary Magdalene, and Joanna, and Mary *the mother* of James, and other *women that were* with them" saw angels at the empty tomb and ran and told the disciples.[159] Mary Magdalene, who must have followed Peter and John back to the empty tomb, actually saw and spoke to Jesus.[160] Jesus then appeared to the disciples and others. Let's see how St. Paul describes the sequence of events.

> I Corinthians 15
>
> 1 Moreover, brethren, I declare unto you the gospel which I preached unto you, which also ye have received, and wherein ye stand;
>
> 2 By which also ye are saved, if ye keep in memory what I preached unto you, unless ye have believed in vain.
>
> 3 For I delivered unto you first of all that which I also received, how that Christ died for our sins according to the Scriptures;

---

[159] Luke 24:1-10.
[160] John 20:1-18.

4 And that he was buried, and that he rose again the third day according to the Scriptures:

5 And that he was seen of Cephas [another name for Peter], then of the twelve:

6 After that, he was seen of above five hundred brethren at once; of whom the greater part remain unto this present, but some are fallen asleep.

7 After that, he was seen of James; then of all the apostles.

8 And last of all he was seen of me also, as of one born out of due time.

> T: How did Jesus appear to over 500 people at once? Let's read one account that picks up as St. Peter discovers the empty tomb:

Luke 24

12 Then arose Peter, and ran unto the sepulchre; and stooping down, he beheld the linen clothes laid by themselves, and departed, wondering in himself at that which was come to pass.

13 And, behold, two of them went that same day to a village called Emmaus, which was from Jerusalem about threescore furlongs.

14 And they talked together of all these things which had happened.

15 And it came to pass, that, while they communed together and reasoned, Jesus himself drew near, and went with them.

16 But their eyes were holden that they should not know him.

17 And he said unto them, What manner of communications are these that ye have one to another, as ye walk, and are sad?

18 And the one of them, whose name was Cleopas, answering said unto him, Art thou only a stranger in Jerusalem, and hast not known the things which are come to pass there in these days?

19 And he said unto them, What things? And they said unto him, Concerning Jesus of Nazareth, which was a prophet mighty in deed and word before God and all the people:

20 And how the chief priests and our rulers delivered him to be condemned to death, and have crucified him.

21 But we trusted that it had been he which should have redeemed Israel: and beside all this, to day is the third day since these things were done.

22 Yea, and certain women also of our company made us astonished, which were early at the sepulchre;

23 And when they found not his body, they came, saying, that they had also seen a vision of angels, which said that he was alive.

24 And certain of them which were with us went to the sepulchre, and found it even so as the women had said: but him they saw not.

25 Then he said unto them, O fools, and slow of heart to believe all that the prophets have spoken:

26 Ought not Christ to have suffered these things, and to enter into his glory?

27 And beginning at Moses and all the prophets, he expounded unto them in all the Scriptures the things concerning himself.

28 And they drew nigh unto the village, whither they went: and he made as though he would have gone further.

29 But they constrained him, saying, Abide with us: for it is toward evening, and the day is far spent. And he went in to tarry with them.

30 And it came to pass, as he sat at meat with them, he took bread, and blessed it, and brake, and gave to them.

31 And their eyes were opened, and they knew him; and he vanished out of their sight.

32 And they said one to another, Did not our heart burn within us, while he talked with us by the way, and while he opened to us the Scriptures?

33 And they rose up the same hour, and returned to Jerusalem, and found the eleven gathered together, and them that were with them,

34 Saying, The Lord is risen indeed, and hath appeared to Simon [Peter].

T: According to verse 16, when Jesus first appeared to the two men on the road to Emmaus, did the men know it was Jesus?

C: No.

T: What does Jesus ask about in verse 17, and why are the two men sad?

C: They know Jesus was killed and now think Jesus' body is missing. [Verses 19 – 24]

T: How did Jesus respond in verse 27 to explain to the men what had happened?

C: He explained the Scriptures concerning the Messiah.

T: Look at verse 31. What happened after Jesus explained the Scriptures regarding the suffering of the Messiah for the sins of Mankind?

C: Their eyes were opened.

T: What does that mean?

C: They recognized Jesus.

T: And then what did Jesus do?

C: He vanished.

T: Verse 32. What did the men feel as Jesus explained the Scriptures to them?

C: Their hearts burned.

T: Now, if similar events happened to about 500 other people after the resurrection, where their hearts were left on fire, what do you suppose happened?

C: The Christians went out and told other people.

T: Told them what?

C: That Jesus was alive.

T: They told others, then, about the <u>Risen</u> Jesus. They saw Jesus after He rose from the dead. Now fast-forward 31 years to 64 A.D. Nero is rounding up Christians to be killed in the Circus Maximus and to be burned for the amusement of his garden party guests. Why don't those Christians recant their belief in the Risen Jesus and save themselves from such horrible deaths? Of the 500 who saw Jesus after the resurrection, could some of the 500 have been among those Nero tortured?

C: Some, maybe.

T: If they were young enough when Jesus rose from the dead, yes. But remember, life expectancy was only 47.5 years on average, so, as St. Paul noted, some had "fallen asleep", meaning they had died, by the time he wrote his letter.[161] I suspect that most of those put to painful death by Nero were second generation Christians, that is, sons and daughters of those who had either seen the Risen Jesus or who knew those who had seen Him, as well as new converts. The question I have for you, though, is, what does the sacrifice of these Christians at the hands of Nero tell us about the early Christians? If they truly believed that Jesus rose from the dead, or actually knew that He did because He appeared to them, I can understand why they suffered such cruelty. If they did not really believe that Jesus rose from the dead and just attended Christian worship services for fellowship and free wine and bread, do you think they would stand firm in their faith when told they would have to dress in animal skins so that they could be torn apart by dogs in the Circus Maximus?

C: They would likely give up the Christian Faith.

T: Right. So the fact that the early Christians were willing to be torn apart by dogs or set on fire under Nero's orders tells us what about them? Were they fools for dying for something they did not believe in or did they really believe in the Risen Jesus?

C: They had to believe in the Risen Jesus.

T: For some of those put to death by Nero, their belief may have come from actually seeing the Risen Jesus; for most others, their belief had to come from hearing about the Risen Jesus from those who saw the Risen Jesus. Hundreds, if not thousands, of Christians died during the Roman persecutions.[162] Were all these people fools for dying for a lord who was not risen from the dead, or did they truly believe that Jesus rose from the dead?

C: They had to believe that Jesus rose from the dead.

T: The people who died for their faith in Jesus are called "martyrs". The fact that there were so many martyrs tells us today that something in the Christian Faith was worth dying for, and that something had to be the Risen Jesus because that is what Christianity is all about. Now let's go forward another 48 years, to 112 A.D. to return to Pliny's letter. Look at *Handout #5*, paragraph 5 and tell me how far the Christian message had gone by 112 A.D.

C: Pliny wrote: "For the matter seemed to me well worth referring to you, especially considering the numbers endangered. Persons of all ranks and ages, and of both sexes are, and will be, involved in the prosecution. For this contagious superstition is not confined to the cities only, but has spread through the villages and rural districts; ...."

T: And precisely 200 years after Pliny wrote Trajan, what event took place that brought Christianity out in the open to where it was no longer illegal?

C: The Battle of Milvian Bridge. (*Handout #6*)

---

[161] St. Paul probably wrote I Corinthians around 53 A.D. – 54 A.D., or ten years before the persecution of Nero.
[162] No precise figure exists for the number of Christians killed by the Romans, but Eusebius chronicled the deaths of many martyrs.

T: So who have we read from to determine that early Christians suffered gruesome deaths under Nero in 64 A.D.? Hint: Look at the source listed on *Handout #4*.

C: Tacitus.

T: Was Tacitus a Christian?

C: No.

T: And who did we read from in *Handout #5* to determine that Christianity had spread to all levels of society by 112 A.D., despite being illegal and punishable by death?

C: Pliny.

T: Was Pliny a Christian?

C: No.

T: So how certain are we that early Christians suffered greatly and took great risks?

C: Very certain.

T: Why?

C: Because non-Christians wrote about their suffering.

T: And if the early Christians were rational people, that is, assuming they weren't crazy, and yet they endured extreme suffering and punishment, what caused them to persevere?

C: Their faith in the Risen Jesus.

T: And how did Christians in the time of Nero in 64 A.D. know that Jesus had risen from the dead? Did Jesus appear to all of them after His resurrection?

C: Not likely, but Jesus may have appeared to their parents and others after He rose from the dead.

T: Then, by 112 A.D., when Pliny wrote Trajan, how did the deaconesses he tortured and killed know that Jesus had risen from the dead?

C: They heard about it from their grandparents?

T: Maybe, or from other Christians whose grandparents saw the Risen Lord. So, <u>how certain can we be that those parents and grandparents of Christians who suffered under the Romans actually saw the Risen Jesus?</u>

C: It is highly likely.[163]

T: There were no news broadcasters with camera crews outside Jesus' tomb on Easter morning to record the stone rolling away and Jesus appearing alive in His resurrected body, so we still have to accept Jesus' resurrection on faith, but we do have the witness of the early Christians who, under immense pressure, would have given up on their faith if they did not truly believe in the resurrection of our Lord.

So, let's summarize the evidence provided by the Roman historians Tacitus and Pliny, as to what they tell us about Jesus:

Was Jesus a real person who lived and walked the earth?

C: Yes.

T: How do we know? Look at *Handout #4*, paragraph 2. What does Tacitus say that indicates he believed Jesus was a real person?

C: "Christus, from whom the name had its origin, suffered the extreme penalty during the reign of Tiberius at the hands of one of our procurators, Pontius Pilatus".

T: And prior to someone being killed, that person had to be ...

C: Alive.

T: Right. And how did Jesus die?

C: He "suffered the extreme penalty during the reign of Tiberius at the hands of one of our procurators, Pontius Pilatus".

T: What does "extreme penalty" imply?

C: Jesus was crucified.

T: From *Handout #4*, paragraph 2, in which region of the Roman Empire did Jesus preach?

C: "... a most mischievous superstition, thus checked for the moment, again broke out not only in Judaea, the first source of the evil, but even in Rome, where all things hideous and shameful from every part of the world find their centre and become popular."

---

[163] While there were martyrs in nearly every major faith on Earth, the only faith in which martyrs claimed to have seen a resurrected prophet is Christianity. Of the major faiths centered on an historical prophet, Christianity is the singular bodiless religion: Mohammed is buried in Medina, Saudi Arabia, Buddha was cremated and his remains sent to locations around present-day China, Confucius was likewise buried in China. Jesus, however, left an empty tomb and, prior to His ascension, actually interacted with disciples in the physical world. While many faiths profess belief in an afterlife, early Christian martyrs professed to having seen, talked to, touched and eaten with their Prophet after His death. These attributes set Christian martyrs apart from all others in that these were verifiable claims to which the early martyrs attested.

T: So Tacitus tells us that Judea was the "first source of the evil" of Christianity. If Judea was the first source, where was Jesus likely preaching?

C: Judea.

T: From the Bible, do we know that Jesus preached in Judea?

C: Yes.[164]

T: From the Bible, do we know that Jesus was crucified by Pontius Pilate?

C: Yes.[165]

T: From the Roman historian Tacitus, do we know that Jesus preached in Judea and was crucified by Pontius Pilate?

C: Yes.

T: Was Tacitus a Christian at the time he wrote the chapter in his *Annals* that you have in front of you as *Handout #4*?

C: No.

T: How do you know Tacitus was not a Christian?

C: He calls Christianity "mischievous superstition".

T: So Tacitus, a non-Christian Roman historian, just confirmed several key elements of our Faith: that Jesus was a real person who preached in Judea and was crucified by Pontius Pilate. Look at *Handout #5*, paragraph 4, last sentence. How did Pliny describe the Christian Faith?

C: A "depraved and excessive superstition".

T: If you were not a Christian, what would you think is the most superstitious element of the Christian Faith? In other words, what, to a non-believer, is the most absurd statement we Christians make about what we believe?

C: That Jesus rose from the dead.

T: There are other statements that would sound absurd to non-believers, such as Jesus' virgin birth, Jesus healing all who were sick, Jesus feeding 5,000 people with two fish and five loaves of bread, but the resurrection tops them all in what seems most outlandish to a non-believer. So what aspect of the Christian Faith do you think Tacitus and Pliny are referring to

---

[164] See, for example, Matthew 19:1, Mark 10:1, and John 4:47.
[165] Mark 15:15: "And so Pilate, willing to content the people, released Barabbas unto them, and delivered Jesus, when he had scourged him, to be crucified."

when they use terms like "mischievous superstition" or "depraved and excessive superstition"?[166]

C: Jesus rising from the dead.

T: Subsequent to Jesus' crucifixion, according to these historians, Jesus' followers spread "superstitions", which we just determined were likely the claims that Jesus rose from the dead. In *Handout #4*, what did Tacitus say happened to those who held to their belief that Jesus rose from the dead?

C: They were killed in the Circus Maximus or burned as human torches.

T: From *Handout #5*, what did Pliny do to those who held to their belief that Jesus rose from the dead?

C: He ordered them killed or tortured until they died.

T: So were these believers crazy for believing in the resurrection of Jesus, or do you think they were willing to die for their belief because they had heard from eyewitnesses, or descendants of eyewitnesses, that Jesus rose from the dead?

C: They knew people who were eyewitnesses.

T: There you have it. Because Jesus' early followers were willing to die for these "superstitions", these followers became our source for "Eyewitness News".[167] These martyrs were the equivalent of first century news reporters, reporting to us many centuries later, as to Jesus' resurrection.[168] And their reporting comes through the fine records of non-Christian Roman historians, such as Tacitus and Pliny.

---

[166] The Latin words for superstition, "superstitio" as used in the passage from Tacitus and "supstitionem" as used in the passage by Pliny, indicated more than just a silly or irrational belief as we use the term today. The Latin definition of superstition was "dread of the supernatural, credulous wonder, anxious credulity" (Tufts Latin Word Study Tool). In the Roman view, then, superstition was a serious threat to their proper religion ("religio").

[167] "Eyewitness News" is the advertising slogan of a major Washington, D.C. television station.

[168] While there are martyrs in many religions, Christianity is unique in that early Christian martyrs professed as empirical fact that they saw, talked to, touched and ate with a person who rose from the dead, Jesus. For faiths that claim an afterlife, their claims cannot be tested as ours can, and the Christian martyrs are one part of the proof. Another consideration is what I call the "Gamaliel test". After Jesus' ascension, when St. Peter and the Apostles were seized for preaching and healing in Jerusalem and brought before the Jewish council (Sanhedrin), a council member named Gamaliel reminded his fellow Jews of previous "prophets" whose followers dispersed soon after the "prophets'" deaths and advised the Sanhedrin to exercise restraint regarding St. Peter, saying, "for if this counsel or this work be of men, it [too] will come to nought: but if it be of God, ye cannot overthrow it" (Acts 5:34-39). The "Gamaliel test", then, is a longevity test: did the Christian claim to resurrection survive the death of its Prophet? We are the living answer to that test!

Confirmand Reference Book First Edition

IX. C.S. Lewis and "Inside Information"

Materials:

1. White boards, markers or equivalent
2. *Mere Christianity*, by C.S. Lewis

Learning Objectives

1. Confirmands will understand how C.S. Lewis uses simple observations about "Fair Play" to assert that a loving but powerful "Something" placed that concept into our "Human Nature", and that "Something" is God.
2. Confirmands will understand that when people do not follow the Rules of Fair Play, their conscience condemns them and they look for God's forgiveness.
3. Confirmands will understand that our role is to tell those looking for forgiveness about the Good News in Jesus, but since we live in "enemy-occupied territory" that rejects that message, we meet in church to listen in to the "secret wireless" message from Scripture to learn how to proclaim the Good News.

T: So far, we've looked at historical records from non-Christians that demonstrate that Jesus existed, preached, and was crucified by Pontius Pilate. Those records also point to the rapid spread of Christianity throughout the Roman Empire and the insistence of early Christians to die for their beliefs. Can you tell me what those early Christians were willing to die for?

C: Their belief that Jesus rose from the dead.

T: Correct. And if Jesus rose from the dead, what does that prove He is?

C: God's Son.

T: But how do you know Jesus is God's Son and not just some person with magical powers?

C: Because Jesus said so? [Said uncertainly]

T: Actually, yes.[169] And Jesus also said that "he that hath seen me hath seen the Father",[170] so if the resurrection demonstrates that Jesus was and is the Son of God, what does the resurrection say about the existence of God?

C: He must be real!

T: Precisely. Up to this point, we established that Jesus rose from the dead by looking at records written by Roman historians. Now, we are going to look at an entirely different approach to figuring out if God, and Jesus, exist: an approach, explained by C.S. Lewis, that looks into your mind and what you know rather than looking at documents written by others. First, though, tell me who C.S. Lewis is.

---

[169] If you need to refer the confirmands to Scriptures that quote Jesus asserting His divinity, you can point to Mark 8:27 and Luke 22:70.
[170] John 14:9.

C: He wrote *The Chronicles of Narnia*.

T: He actually wrote many books, some with Christian themes, like the *Narnia* series, others on different topics such as science fiction and literature. He was a professor at Oxford University and lived in England during the First and Second World Wars. What was the title of the most popular of the chronicles in the *Narnia* series?

C: *The Lion, the Witch and the Wardrobe*.

T: That was made into a movie. Do you remember how the movie version of *The Lion, the Witch and the Wardrobe* starts? What is the first scene you see?

C: A bombing raid.

T: The movie opens in the cockpit of a Luftwaffe bomber as it begins to drop its bombs on London during the Blitz of 1940. To protect their children from the bombs, British parents sent them into the country, away from cities, and that is why, in Lewis' *Narnia* fantasy, the Pevensie children are sent to live with Professor Digory Kirke, where Lucy Pevensie finds the wardrobe. In 1940, during the bombing Blitz of London, what war was going on?

C: World War II.

T: Right. While the story of the Pevensie children is fiction based on real events, what really did happen in World War II was that the British Broadcasting Corporation asked C.S. Lewis to give a series of radio broadcasts, much like today's podcasts only broadcast over radio waves to radio sets in people's homes. Most people did not have televisions at that time, so imagine everyone gathered around a big box with vacuum tubes and speakers, an early version of a car radio, to listen to the radio programs. Lewis' broadcasts, though, were not about the war specifically; instead, BBC asked him to talk about the Christian Faith. After giving a series of radio talks, Lewis published each set. He later collected the sets into a book, the book in your hands now, called *Mere Christianity*. Turn to the Preface and tell me in which years Lewis gave the radio talks.

C: 1942, 1943 and 1944. [From the first sentence of the Preface]

T: So Lewis' radio talks began in 1942, when Nazi Germany had reached the peak of its power, having pushed the British out of much of North Africa, having captured France and having forced the Russians to retreat far into their country.[171] The radio talks continued into 1944 when British, American and Canadian forces invaded Normandy, in France, and began to push the Germans back. That invasion is referred to as "D-Day". During the years leading up to D-Day, people in England came to learn about the brave resistance fighters in France. These were French men and women who were staging raids and blowing up bridges and supply depots to disrupt the German forces that were occupying most of their country. Just days before the Allied invasion of the beaches of Normandy, the French resistance received instructions by radio to launch a series of attacks on railroads and rail stations to slow German reinforcements that would likely be sent to Normandy once the invasion began. The

---

[171] This section is a long narrative. If you have a confirmand who paid attention during his/her history classes and can describe events in World War II, invite that confirmand to narrate events from 1942 to 1944.

British called the radio a "wireless" because, unlike a land-line telephone, a person could talk to another person without the use of wires. In order to receive instructions over the wireless, though, the French resistance fighters had to gather in secret places. Why did they meet in secret?

C: Because their country was occupied by the Germans.

T: The resistance fighters were in enemy-occupied territory and, if they were caught, they would likely be executed by the Germans. Many of the secret meeting places were equipped with a wireless so that the resistance leaders could communicate with resistance fighters. The broadcasts to the resistance fighters originated in England and were coded so that the Germans, who were no doubt listening, could not understand. I want you to keep in mind what was going on when Lewis gave his radio talks because his examples will refer to events during this period of World War II. Now turn to the cover page of Book One and read the title.

C: "Right And Wrong As A Clue To The Meaning Of The Universe"

T: So, after we finish with our discussion today, what are we going to have a clue to?

C: The meaning of the universe!

T: That's a pretty big claim; let's see if Lewis delivers.

Read the first two paragraphs of Book One, Chapter 1, "The Law of Human Nature".

T: OK, first, when Lewis talks about the "rules of football", to which sport is this British theologian referring?

C: Soccer, which in Europe is called "football".

T: Right. Soccer has certain rules. Can you tell us a few?

C: No one except the goalie can use his hands while on the field; if one team member kicks the ball out past one of the touchlines, the other team gets a throw-in from off-field; etc.

T: If a soccer team shows up for a game but refuses to follow the rules, is that considered fair?

C: No!

T: And if all the teams cheat, there is chaos because no one is following the rules. So we need both teams and all members of each soccer team to agree to follow the rules, or we can't play the game! Lewis also talked about the "Rule of fair play or decent behaviour";[172] what would those rules mean to you if you were on the soccer field? What if someone trips and lands face first in the pitch right next to you; what would you do?

---

[172] From the second paragraph of Book One, Chapter 1, *Mere Christianity*, by C.S. Lewis copyright © C.S. Lewis Pte. Ltd. 1942, 1943, 1944, 1952, p. 4. Extract reprinted by permission.

C: Offer him a hand to get up.

T: Even if he was on the other team?

C: Yes.

T: Why would you help an opposing team member get up?

C: Because it's the right thing to do.

T: Precisely. That's implementing the "Rule of Fair Play". But there is a difference between the rules of soccer and the Rule of Fair Play. Where, today, can I find the official rules of soccer?

C: On FIFA's website.[173]

T: Where can I find the Rule of Fair Play?

C: (Silence)

T: Maybe a soccer coach has written a book on fair play, but there is no official version of those rules.[174] Yet, most of you already knew the Rule of Fair Play. Lewis is going to call the Rule of Fair Play the "Law of Nature" because "everyone knew it by nature and did not need to be taught it."[175] So if you are obeying the Law of Nature, are you doing the Right thing or the Wrong thing?

C: The Right thing.

T: By the converse, then, if you do not obey the Law of Nature, you are doing …

C: The Wrong thing.

T: So the Law of Nature points us to what we believe to be the Right thing to do and what we believe to be the Wrong thing to. That is, the Law of Nature gives us a sense of Right and Wrong. The Rule of Fair Play, which is a Law of Nature, essentially says "Treat others as you would have them treat you". Have you heard that before? What name do people today give this rule?

C: The Golden Rule.

---

[173] Rules are actually promulgated by The International Football Association Board ("IFAB") and can be found at http://resources.fifa.com/mm/document/footballdevelopment/refereeing/02/79/92/44/laws.of.the.game.2016.2017_neutral.pdf.

[174] The IFAB does have rules governing "unsporting behaviour" (see the previous cite), but those rules generally only proscribe bad behavior (playing in a dangerous manner or spitting on an opponent) and do not cover conduct that we consider good sportsmanship.

[175] From the fifth paragraph of Book One, Chapter 1, *Mere Christianity*, by C.S. Lewis copyright © C.S. Lewis Pte. Ltd. 1942, 1943, 1944, 1952, p. 5. Extract reprinted by permission.

T: Are there other examples of the Rule of Fair Play, or Golden Rule, besides soccer or sports? What if someone cuts in front of you in a line? If they did not have permission, would you be upset?

C: Sure.

T: But if I told you there was no written law on line-cutting, why are you upset when someone cuts in front of you?

C: Because it's not fair!

T: Right: the Rule of Fair Play comes into effect and you get mad because someone is not obeying the Rule. But who taught you the rule on line-cutting?

C: Our parents? Teachers? Friends?

T: They may have helped you understand the impact and repercussions of cutting in front of someone else, but the sense you have that cutting is just not Right is just that: a sense within you that you've had since you were old enough to have any memories at all. So the question Lewis puts to us is: where does this sense of Right and Wrong, that is the Law of Nature, come from? Jump to Chapter 4, "What Lies Behind the Law", and go to the fourth and fifth paragraphs:

> [Selected sentences are shown here for emphasis.[176] Confirmands should read the entire fourth paragraph and the first three sentences of the fifth paragraph.]
>
> The position of the question is like this. We want to know whether the universe simply happens to be what it is for no reason or whether there is a power behind it that makes it what it is. ... The only way in which we could expect it to show itself would be inside ourselves as an influence or a command trying to get us to behave in a certain way. ... The only packet I am allowed to open is Man. When I do, especially when I open that particular man called Myself, I find that I do not exist on my own, that I am under a law; that somebody or something wants me to behave a certain way. ... But I should expect to find that there was, so to speak, a sender of letters in both cases, a Power behind the facts, a Director, a Guide.
>
> Do not think I am getting faster than I really am. I am not yet within a hundred miles of the God of Christian theology.[177] All I have got to is a Something which is directing the universe, and which appears in me as a law urging me to do right and making me feel responsible and uncomfortable when I do wrong.

T: In the fourth paragraph, Lewis is talking about whether the universe has meaning, then in the fifth paragraph, he comes down to what makes us comfortable or uncomfortable. Let's

---

[176] From the fourth and fifth paragraphs of Book One, Chapter 4, *Mere Christianity*, by C.S. Lewis copyright © C.S. Lewis Pte. Ltd. 1942, 1943, 1944, 1952, pp. 24-26. Extract reprinted by permission.
[177] Actually, I think Lewis is being very crafty and disarming here. Once a person accepts his premise in the next sentence, that person is well on the way toward accepting God!

take these in reverse order. What did we just call the "law urging me to do right and making me feel responsible and uncomfortable when I do wrong"?

C: The Rule of Fair Play or the Law of Nature.

T: Right. We said the Rule of Fair Play was a Law of Nature. Why is it a Law of Nature? [Point to the phrase you wrote on the board.]

C: Because "everyone knew it by nature and did not need to be taught it." [from Chapter 1, fifth paragraph]

T: So if you don't need to be taught it, and everyone knows it, how did the Rule of Fair Play get inside you?

C: God?

T: Read the first three sentences again from the fifth paragraph.

C: [Reads from paragraph again.]

T: At this point, Lewis is just referring to a Being that puts the Rule of Fair Play into you. From the third sentence, what does he call that Being? [Hint: it's capitalized!]

C: A "Something".

T: And if that Something can implant a rule into your conscience and everybody else's collective conscience, how powerful is that Something?

C: Very.

T: Hence, Lewis concludes that the Something is "directing the universe" since the Something has the power to implant the Rule of Fair Play into all people.[178] Now let's return to the preceding paragraph and his statement: "We want to know whether the universe simply happens to be what it is for no reason or whether there is a power behind it that makes it what it is." From what we know inside each of us, we know that a Something has the power to direct the universe. So does the universe simply happen to exist for no reason or is there "a power behind it that makes it what it is"?

C: There must be a power – the Something.

T: We can now conclude that this powerful Something created the universe and put the Rule of Fair Play into each of us. Do you suppose, then, that this Something believes in the Rule of Fair Play?

---

[178] Note that Lewis never asserts that all people follow the Rule of Fair Play. Indeed, he asserts that "there are two odd things about the human race. First, that they are haunted by the idea of a sort of behaviour they ought to practise, what you might call fair play, or decency, or morality, or the Law of Nature. Second, that they did not in fact do so." (Book One, Chapter 3, first paragraph of *Mere Christianity*, by C.S. Lewis copyright © C.S. Lewis Pte. Ltd. 1942, 1943, 1944, 1952, p. 16. Extract reprinted by permission.)

C: Yes.

T: Why?

C: Because the Something thought it was important enough to put in each of us.

T: However, do you always follow the Rule of Fair Play? Do you treat your neighbor as you would want them to treat you?

C: No.

T: We fail to consistently follow the Rule of Fair Play. The Something that designed the universe and put the Rule of Fair Play into us also allowed us to override it. In other words, the Something did not make us robots that had to obey all commands; the Something gave us what?

C: A choice.

T: And when we choose wrongly, and do not follow the Rule of Fair Play, do we make the Something unhappy?

C: I suppose so.

T: Well, the Something created the Rule of Fair Play, put the rule into you and every other human, and designed the universe around it. Then you go and ignore the rule and fail to treat another person fairly. At that point, are you with the Something or apart from the Something?

C: Apart.

T: But the Something must care about you or else why go to the trouble of designing the universe, so the Something wants you back after you turn away. When a person does not follow the Rule of Fair Play and hurts you and then comes back and apologizes, what should you do?

C: Forgive that person.

T: Indeed, if that person apologized sincerely, then your forgiveness is part of the Rule of Fair Play: it's fair that when someone apologizes that you forgive that person. So when you turn away from the Something and do not follow the Rule of Fair Play and then come back and apologize, does that make the Something happy?

C: Yes.

T: What would you expect the Something will do about the wrong things you do if you apologize? [Hint: the answer is the same as if someone apologized to you for doing wrong.]

C: The Something will forgive you.

T: So now let's fill out the obvious names that our Faith attaches to these roles. Who is the Something?

C: God.

T: Why is it God?

C: Because He created the universe, and He placed the Rule of Fair Play in us.

T: Even more than that. Remember, we determined that the Something was governed by the same Rule of Fair Play that we have in us. The Rule of Fair Play, the Golden Rule, is a part of love we have for each other and for our Creator and that our Creator has for us. So when we disobey the Rule of Fair Play and then repent and turn back, what must God do?

C: Forgive us.

T: And who told us that God forgives us?

C: Jesus.

T: And the prophets too, but Jesus could speak directly, as a part of God – remember the Trinity! Now go to the last paragraph of Book One.

[Turn to the last paragraph of Book One, Chapter 5, "We Have Cause to Be Uneasy".[179] Important sentences are below.]

When I chose to get to my real subject in this roundabout way, I was not trying to play any kind of trick on you. I had a different reason. My reason was that Christianity simply does not make sense until you have faced the sort of facts I have been describing. Christianity tells people to repent and promises forgiveness. It therefore has nothing (as far as I know) to say to people who do not feel that they need forgiveness. It is after you have realized that there is a real Moral Law, and a Power behind the law, and that you have broken that law and put yourself wrong with that Power – it is after this, and not a moment sooner, that Christianity begins to talk.

Of course, I quite agree that the Christian religion is, in the long run, a thing of unspeakable comfort. But it does not begin in comfort; it begins in the dismay I have been describing, and it is no use at all trying to go on to that comfort without first going through that dismay.[180]

---

[179] *Mere Christianity*, by C.S. Lewis copyright © C.S. Lewis Pte. Ltd. 1942, 1943, 1944, 1952, pp. 31-32. Extract reprinted by permission.
[180] The reference in the last sentence of this paragraph to "pre-war wishful thinking about international politics" was Lewis' comment about the failure to appease Hitler prior to World War II as Nazi troops expanded into surrounding territories without British or French military intervention. Such intervention would have been costly in both funds and human lives, but it may have forced Hilter's hand before he was ready to launch his intended campaign in 1939. Regardless, the Allied Powers chose to think that if they just gave Hitler a little more territory, he would be satisfied and, in doing so, the Allies

T: What must happen before "Christianity begins to talk"? [Hint: read the part of the sentence that precedes that statement.]

C: You must realize that there is a Moral Law and that you have broken that law.

T: Here, Lewis is using the broader term, "Moral Law", to include the Rule of Fair Play. It is only when you realize that the Moral Law is real, that there is "a Power behind the law, and that you have broken that law and put yourself wrong with that Power" that you need to repent. When you need to repent, but you haven't yet, how happy are you?

C: Not very happy.

T: To use Lewis' term, you are in a state of "dismay", and you are not comfortable. But that discomfort from the dismay nags at you and drives you to do what?

C: Repent.

T: And to repent, you seek out a faith that speaks to repentance. What faith is that?

C: Christianity.

T: Other world faiths call for some form of repentance, though. Why Christianity?

C: [Lots of different answers.]

T: What separates us from all other religions? Ours is based on a person who claimed to be part of God yet lived among us and sacrificed Himself for us. There may be repentance within other faiths, but ours is the faith that has a Person who is part of the Something who put the Rule of Fair Play into us and showed us by His words and His example of dying on the cross how to restore our relationship with that Something. And that Something is …

C: God.

T: Now let's look at what Lewis did in this section of *Mere Christianity*. He discussed how the concept of Right and Wrong is a clue to the meaning of the universe, but did he cite to any Scripture from the Bible?

C: No.

T: Did he quote from non-Christian historians such as Titus and Pliny the Younger?

C: No.

---

chose the (short-lived) comfort of wishful thinking over truth. Lewis hoped that, with World War II having laid bare the fallacy of appeasement, we could speak the truth in our Faith that comes with the painful cost of repentance rather than the comfortable sounding "soft soap and wishful thinking" that repentance is no longer as important. Lewis concluded that looking for comfort first, rather than truth, eventually leads to despair.

T: Did he show pictures of stone engravings or religious sites?

C: No.

T: Where did Lewis start his discussion?

C: The Rule of Fair Play.

T: To get that Rule, where did Lewis look?

C: Within us. At our conscience.

T: He uses what he calls "inside information".[181] Lewis gets us to God and Jesus by looking only at what a person can see when that person looks at himself or herself. That, my friends, is the genius of Lewis! Now, let's look at what Lewis says about the Christian Church. Remember in our first session what we found out when we studied the Garden of Eden. In the Garden, who convinced Adam and Eve to eat from the Tree of Knowledge of Good and Evil?

C: The serpent.

T: And what happened after they ate from the tree?

C: Man was separated from God.

T: Also, Evil, along with the serpent, also known as the Devil, came into this world. Lewis sees our current condition as the forces of God fighting the forces of the Devil. Think of the *Narnia* series; what forces were fighting each other?

C: The forces of Aslan fought the forces of the evil witch, Jadis.[182]

T: Lewis sees our world as he depicted Narnia under the control of Jadis, and we are the Pevensie kids walking through a country controlled by an evil power. Turn to Book Two, titled "What Christians Believe", and go to the last paragraph of Chapter 2, "The Invasion".

[Selected sentences from the last paragraph of Book Two, Chapter 2.][183]

Enemy-occupied territory – that is what this world is. Christianity is the story of how the rightful king has landed, you might say landed in disguise, and is calling us all to take part in a great campaign of sabotage. When you go to church you are really listening-in to the secret wireless from our friends: that is why the enemy is so anxious to prevent us from going.

---

[181] *Mere Christianity*, by C.S. Lewis copyright © C.S. Lewis Pte. Ltd. 1942, 1943, 1944, 1952, p. 23. Extract reprinted by permission.
[182] For a plot summary, see Sec. V.B.c.
[183] *Mere Christianity*, by C.S. Lewis copyright © C.S. Lewis Pte. Ltd. 1942, 1943, 1944, 1952, p. 46. Extract reprinted by permission.

T: Who is the "rightful king" who has landed?

C: Jesus.

T: When Lewis refers to listening in on the secret wireless and performing acts of sabotage, what was going on in 1942 that was similar to this?

C: The French resistance.

T: So we are the resistance fighters. What is the secret wireless that we are listening to when we go to church?

C: The Bible. [The Holy Spirit would also be an acceptable answer.]

T: And the discussions regarding the Scriptures in that Bible, either in the form of the sermon during the service or in Sunday School discussions. What are the acts of sabotage that we do that will hurt the Devil?

C: Helping others in need, sharing our faith, spreading God's Word, etc.

T: And living God's Word by following the Rule of ...

C: Fair Play.

X. The Church

Learning Objectives

1. Confirmands will understand that the gods of first century A.D. religions were capricious, so there was no use for application of reason and little incentive to seek a better life.
2. Confirmands will understand that Christianity fostered reason to explore the meaning of Scripture, and that use of reason expanded to secular pursuits of advancements in communication, agriculture and technology, allowing people to produce and sell excess goods, thereby expanding capitalism.
3. Confirmands will learn the origins of Apostolic Succession.
4. Confirmands will understand that the break between the Church of England and the Roman Catholic Church had its roots in the Protestant movement that had already been underway in Continental Europe before the reign of Henry VIII.
5. Confirmands will understand that the American Revolution caused a break between the Church of England and the former British colonies that required a significant act of charity on the part of Great Britain to allow the ordination of American bishops.
6. Confirmands will understand that the Constitutions for the United States and for the Episcopal Church were developed in parallel time and proximity, and that there are similarities in the structure of the US government and the Episcopal Church.

Author's Note

The building blocks of the Anglican Faith have traditionally been described as Scripture, tradition and reason.[184] In Sec. VIII.A., we discussed the authority of Scripture. In this section, we will discuss tradition and reason.[185] The former is rather straight-forward, and we will begin with the Early Church and follow through to the formation of the Episcopal Church in the United States. The concept of reason, though, is more nuanced in its development within the Church and in its application. Here, Professor Stark's book, *The Victory of Reason*, is on-point. He describes how early Christians who emerged from the ruins of the Western Roman Empire and who used reason to debate and interpret Scripture applied the same reasoning skills to other areas, from art to science to many other fields, and Western Civilization experienced some of its greatest advances. The advances were so great that the Medieval Church needed to hire professional managers for its monastic estates to allow the clergy to focus on more spiritual matters. In turn, the professional managers produced surplus goods and services that were traded in free markets, giving rise to an evolved form of capitalism with entities employing human and physical capital (the former called "free labor" and the latter referred to as "capital goods") under professional management. Professor Stark's research

---

[184] These building blocks trace back to the late-sixteenth century publication of Richard Hooker's *Laws of Ecclesiastical Polity*, in which he "denies the Puritan assertion that the Bible is the *only* source of authority; in his view Reason and Tradition are the other sources, and Reason serves to interpret both Scripture and Tradition." James Thayer Addison, *The Episcopal Church in the United States, 1789-1931* (Archon Books, 1969), p. 11.

[185] Also, we will apply all three building blocks in an exercise in Sec. XI.A.

traces the origin of capitalism with professional management to ninth century Catholic monastic estates and refers to this structure as "religious capitalism".[186]

Indeed, the concept of professional management of resources is well-grounded in the New Testament Gospels of Matthew and Luke. In each of those Gospels, Jesus tells parables to illustrate aspects of the Kingdom of Heaven that are set in such a management structure.

In Matthew 25:14-30, a wealthy man distributes talents (each equivalent to several year's wages for a laborer) to three servants, based upon their abilities, each empowered to manage the investment of those funds: one received five talents, another received two talents and the last received one talent. Since these servants perform managerial functions, I will refer to servants in this capacity as "managers". The first two managers doubled the number of talents assigned, and Jesus tells us that the wealthy man responds to each, "Well done, thou good and faithful servant: thou hast been faithful over a few things, I will make thee ruler over many things: enter thou into the joy of thy lord" (versus 21 and 23). However, the third manager buried his talent because he was afraid of risking it to earn a return on investment, and, upon being told, the wealthy man scolded the third manager for failing to perform the bare minimum and place his talent with the money lenders who would have paid interest on the investment. For his failure, the wealthy man directs that the third manager's talent be taken away from him and be given to the first manager. Jesus concludes the parable with the wealthy man saying, "For unto every one that hath shall be given, and he shall have abundance: but from him that hath not shall be taken away even that which he hath. And cast ye the unprofitable servant into outer darkness: there shall be weeping and gnashing of teeth." (versus 29-30). In this parable, then, we see Jesus acknowledge and use to teach from a professional management structure with, what we would label today, a "performance-based compensation system". Moreover, since the manager who succeeded was not only rewarded but allowed to keep his reward,[187] and because there is no description of a social safety net for the manager who failed, this parable is set in a pure capitalist system. Presumably, Jesus observed this management system in practice at the time, although He may have embellished with rather dire consequences for failure so that He could emphasize His point about the Kingdom of Heaven!

In Luke, we have three parables that illustrate professional management structures. One parable, in Luke 19:11-28, closely tracks the Matthew parable of the talents above and so will not be repeated here. In the parable of the Faithful and Wise Steward, Luke 12:42-48, Jesus contrasts a good manager who is given charge of the household by its owner and gives the servants "their portion of meat in due season" with a manager who beats the servants and is drunk. Jesus concludes the parable with a saying similar to that of the Matthew parable, "For unto whomsoever much is given, of him shall be much required: and to whom men have committed much, of him they will ask the more." Then, in Luke 16:1-13, Jesus presents a parable with an interesting twist on the professional management structure in that an incompetent manager who is about to be fired by his master exhibits cunning by using his authority to open doors for his next career move. The cunning manager asks those who trade with his

---

[186] Stark's discussion of capitalism and religious capitalism is found on pp. 55-61 of *The Victory of Reason*.
[187] The reward was the ability of the manager with ten talents to invest the eleventh talent with the others to earn a greater return on the increased capital available. As explained in the following paragraph, this compensation system would allow the manager to share the earnings from capital investment with his master when those earnings cleared a predetermined hurdle rate of return.

master to reduce the amounts they owe so as to curry favor. Presumably, the debt reductions authorized by the manager came out of his share of the profits because the master, upon hearing what the manager did, commended the manager (it is not clear whether the manager's plan kept him from being fired, though). Jesus' point of this parable was to use earthly riches to gain heavenly rewards: "Make to yourselves friends of the mammon of unrighteousness; that, when ye fail, they may receive you into everlasting habitations" (verse 9). He adds that, if you are "faithful in the unrighteous mammon", God will trust you with "true riches" (verse 10). Finally, Jesus warns that, "No servant can serve two masters: for either he will hate the one, and love the other; or else he will hold to the one, and despise the other. Ye cannot serve God and mammon" (verse 13).

These parables inform us that professional management structures in a capitalist economic system existed in the Roman Empire at least as early as first century AD and that Jesus found them useful in explaining spiritual concepts. After introducing the concept of reason in the next subsection, the following subsection will pick up with the fall of the Roman Empire to illustrate some of the advances born of reason and using professional management structures. We will not discuss the parables above, but I provide them for context on the origins of professional management later employed by the Early Church.

A. The Rise of Reason

> T: Let's return to the Roman Empire before Constantine legalized Christianity. What belief system was the official religion of the state?
>
> C: Worship of many gods.
>
> T: The Romans borrowed many of their gods from other cultures. Where did most of the Roman gods come from?
>
> C: The Greeks.[188]
>
> T: Let's take a closer look at the Greco-Roman gods, starting with the Family Tree of the Greek gods.

---

[188] From F.W. Kelsey, *An Outline of Greek and Roman Mythology*, pp. 12-13: "In Mythology, as in literature and the arts, the Romans borrowed freely from other nations. At an early time they were no doubt much influenced by contact with the neighboring Etruscans. In the Republican period their relations with the Greeks became close, first through the Greek colonies in Magna Graecia, then through commercial and political connections with the cities of Asia Minor and Greece. The worship of many Greek divinities was introduced. With these came the whole body of Greek mythology. In many instances a Greek god was identified with a Roman and the myths of the one ascribed to the other. As educated Romans became saturated with the Greek culture, the Greek myths came to be as familiar to them as their own, and consequently occupy as prominent a place in the Roman literature as in the Greek."

Handout #7: Greek Mythology

Greek Gods Family Tree

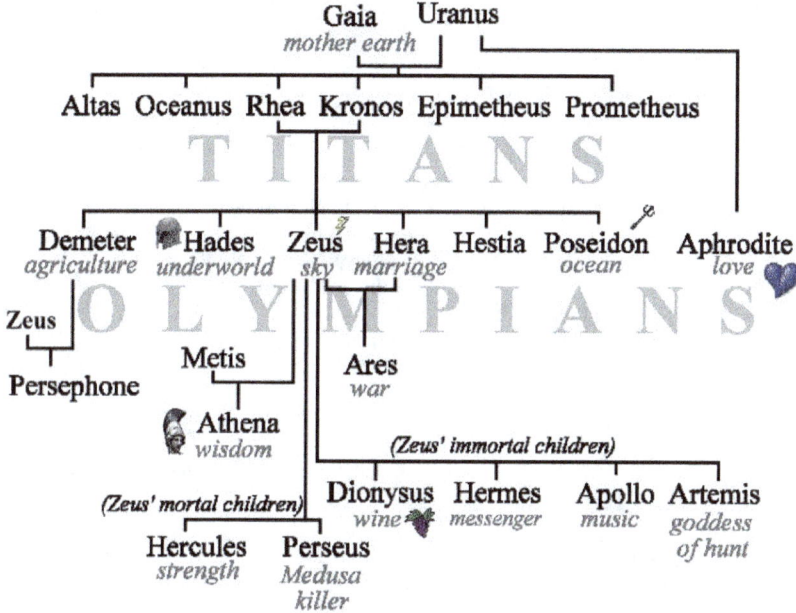

Source: http://jonesworldhistory.weebly.com/unit-2-greek-and-roman-empires.html, licensed under a Creative Commons Attribution 4.0 International License.

The family tree of the Greek gods tells a story of jealousy. The Titans were the children of Sky and Earth: Uranus and Gaia. But Uranus was jealous of his children, so he stuffed them into the earth. Kronos, though, ambushed Uranus and freed his siblings. Kronos then married his sister, Rhea, who gave birth to the Olympians – gods who lived on Mount Olympus. However, Kronos, like his father, became jealous of his children and swallowed them all except Zeus, whom Rhea managed to hide in a cave on the island of Crete. Zeus later defeated his father and became the ruling god. Zeus married Metis first, then Hera, but Metis he swallowed when she was pregnant with Athena fearing she would have a son who would overthrow him! Athena, then, was born from Zeus' head since Metis was still inside him. Zeus' marriages were mere formalities, though, since he fathered many other children from other goddesses and human women.

The Greek gods also toyed with humans, especially when the gods were upset. Artemis, for example, was bathing in a stream when a human, a hunter named Actaeon out hunting with his dogs, came by and saw her. Offended that Actaeon saw her without clothes, Artemis turned Actaeon into a stag (a male deer) so that Actaeon's dogs would turn on him and tear him apart.

On the plus side, though, Greek gods could help humans. The poet Homer, in his epic story *The Iliad*, gave an account of Apollo helping the Trojans when the Greeks were besieging Troy. Apollo's help was not out of pity for the humans, however. The Greek king, Agamemnon, had kidnapped the daughter of a priest of the Temple of Apollo in Troy, and Apollo was angry, so Apollo sent a plague to attack the Greeks. The Greeks retreated, but in the end, though, the Greeks out-smarted the Trojans by leaving behind a "gift", a wooden horse full of soldiers, that opened the gates of Troy and let in the Greek army.

In Greek mythology, humans, then, were mere inconveniences or entertainment to the gods they worshiped. Homer composed a hymn to Apollo that expressed this sentiment, and part of that hymn's lyrics state:

> And straightway music and singing beguile the immortals.
> All the Muses together, voice answering heavenly voice,
> Hymn the undying gifts of the gods and the sufferings of men,
> Who, enduring so much at the hands of the gods everlasting,
> Live heedless and helpless, unable to find for themselves
> Either a cure for death or a bulwark against old age.
>
> *Hymn to Apollo* 3.188-192

For further background, an excellent synopsis of Greek mythology is available at: http://faculty.gvsu.edu/websterm/Greekhistory&gods.htm.

T: So if you worshipped the Greek gods, or their Roman counterparts, and you prayed to one or more of those gods for help, what could happen?

C: [Many answers] Nothing. Something bad. Something good, but only if that god could gain from helping you.

T: Do you think the Greco-Roman gods cared much for us humans?

C: No.

T: Do you think there was any love between Greco-Roman gods and humans?

C: No.

T: Did a worshipper of Greco-Roman gods have any means by which he/she would figure out whether a given god would provide help? Or, asked another way, if these Greco-Roman gods didn't care much about humans, was there any purpose for a worshipper to even try to figure out how to get the gods to help?[189]

---

[189] From Acts 17:16-34, we read that when St. Paul was in Athens, he encountered Epicurean and Stoic philosophers at Mars Hill and gave a fascinating critique of their gods. He pointed out that they were so lacking in their understanding of their gods that they had a statue titled "TO THE UNKNOWN GOD" in case they missed one; St. Paul then stated that his God was the God the Greeks had over-

C: No. Those gods didn't care, so what's the use.

T: Apparently there were plenty of ways to upset the gods, such as Agamemnon kidnapping the daughter of a priest of Apollo, but if a Greco-Roman god helped someone, as Apollo helped the Trojans, that was either sheer luck or the god had another motive. We spent a fair amount of time in this course studying Scripture to determine what God wants us to do and find out how God helps us. Do you think there was any reason for a worshipper of Greco-Roman gods to study the myths and literature, of which there was a lot, to determine how one of those gods would help?

C: No.[190]

T: When we study Scripture as we have in this course, we use our minds to build a picture from the words of Scripture to show us what God wants us to become. We do that by looking at what various writers from the Old and New Testament wrote, what Jesus said and what His disciples later wrote. This process of studying Scripture is called the application of REASON: the use of our minds to infer from information we have to answer a question. Christians use reason to discern from Scripture, our "information", to answer the "question" of what is God's vision for us. This use of reason would be worthless to a Greco-Roman god worshipper because there were no laws governing the conduct of those gods and therefore nothing to discern that would help that worshipper. Our God, though, has laws, called "covenants", that He entered into with us, and we can study those covenants and discern how God wants us to live.[191]

B. Christianity and "Religious Capitalism"

T: Remember our discussion of the Battle of Milvian Bridge? Who can tell me what happened?

C: Constantine won using shields painted with a Christian symbol.

T: Before Constantine won, was Christianity a legal religion in the Roman Empire?

C: No.

T: After Constantine's victory, what did he do about Christianity?

C: He made it legal.

---

looked (vs. 23). Moreover, St. Paul rejected the Greek concept that gods needed to be served by human hands; the God who made the universe did not need human help (vss. 24-25). St. Paul's critique, then, highlights how incomplete and contradictory was the Greek belief system.

[190] Unquestionably, there were many reasons for the ancients to study the god myths as a means to make sense of their world, and often to seek help, but those myths did little to provide assurance that help would come.

[191] Also, any religion that does not allow for open debate of its tenants and insists on strict adherence to a set of unchallengeable beliefs would close out the use of reason. You may wish to raise this premise as well.

T: Constantine, as Emperor of the Western Roman Empire, and Licinius, Emperor of the Eastern Roman Empire, agreed to issue the Edict of Milan in 313 A.D. that gave Christianity legal status throughout the Empire. Soon afterwards, in 325 A.D., since Christians no longer needed to hide, Church leaders gathered at a meeting in Nicaea, a town in the same province Pliny the Younger governed 200 years earlier,[192] to establish the principles of our Faith. The product of that meeting in Nicaea was a creed that sets out those principles, which we say in most of our church services today. Does anyone know what that creed is called?

C: [With a look of revelation] The Nicene Creed!

T: So we are up to the year 325 A.D. How much longer did the Roman Empire exist after that point in time? Look at panels XI and XII of the *Timechart* and see.

The *Timechart* shows the massive brown area that represents the Roman Empire beginning to break apart before 400 A.D. The beginning of the end of Rome's dominance likely began with the settlement of large Germanic tribes on Roman territory, starting around 375 A.D. Those tribes were so large that Rome could not force them to integrate into Roman society, and those tribes created semi-autonomous states within the Empire. Military collapse arrived in 410 A.D. when one of those tribes actually sacked Rome. The formal end of the Western Roman Empire came when Odoacer (shown in yellow in the lower part of Panel XII) deposed the last emperor in 476 A.D. The Eastern Empire survived for another millennium. From this point forward, though, we will focus on the rise of new countries from the breakup of the Western Empire, especially Britain near the top of the timeline.

T: As the Roman Empire is breaking apart, when does the *Timechart* show Rome abandoning Britain? [Direct attention to Panel XII, under the title "Britannia"]

C: In 426 A.D.

T: At that point, it was pretty much every-man-for-himself. Look further to the right and you will see numerous small kingdoms established over the next century.[193] Indeed, by the year 500 A.D., the entire western part of the Roman Empire had fractured. Some historians labeled the period that follows the breakup of the Western Roman Empire as the "Dark Ages". What have you been told about what happened during the Dark Ages to make them so "dark"?

C: [Many answers] People starved. Disease spread. Civilization did not advance.

T: What about technology? Were there any major technological advancements during the Dark Ages?

C: No.

---

[192] Bythnia, in present-day northwestern Turkey.
[193] You may want to point out King Arthur Pendragon, shown in yellow from 500 – 542 A.D. He was cited in a wide range of literature spanning many centuries, most famous of which was *Le Morte d'Arthur* by Sir Thomas Mallory, first published in 1485. Arthur's dream of uniting the Britons, though, did not begin to come to pass for another three centuries when Egbert brought some of the kingdoms together through conquest and bribery.

Confirmand Reference Book First Edition

> T: When, according to the "Dark Ages version of events", did technological innovation begin?
>
> C: Some time much later. Not until the Renaissance.
>
> T: Actually, advancements in technology and government began much earlier than you think. Let's look at research performed by social scientist Rodney Stark.

In Stark's book, *The Victory of Reason*, turn to page 35 and read paragraphs to the break on page 37. Important passages:

> For the past two or three centuries, every educated person has known that from the fall of Rome until about the fifteenth century Europe was submerged in the "Dark Ages"[194]—centuries of ignorance, superstition, and misery—from it was suddenly, almost miraculously rescued, first by the Renaissance and then by the Enlightenment. But it didn't happen that way. Instead, during the so-called Dark Ages, European technology and science overtook and surpassed the rest of the world! [Footnotes omitted.][195]

To illustrate these points, continue to read the following section on "Technical Progress" and the first three paragraphs of "Innovations in Production".

> T: The point about paper is instructive. The pulping process was invented in China in the second century A.D. during the Han Dynasty [found at the very bottom of Panel XI of the *Timechart*]. Certainly, the Chinese understood waterpower at that time, but despite having a 1,000-year lead on the Europeans, they did not develop a means to mechanize the production of paper using waterpower, or anything else. What did the mass production of paper allow people to do?
>
> C: Print books!
>
> T: And with the printing of books, you could spread what?
>
> C: Knowledge.
>
> T: Now let's take a look at agriculture.

Turn to page 42 and read the two complete paragraphs on that page, and refer to the following handout.

---

[194] Stark published this statement in 2005. Subsequently, due to research by other scholars in addition to Stark, the "Dark Ages" moniker, if used at all, attached only to the first 500 years after the fall of Rome, until about 1000 A.D., in recognition of evidence that substantial development occurred after that period. Still, Stark cites evidence in his book of significant technological advances starting in the eighth century (with crop rotation – page 42), so perhaps it would be best to relegate the term to the status of "myth"!

[195] Excerpts from p.35 of *The Victory of Reason: How Christianity Led to Freedom, Capitalism, and Western Success*, by Rodney Stark, copyright © 2005 by Rodney Stark. Used by permission of Random House, an imprint and division of Penguin Random House LLC. All rights reserved.

Handout #8:

Two-Field and Three-Field Systems

Roman System

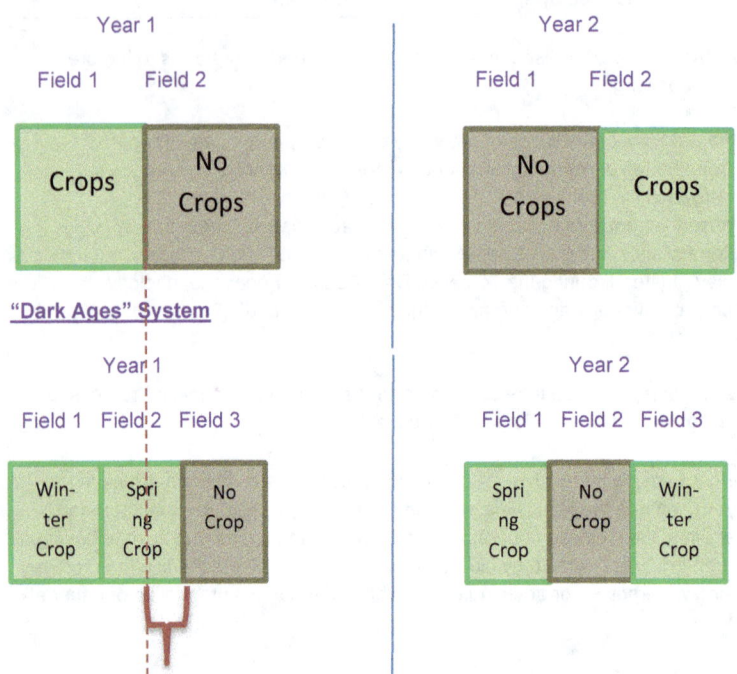

"Dark Ages" System

Extra crops grown during the "Dark Ages" compared to Roman System

Key:
Winter crops: wheat
Spring crops: oats, legumes (peas and beans), vegetables

Adapted from: Stark, *The Victory of Reason: How Christianity Led to Freedom, Capitalism and Western Success*, Random House, 2006, p. 42.

T: When did the three-field system first appear?

C: In the eighth century.

T: And what did that system do for food production?

C: It expanded it by planting more crops.

T: How did the three-field system differ from the Roman two-field system? What was the spring field planted with?

C: Oats, legumes and vegetables.

T: Stark does not explain this in the passage we just read, but how did Europeans discover that legumes helped restore nutrients to the land? In 700 A.D., was there a government-run laboratory that conducted soil tests?

C: No – farmers just had to use trial and error.

T: Probably. It could be that some farmers reported that fields planted with beans did not need to be rotated as frequently; that is, the legume fields did not need to lay fallow as often. Then others took that information and incorporated it into the old Roman system to develop the three-field method. Now, look back at our definition of reason:

REASON: the use of our minds to infer from information we have to answer a question.

T: What was the "question", or problem, that the farmers had?

C: How to produce more food.

T: What was the "information" the farmers had that would allow them to produce more food? [Look to the Spring Crops on the handout.]

C: That legume fields did not need to lay fallow as often.

T: So "Dark Ages" farmers used reason to infer from legume fields that they could rotate crops over three fields instead of two and thereby produce more food. This is the same use of reason we employed earlier to take information from Scripture to gain a better picture of God. So, speaking generally, not just about Christianity, but any religion that encourages the use of our minds to interpret holy writings will encourage the use of reason. And if a religion encourages the use of reason, do followers of that religion apply reason to other areas, such as improvements in technology?

C: Yes.[196]

T: If the three-field system were the only advancement, I'd likely attribute this development to luck or other causes, but when you stack the three-field agricultural advancement with the mass production of paper and others that Stark describes, I start to ask, "is there a connection?" Turn to page 54 and read the last paragraph that continues to page 55.

T: Why did Christianity teach, as Stark asserts, that "progress was 'normal' and that 'new inventions would always be forthcoming'"?

C: Christianity taught the use of reason.

---

[196] Another necessary condition is a form of government that provides a rule of law whereby producers can retain and reinvest the profits of their production. Autocratic governments that confiscate the fruits of production, either through high taxes or direct seizure, provide no incentive to advance technology. The autocratic dynasties of China were likely responsible for the failure to develop paper and other technologies.

T: Stark also said that Medieval Europeans invented "better ways to get things done." Turn to page 57 and read the first two paragraphs under "The Rise of Religious Capitalism" to see what he is talking about.

T: From the first paragraph, what was the attitude of early church fathers toward commerce when Christianity was not a legal religion in the Roman Empire?

C: They thought it was beneath them, lower class.

T: And that was also the opinion of Roman high society, which looked down upon tradesmen and shopkeepers. Then after Constantine's conversion, and the Edict of Milan, what changed?

C: Attitudes towards commerce began to change.

T: Who was Augustine? [Look to Augustine on the *Timechart* – his bar spans Panels XI and XII in the top third section – and read his description.]

C: "Most famous of the Latin Fathers."

T: Look on the *Timechart* back to the left of Augustine and you will see several early church writers identified as either Greek or Latin in parentheses to let you see the language used in their writings. Augustine was a bishop of Hippo, located in North Africa, and he wrote a lot! In the first sentence of the second paragraph, how did Augustine describe what sets the price of goods and services?

C: A combination of the seller's costs and the buyer's desire for the item being sold.

T: And is that definition still true today?

C: Yes.

T: Further in that paragraph we read about monastic estates – large areas of land farmed by Christian monks – that were able to specialize in particular crops or products and trade their excess crops and products with others. So here we see the beginnings of an economy where people who produced extra wheat could sell or trade with people who produced extra vegetables, or perhaps for tools and supplies, at prices set through negotiation between buyer and seller. What economic system did I just describe? [Hint: see the last two sentences of the second paragraph.]

C: Capitalism

T: Since it was developed by Christian monks, it is sometimes referred to as "Religious Capitalism". And how did the Christian monks produce excess crops?

C: The three-field system.

T: Along with advancements in the use of horses and plows. And how did the Christian monks figure out that legumes would allow them to rotate crops over three fields?

C: Trial and error. Reason.

T: Now take a guess as to where the monks learned about the use of reason. What did monks read a lot of and discuss frequently among themselves?

C: Scripture.

T: Scripture of which religion?

C: Christianity.

T: So we have the following chain of events:

Christianity →

Reason to understand Scripture →

Reason to apply technology →

Excess production →

Religious Capitalism

C. Apostolic Succession

T: Now, let's go back to the Council of Nicaea in 325 A.D. At that time, the Western Roman Empire had just over a hundred years of life left before it would break apart; the Eastern Empire would last another thousand years. But the breakup of the Western Empire was not bad news by any means. The Roman Empire existed to serve the interests of its rulers by living off the wealth of its conquered territories. When the Empire collapsed in Western Europe, its people were free to pursue their own interests, and Christians built a church centered in Rome called the Roman Catholic Church. Who is the head of the Roman Catholic Church?

C: The Pope.

T: Where did the early Roman Catholic Church get the idea that one person would be the leader of its church and who would that person be? Let's look at a conversation Jesus had with his disciples:

> Matthew 16
>
> 13 When Jesus came into the coasts of Caesarea Philippi, he asked his disciples, saying, Whom do men say that I the Son of man am?
>
> 14 And they said, Some say that thou art John the Baptist: some, Elias; and others, Jeremias, or one of the prophets.
>
> 15 He saith unto them, But whom say ye that I am?

16 And Simon Peter answered and said, Thou art the Christ, the Son of the living God.

17 And Jesus answered and said unto him, Blessed art thou, Simon Barjona: for flesh and blood hath not revealed it unto thee, but my Father which is in heaven.

18 And I say also unto thee, That thou art Peter, and upon this rock I will build my church; and the gates of hell shall not prevail against it.

19 And I will give unto thee the keys of the kingdom of heaven: and whatsoever thou shalt bind on earth shall be bound in heaven: and whatsoever thou shalt loose on earth shall be loosed in heaven.

T: Our Roman Catholic brothers and sisters in Christ point to verse 18 as evidence that Peter was to be the first pope. Explain what in verse 18 supports that view?

C: Jesus said that Peter is the rock upon which He will build His Church.

T: As you can imagine, other Christian denominations disagree with that interpretation. Here is verse 18 from the Amplified Bible,[197] which expands on the Greek words used in the original text [Teacher reads this text]:

> Matthew 16:18 (AMP)
>
> And I tell you, you are Peter [Petros, a small or detached stone], and on this rock [petra, bedrock or a huge rock] I will build My church, and the gates of Hades (death) shall not overpower it [by preventing the resurrection of the Christ]. [Footnotes omitted.]

From the Amplified translation, then, if Peter is a large piece of rock that is part of an even bigger piece of rock upon which Jesus will build His Church, what is the "petra" or huge piece of rock likely to be? To answer that question, who, in addition to Peter, is listening to Jesus when He says these words? [Hint: Look at verse 13.]

C: His disciples.

T: Right. So if Peter is a large rock, who is the huge rock?

C: The disciples.

---

[197] Scripture quotations marked (AMP) are taken from the Amplified Bible, Copyright © 1954, 1958, 1962, 1964, 1965, 1987 by The Lockman Foundation. Used by permission.

T: Protestants, such as our church, believe that Jesus was not just going to build His Church on Peter alone but on the foundation of all His disciples. That said, Peter was clearly an important leader in the Early Church.[198] But I want to focus on the role of Jesus' disciples after Jesus ascended into Heaven.

> Acts 6
>
> 1 And in those days, when the number of the disciples was multiplied, there arose a murmuring of the Grecians against the Hebrews, because their widows were neglected in the daily ministration.
>
> 2 Then the twelve [apostles] called the multitude of the disciples unto them, and said, It is not reason that we should leave the word of God, and serve tables.
>
> 3 Wherefore, brethren, look ye out among you seven men of honest report, full of the Holy Ghost and wisdom, whom we may appoint over this business.
>
> 4 But we will give ourselves continually to prayer, and to the ministry of the word.
>
> 5 And the saying pleased the whole multitude: and they chose Stephen, a man full of faith and of the Holy Ghost, and Philip, and Prochorus, and Nicanor, and Timon, and Parmenas, and Nicolas a proselyte of Antioch:
>
> 6 Whom they set before the apostles: and when they had prayed, they laid their hands on them.
>
> 7 And the word of God increased; and the number of the disciples multiplied in Jerusalem greatly; and a great company of the priests were obedient to the faith.

T: So, when the Church was growing rapidly, what did the twelve apostles do to increase the number of ministers?

C: They found more people to help them.

T: Once they found the seven mentioned in the passage we just read, what does verse 6 say the apostles did next?

---

[198] For example, the Book of Acts shows that Peter is the first to speak to the multitudes on the day of Pentecost (Acts 2:14), he performs the first recorded healing miracle after Jesus' ascension (Acts 3:6-7), and when Cornelius the centurion sees a vision that will lead to his conversion, God instructs him to look for Peter in the town of Joppa (Acts 10:5).

C: The apostles prayed and then laid their hands on them.

T: If you were to continue reading in the Book of Acts, you would learn more about the first of the seven, Stephen. In addition to taking care of widows and the poor, Stephen preached to the Jews in Jerusalem and then was stoned to death because he accused them of rejecting Jesus as God's Son.[199] Then you would read of the second of the seven, Philip, who preached about Jesus to the people of Samaria.[200] So, after the apostles laid hands on the seven, what did the seven do?

C: They took care of the poor and preached about Jesus.

T: The apostles laid hands on the seven and sent them out to preach, and the apostles themselves later left Jerusalem to preach,[201] and, collectively, they found others who were willing to preach, and so on and so on. They retained the practice of laying on of hands, though, from one generation to another. Before the Edict of Milan, however, how risky was it for these early Christian ministers to preach the Word of God openly?

C: Very risky because Christianity was not legal.

T: After the Edict of Milan, when Christian ministers could speak openly, they gathered in Nicaea to hold a council. Who do you suppose likely showed up? Christian ministers certainly came, but how did these people know they were ministers?

C: People followed them.

T: That would be a good clue, but there's more. Look back at Acts 6:3. The apostles wanted "men of honest report, full of the Holy Ghost and wisdom". So there was some screening process. Then, looking at Acts 6:6, what action did the apostles take that signaled to the church that these seven had been chosen?

C: The apostles laid hands on the seven.

T: And the apostles laid hands on others, who laid hands on others, and so on. So, those who came to Nicaea in 325 A.D. knew they were ministers because ...

C: Someone had laid hands on them.

T: That was true for at least some of the attendees at Nicaea who were referred to as "bishops".[202] And for those bishops at Nicaea who could say they had someone lay hands on them, and that someone had someone else lay hands on him, and that someone had someone else lay hands on him, how far back did this line go? Who originated the laying on of hands?

---

[199] Acts 6:8 – 7:60.
[200] Acts 8:4-24. Philip then encountered the Ethiopian eunuch on the road to Gaza (Acts 8:25-40), which we will cover in the discussion of Holy Baptism in Sec. XI.C.a.
[201] The Temple History discussion in IV.A. described the diaspora of Jews after the revolt of 68 A.D. – 70 A.D.
[202] St. Athanasius, who was present at the Council of Nicaea, stated in his letter, *Ad Afros*, that 318 bishops attended.

C: The apostles.

T: So, we refer to this line of bishops who received the laying on of hands as the "Apostolic Succession": each bishop can trace this line of previous bishops back to the first bishops, the apostles of Jesus.[203] Who is going to confirm you?

C: A bishop.

T: That bishop, too, can tell you the names of the bishops who performed the laying on of hands and, with reference to some documents, who laid hands on those bishops, and who laid hands on them until you reach the beginning. And who will be named at the beginning?

C: The apostles of Jesus.

D. The Protestant Reformation

T: There are bishops who oversee other bishops. They are called archbishops. We do not have an archbishop in the Episcopal Church in the U.S. but rather use the term "Presiding Bishop". In other countries, there is at least one archbishop. In England, there are two archbishops, one in York and another in Canterbury. Recall that earlier in this course we read from the first Book of Common Prayer published in England in 1549. Look at the *Timechart*, Panel XIV, and tell me who was king of England in 1549?

C: Edward VI.

T: Edward had been king for only a few years when the book was published, but the first Book of Common Prayer represented a major shift in Christianity because the book, and the Church that used it, did not acknowledge any role for the Roman Catholic Pope. To see how this came to pass, look back at the *Timechart* and tell me which king preceded Edward VI.

C: Henry VIII.

T: He was Edward's father. And what does the *Timechart* list under Henry VIII?

C: The names of six women.

---

[203] Former Archbishop of Canterbury Michael Ramsey argued that the doctrine of Apostolic Succession did not come into existence until St. Augustine of Hippo in the early fifth century A.D. (Ramsey, *The Gospel and the Catholic Church*, 1936, p. 70). The recorded practice of one bishop succeeding another, though, predates that time. I invite anyone interested to examine the writings of Cyprian from the third century, especially his Epistle 66 at v. Keep in mind that much of this discussion takes place in the context of whether a minister is properly ordained if the officiant is or is not a successor to the apostles. That discussion, though, is well beyond the scope of this course. The Chicago-Lambeth Quadrilateral of 1886, 1888 established the "Historic Episcopate" as "essential to the restoration of unity among the divided branches of Christendom". See also The Episcopal Church's website at http://www.episcopalchurch.org/library/glossary/historic-episcopate. All we need to accomplish here, though, is to establish that the bishop who confirms the confirmands draws upon a spiritual authority to do so beginning with the apostles and passed down through successors.

T: They were Henry's wives. Who was the first wife and what does the *Timechart* say after her name?

C: Catherine, divorced.

T: In order to get a divorce in that time, a king had to appeal to the Roman Catholic pope for permission. The pope, though, refused. So what do you think Henry did to get his divorce? Look at what is written directly above Henry VIII on the *Timechart*.

C: It says "Head of the Church"

T: Henry was not just king of England, he asserted he was also Head of the Church in England, so he pulled the Church of England out of the Roman Catholic Church. Of the bishops in England, who were the highest-ranking at that time?

C: Archbishops of York and Canterbury.

T: And of those two, the Archbishop of Canterbury position was the oldest because it traced its beginning to St. Augustine 1000 years earlier. So Henry looked to the Archbishop of Canterbury, who was a man named Thomas Cranmer, to grant him a divorce. If a divorce was all that happened, however, I don't think we'd be talking about it much today. But there was a lot of discontent with the Roman Catholic Church at that time; those who were not happy with the Roman Catholic Church were called "Protestants" because they were protesting positions taken by that Church. On the *Timechart*, look directly above Henry VIII and you will see the drawing of a monk holding a book. Who is he?

C: Martin Luther.

T: What else is written after his name?

C: At Worms, 1521

T: Luther had written a list of complaints, 99 to be exact, against the Roman Catholic Church and its pope in 1517. Chief among these complaints was that the Roman Catholic Church sold forgiveness of sins for donations to the Church. Luther thought selling forgiveness was wrong, but the pope excommunicated him, which meant Luther could no longer receive communion, and effectively he was banned from the Church. At Worms in 1521, Luther was declared an outlaw, but he escaped to a friendly part of Germany and set about building a new church in 1525. Today, what is the name of the Church Luther built?

C: The Lutherans.

T: So by the time Henry VIII gets a divorce in 1533 by pulling the Church of England away from the Roman Catholic Church, the Lutheran Protestants in Germany were already building their church. Also, Thomas Cranmer, while serving as an ambassador for King Henry, had extensive contact with the Lutherans.[204] So the break in England gave the Lutheran-minded reformers there the chance to build their church too. Archbishop Cranmer, with the help of other reformers, then developed the Book of Common Prayer, which we read from earlier in

---

[204] Cranmer even married a relative of one of the chief Lutheran reformers, Andreas Osiander.

this course [Section I.C.], that was published soon after Henry's death in 1549. So here are the key dates:

1517 – Luther wrote his 99 Theses [the complaints against the Roman Catholic Church]

1521 – Luther excommunicated and declared an outlaw at Worms

1525 – Luther began to draft the faith principles for the Lutheran Church

1533 – Henry VIII broke with the Roman Catholic Church, separating the Church of England

1549 – First Church of England Book of Common Prayer published

E. The American Revolution

T: Now let's jump forward about 50 years. The British set up colonies in the New World, starting with the settlement of Jamestown in Virginia in 1607. What church did the British bring to America? The Roman Catholic Church?

C: No, the church founded by Henry VIII.

T: Called the "Church of England", even when that Church came to the British colonies in America.[205] The colonists, at first, considered themselves British, so worshiping in a Church of England church was not unusual. By the time of the Revolution, however, what changed about the Americans' attitude regarding the English?

C: The Americans thought they were being treated unfairly about taxation and rights.

T: For those of you who paid attention during history class, who won the American Revolution?

C: We did!

T: Where was the final, decisive siege that spelled the end of British rule in the Americas?

C: Yorktown.

T: What caused the British forces at Yorktown to surrender?

C: The French fleet showed up, and the French were allied with the Americans.

T: That year was 1781. By 1783, the British formally surrendered with the Treaty of Paris. While that treaty addressed issues relating to war and commerce, it neglected to address is-

---

[205] See "Jamestown excavation unearths four bodies — and a mystery in a small box", *The Washington Post*, July 28, 2015.

sues relating to the Church in America. There was one big problem when we broke with England during the American Revolution: there were no bishops in America! Who is going to confirm you?

C: The bishop.

T: We haven't covered this yet, but if a bishop is needed to confirm you, who do you think is needed to ordain a priest?

C: A bishop.

T: Right. And it takes a minimum of three bishops to consecrate a new bishop.[206] So, in 1783, where would someone in America have to go to be ordained a priest?

C: England.

T: Yes – the country we just fought a war with and won! To give you a sense of how sore the British were at the loss of their colonies in America, when painter Benjamin West tried to produce a portrait of the signing of the Treaty of Paris, the British representatives refused to sit for the portrait, so part of his painting is unfinished!

Benjamin West, *The Signing of the Treaty of Paris*, 1783, public domain.

---

[206] BCP, p. 511.

What we needed were bishops in America. Why didn't the priests and lay people in America just hold an election and choose three priests to become bishops? [Hint: There is something all bishops need to trace back to the apostles of Jesus.]

C: They needed laying on of hands.

T: Why was laying on of hands important?

C: Bishops have to come from a chain of bishops going back to the Apostles.

T: That's called Apostolic Succession, and to maintain the Apostolic Succession, an American priest desiring to be consecrated a bishop had not only to go to England to find bishops willing to lay hands on him, but, at the time, he had to swear allegiance to the English King, called the "Oath of Supremacy". One American priest, Samuel Seabury, who was elected bishop by the clergy in Connecticut, found some Scottish bishops willing to consecrate him as bishop in 1783, but the problem was not officially resolved until 1786 when the British Parliament passed the Consecration of Bishops Abroad Act. That act allowed the Archbishop of Canterbury or the Archbishop of York, with other bishops assisting, to consecrate bishops from countries outside the control of the King.[207] Now think about what happened here. How any years had passed since the siege of Yorktown in 1781 to passage of the Consecration of Bishops Abroad Act in 1786?

C: 5.

T: And from the signing of the Treaty of Paris in 1783 to passage of the Consecration of Bishops Abroad Act in 1786?

C: 3.

T: And, judging from Benjamin West's unfinished painting of the signing of the treaty, how mad do you think the British were about the loss of the American colonies?

C: Really mad!

T: I doubt they were any less mad in 1786 than they were in 1783. So in spite of being really mad about losing the colonies, the British Parliament did something truly remarkable to help the Church in the newly formed United States. What was that?

C: They passed an act that allowed our bishops to be consecrated.

---

[207] The relevant portion of the Consecration of Bishops Abroad Act of 1786: "... Be it enacted by the King's most excellent Majesty, by and with the advice and consent of the Lords Spiritual and Temporal and Commons in this present parliament assembled ... it shall and may be lawful to and for the Archbishop of Canterbury, or the Archbishop of York, for the time being, together with such other Bishops as they shall call to their assistance, to consecrate persons being subjects or citizens of countries out of his Majesty's dominions, Bishops for the purposes aforesaid, without the king's license for their election ... and without requiring them to take the oaths of allegiance and supremacy, and oath of due obedience to the Archbishop for the time being." Episcopal News Service, July 7, 2010, *July 18 bulletin inserts recall first presiding bishop.*

T: Why do you think the British would want to help the very people who fought against them only a few years earlier?

C: They saw we needed bishops.

T: Parliament put the interests of spreading the Christian Faith over their own resentment about losing the American Revolution![208] Soon, three more American bishops were consecrated in England: William White, Samuel Provoost, and James Madison – author of many of the Federalist Papers and the Bill of Rights, as well as our fourth president. With a minimum of three bishops needed to consecrate another bishop, the four new American bishops consecrated other American bishops without having to send them to England. Now, let's see what happened after the first four bishops were consecrated:

In *Handout #9* following, you can identify who was present for the consecration of the first four American bishops, then step through the consecration of others to see how American bishops were consecrating other American bishops.

Handout #9

Early Bishops of the Protestant Episcopal Church of the United States

The number references the sequence of consecration. "Diocese" refers to the diocese for which the individual was ordained. Note, this does not mean it was the only diocese that bishop presided over. For example, the Diocese of Delaware was under the supervision of the Diocese of Pennsylvania under William White. "PB" refers to whether the bishop became a Presiding Bishop in the Protestant Episcopal Church of the United States and, if so, which number in the sequence.

Under consecrators, one finds numbers (and/or letters) referencing previous bishops on the list. If a series of letters is under "Consecrators," then the consecrators were bishops/archbishops from outside of the Protestant Episcopal Church of the United States:

KIL = Robert Kilgour, Primus and Bishop of Aberdeen
MAR = William Markham, Archbishop of York
MOO = John Moore, Archbishop of Canterbury
MOS = Charles Moss, Bishop of Bath and Wells
PET = Arthur Petrie, Bishop of Moray and Ross
POR = Beilby Porteus, Bishop of London
SKI = John Skinner, bishop coadjutor of Aberdeen
THO = John Thomas, Bishop of Rochester

---

[208] To me, this is one of the most remarkable corporate acts of Christian Charity by one nation toward another. Feel free to elaborate on this topic as you see fit.

Confirmand Reference Book First Edition

No.	Bishop	Consecrators	Year	Diocese	Notes
1	Samuel Seabury	KIL PET SKI	1784	I Connecticut, I Rhode Island	PB2
2	William White	MOO MAR MOS	1787	I Pennsylvania	PB1 & PB4
3	Samuel Provoost	MOO MAR MOS	1787	I New York	PB3
4	James Madison	POR MOO THO	1790	I Virginia	
5	Thomas John Clagett	1 2 3 4	1792	I Maryland	
6	Robert Smith	2 3 4	1795	I South Carolina	
7	Edward Bass	2 3 5	1797	I Massachusetts, II Rhode Island[N 1]	
8	Abraham Jarvis	2 3 7	1797	II Connecticut	
9	Benjamin Moore	2 5 8	1801	II New York	
10	Samuel Parker	2 5 8	1804	II Massachusetts	
11	John Henry Hobart	2 3 8	1811	III New York	
12	Alexander Viets Griswold	2 3 8	1811	Eastern Diocese (simultaneously III Massachusetts, III Rhode Island and I New Hampshire).[N 2]	[N 3] PB5
13	Theodore Dehon	2 8 11	1812	II South Carolina	
14	Richard Channing Moore	2 11 12	1814	II Virginia	
15	James Kemp	2 11 14	1814	II Maryland	
16	John Croes	2 11 15	1815	I New Jersey	

17	Nathaniel Bowen	2 11 15	1818	III South Carolina		
18	Philander Chase	2 11 15	1819	I Ohio, I Illinois (Chicago)	IN 4I	PB6
19	Thomas Church Brownell	2 11 12	1819	III Connecticut		PB7

To obtain the most up-to-date list that continues to the present day go to: https://en.wikipedia.org/wiki/List_of_bishops_of_the_Episcopal_Church_in_the_United_States_of_America

F. The Protestant Episcopal Church in the USA

T: Think back to your American history studies regarding the development of our Constitution. Immediately after the American Revolution, our country did not have the constitution we have today. What document established the first US government?

C: Articles of Confederation.

T: How well did the Articles of Confederation work?

C: Not well. Government was too weak.

T: The federal government had very little power compared to the states. By 1787, problems with the Articles of Confederation were apparent, and states sent 55 delegates to meet in Philadelphia to draft a new constitution. What was the name of that meeting?

C: The Constitutional Convention.

T: The product of that convention was a federal government with more power, but there were checks and balances using three branches of government. What were, and are, the three branches of our government?

C: Legislative, executive, and judicial.

T: Of the delegates at the 1787 Constitutional Convention in Philadelphia, about 32, or 57%, were Episcopalians; many of these were signers of the Constitution.[209] Where in Philadelphia was the Constitutional Convention held?

---

[209] Episcopalian headcounts vary. For example, see https://www.redlandsdailyfacts.com/2019/07/04/professing-faith-the-religious-foundations-that-bolstered-the-declaration-of-independence/ and compare to http://candst.tripod.com/tnppage/qtable.htm. Assigning religious affiliation is difficult because identifying a delegate's religion is a matter of some interpretation. For example, Benjamin Franklin, who was baptized as an Anglican and is counted as an Episcopalian delegate, was a Deist who doubted the divinity of Christ, but he was buried in the Episcopal cemetery at Christ Church, Philadelphia.

C: Independence Hall.

T: A few blocks from Independence Hall is an Episcopal church named Christ Church. In that church's burial ground you will find five signers of the Declaration of Independence and three signers of the Constitution. The rector of Christ Church was William White. Where have we seen his name before?

C: He was one of the early bishops. [*Handout #9*]

T: Rev. White hosted a meeting of bishops, clergy and laity in Philadelphia in 1789 to approve a constitution for the newly formed Protestant Episcopal Church in the United States of America –PECUSA. Given the large number of Episcopalians who met in Philadelphia just two years earlier to draft the US Constitution, how many branches of government would you expect to see in the PECUSA Constitution?

C: Three.

T: You would be right, but the allocation of power among those branches is very different from the US Constitution. Under the US Constitution, the three branches provided checks and balances. In the PECUSA Constitution, the legislative branch holds most of the power. Here is how the three PECUSA branches break out:

General Convention

Presiding Bishop

Ecclasiastical Courts

Which of the above do you suppose is the legislative branch?

C: General Convention.

T: Right. General Convention meets once every three years and consists of two houses:

General Convention  House of Bishops

House of Deputies

How many houses are in the US Congress?

C: Two.

T: To get a bill passed in the US Congress, who has to approve that bill?

C: The House of Representatives and the Senate.

T: To pass legislation or resolutions at General Convention, guess which houses need to approve.

C: The House of Bishops and the House of Deputies?

T: Right, with a twist. The House of Deputies consists of lay deputies, who, like us, are not ordained, and of priests and deacons, who are ordained. If requested, the House of Deputies will vote by order: the lay persons will cast their votes separately from the priests and deacons, then the measure must pass both orders to move to the House of Bishops for final approval.

Let's look at the Presiding Bishop next. The Presiding Bishop is elected by the House of Bishops, so not everyone gets to vote on that office – just bishops. But the Presiding Bishop does not have powers similar to the US President. What if the US Congress passes a bill the President does not like? What can the President do?

C: Veto the bill.

T: And to turn a bill into law, the President must ...

C: Sign the bill.

T: The Presiding Bishop cannot veto measures passed by General Convention, nor is it necessary for the Presiding Bishop to sign off on any measure approved by General Convention. The Ecclasiastical Courts are also very limited in that they function principally to discipline clergy for various offenses but cannot overturn legislation, as is the case with the US Supreme Court. So what branch runs the Episcopal Church?

C: The legislative: General Convention.

T: But how easy is it, do you think, to get agreement between the House of Bishops and the House of Deputies, when the House of Deputies may need separate approval from the clerical and lay orders?

C: Not easy, and it seems like it takes a lot of effort

T: This is the structure we have today. Bishops are elected by each diocese to serve until they retire, and, for each General Convention, individual clergy and lay deputies are elected by each diocese as well.

Confirmand Reference Book First Edition

XI. The Creeds and the Sacraments

Learning Objectives for Subsections A and B

1. Confirmands will learn how the Nicene Creed was developed to refute heresies and understand how to use Scripture to determine what is heretical.
2. Confirmands will understand the differences between the Nicene and Apostles' Creeds and why Jesus had to pay for our sins in Hell.

A. The Nicene Creed

T: Turn to page 358 of the Book of Common Prayer. Just past the sermon, what comes next in the Holy Eucharist?

C: The Nicene Creed.

T: Where did the Nicene Creed get its name?

C: The Council of Nicaea.

T: Go to the *Timechart* and find the Council of Nicaea. Remember, it took place soon after the Battle of Milvian Bridge and the Edict of Milan. When did those events occur?

C: 312 and 313 A.D.

Note that the *Timechart* entry labels the Council of Nicaea as the "First Ecumenical Council" and uses the name "Nice" for its location.

T: When was the Council of Nicaea?

C: 325 A.D.

T: According to the *Timechart*, who attended the council?

C: 318 bishops and 2,048 ecclesiastics.

T: An "ecclesiastic" is another name for priest or deacon: someone who belongs to a religious order. This gathering at Nicaea was important, not just because it was the first council. What were Christians able to do in 325 A.D. that they had not been able to do previously?

C: Meet in public.

T: What allowed Christians to meet and worship without fear of prosecution?

C: The Edict of Milan.

T: We divide the Nicene Creed into three paragraphs. Look at the first sentence of each paragraph and tell me who is described in each paragraph.

> C: God in the first paragraph; Jesus Christ in the second; the Holy Spirit in the third.
>
> T: OK, but the creed in front of you now is not the creed that was originally drafted at the Council of Nicaea. Take a look at *Handout #10*, and read the creed as written in the Original Nicaea Creed column.

Handout #10: Evolution of the Nicene Creed

The following table indicates by [square brackets] the portions of the 325 A.D. text that were omitted or moved in 381 A.D., and uses *italics* to indicate what phrases, absent in the 325 A.D. text, were added in 381 A.D.

Original Nicaea Creed (325 A.D.)	Constantinople Creed (381 A.D.)
We believe in one God, the Father Almighty, Maker of all things visible and invisible.	We believe in one God, the Father Almighty, Maker of *heaven and earth, and* of all things visible and invisible.
And in one Lord Jesus Christ, the Son of God, begotten of the Father [the only-begotten; that is, of the essence of the Father, God of God,] Light of Light, very God of very God, begotten, not made, being of one substance with the Father;	And in one Lord Jesus Christ, the *only-begotten* Son of God, begotten of the Father *before all worlds (æons),** Light of Light, very God of very God, begotten, not made, being of one substance with the Father;
By whom all things were made [both in heaven and on earth];	by whom all things were made;
Who for us men, and for our salvation, came down and was incarnate and was made man;	who for us men, and for our salvation, came down *from heaven*, and was incarnate *by the Holy Ghost of the Virgin Mary*, and was made man;
He suffered, and the third day he rose again, ascended into heaven;	he *was crucified for us under Pontius Pilate, and* suffered, *and was buried*, and the third day he rose again, *according to the Scriptures, and* ascended into heaven, *and sitteth on the right hand of the Father*;
From thence he shall come to judge the quick and the dead.	from thence he shall come *again, with glory*, to judge the quick and the dead;
	whose kingdom shall have no end.
And in the Holy Ghost.	And in the Holy Ghost, *the Lord and Giver of life, who proceedeth from the Father, who*

with the Father and the Son together is worshiped and glorified, who spake by the prophets.

In one holy catholic and apostolic Church; we acknowledge one baptism for the remission of sins; we look for the resurrection of the dead, and the life of the world to come. Amen.

[But those who say: 'There was a time when he was not;' and 'He was not before he was made;' and 'He was made out of nothing,' or 'He is of another substance' or 'essence,' or 'The Son of God is created,' or 'changeable,' or 'alterable'— they are condemned by the holy catholic and apostolic Church.]

- *Æons* are an immeasurably long period of time; ages. The last italicized words were dropped from later versions of the creed.

Source: **Creeds of Christendom, with a History and Critical notes. Volume I. The History of Creeds, by Philip Schaff, pp. 28-29 (public domain).**

T: The version we use today was actually developed 56 years after the Council of Nicaea at the Council of Constantinople. However, we still name the creed after the Council of Nicaea because it originated there. We'll call the creed in the left-hand column the "Original Nicene Creed" and the creed on the right side, which is very close to the creed in the Book of Common Prayer, the "Constantinople Creed". Look at the last, long paragraph in brackets in the Original Nicene Creed column. Does that paragraph, which was largely discarded in the Constantinople Creed, look like a statement of what we believe to you?[210]

C: No. It looks like a statement of what we don't believe.

T: So, at least in 325 A.D., there must have been people around who said, "There was a time when he was not" and "He was not before he was made", and so forth. Insert the word "Jesus" every time you see "He" and read that paragraph.

C: "There was a time when Jesus was not", "Jesus was not before Jesus was made", "Jesus was made out of nothing," and "Jesus is of another 'substance' or 'essence'".

---

[210] The last paragraph, referred to as the "anathema", was placed in this creed to oppose the beliefs of Arias and his followers at the council. (Creeds of Christendom, with a History and Critical notes. Volume I. The History of Creeds, by Philip Schaff, p. 25, public domain.) We will read more of Arias later in this section.

> T: Let's take the first two: "There was a time when Jesus was not" and "Jesus was not before Jesus was made". Turn to the first chapter of the Gospel of John:

John 1

1 In the beginning was the Word, and the Word was with God, and the Word was God.

2 The same was in the beginning with God.

3 All things were made by him; and without him was not any thing made that was made.

4 In him was life; and the life was the light of men.

5 And the light shineth in darkness; and the darkness comprehended it not.

6 There was a man sent from God, whose name was John.

7 The same came for a witness, to bear witness of the Light, that all men through him might believe.

8 He was not that Light, but was sent to bear witness of that Light.

9 That was the true Light, which lighteth every man that cometh into the world.

10 He was in the world, and the world was made by him, and the world knew him not.

11 He came unto his own, and his own received him not.

12 But as many as received him, to them gave he power to become the sons of God, even to them that believe on his name:

13 Which were born, not of blood, nor of the will of the flesh, nor of the will of man, but of God.

14 And the Word was made flesh, and dwelt among us, (and we beheld his glory, the glory as of the only begotten of the Father,) full of grace and truth.

T: St. John wrote that "In the beginning was the Word, and the Word was with God, and the Word was God." The "Word", then, is not something printed with letters on a piece of paper. According to verse 14, what, or rather who, was the "Word"?

C: Jesus.

T: How do you know the Word was Jesus?

C: Verse 14 says that "the Word was made flesh, and dwelt among us", and that He was "the only begotten of the Father".

T: Did Jesus became flesh and did He live among us, and did Jesus say He was God's Son?[211]

C: Yes.

T: Now look at verse 10: "He was in the world, and the world was made by him, and the world knew him not." Focus on the middle part of the sentence: "the world was made by him". I thought the Book of Genesis said the world was created by God. Now St. John says the world was made by Jesus. What gives?

C: Maybe they were together?

T: Look back at verse 1: "In the beginning was the Word, and the Word was with God, and the Word was God."

C: Jesus was with God when the world was made.

T: Remember when we talked about the Trinity: Jesus and God are one, along with the Holy Spirit. Since all three are one, then all three were together at the beginning of time and the creation of our world. Now look back at *Handout #10* and the last paragraph of the Original Nicene Creed: "But those who say: 'There was a time when he was not;' .. are condemned by the holy catholic and apostolic Church." Why were the early Church fathers so concerned about people saying, "There was a time when Jesus was not" and "Jesus was not before Jesus was made"? If Jesus was with God from the beginning of time, was there ever a time when Jesus "was not"?

C: No.

T: And was there a time when Jesus "was not before he was made," implying that Jesus did not exist before He was born?

---

[211] As to Jesus' claim of Godhead, see, for example, Luke 22:70.

C: No, for the same reason.

T: What about the phrases, "'He was made out of nothing,' or 'He is of another substance' or 'essence'"? Verse 14 says, Jesus "was made flesh, and dwelt among us." If Jesus had been made of some substance or essence other than our flesh, what would he have been made of?

C: Don't know. Maybe a ghost?

T: A ghost, a supernatural being, who knows? But think back to the Old Covenant between God and Abraham. Was Abraham a ghost, a supernatural being, or a Man?

C: Abraham was a Man.

T: If you followed the Old Testament Law under the Abrahamic Covenant, you received blessings, but if you did not follow the Old Testament Law and its 613-odd commandments, what did you receive?

C: Curses!

T: And by dying on the cross for us, what did Jesus do about the curses?

C: He got rid of them.

T: He did that by taking our sins upon Himself, which He could do because Jesus was a Man living under the Abrahamic Covenant and the Old Testament Law. If Jesus had been a supernatural being and not a Man, could He have taken upon Himself the sins of Man?

C: [Pondering]

T: Remember, Jesus had to be the perfect scapegoat: someone who knew no sin but could carry our sins upon Himself. So, what type of being had to die on the cross to save Man?

C: A Man!

T: And if a supernatural being who was not a Man, died on the cross, who would be saved?

C: Supernatural beings?

T: If they existed, maybe, but certainly not Man. Explain why, then, did the early Church fathers get so upset when someone said that Jesus was from some substance or essence other than human flesh? If Jesus had been a supernatural being, would we humans be saved?

C: No.

T: And that's the rub. Those gathered at the Council of Nicaea in 325 A.D. had to wrestle with these issues, literally. One of the bishops in attendance at the council, named Arias, believed Jesus held a position lesser than God, and he probably believed some of the statements made in the last paragraph of the Original Nicene Creed that were condemned by the council. One of the folktales from that council meeting is that, while Arias was speaking, a bishop named Nicholas became very upset. Nicholas was later sainted due, in part, to his care for the poor.[212] Does anyone know how St. Nicholas is more widely known today?

C: As Santa Claus.

T: Well, at the Council of Nicaea, St. Nicholas purportedly punched Arias in the face![213] If Santa Claus got into fist fights at the Council of Nicaea, how intense do you think the debate was?

C: Heavy!

T: Now think. How do you know the Council of Nicaea determined that statements like, "There was a time when Jesus was not" and "Jesus was not before Jesus was made" were not correct? Where did we just look to find our answers? [Hint: it's open in front of you now!]

C: The Bible.

T: Today, if you hear something about the Christian Faith, and you want to check out whether the statement agrees with the principles of our Faith, what source do you go to?

C: The Bible.

T: You're actually using more than the just the Bible. You're using the thing that resides between your two ears – what's that called?

C: Your brain.

T: So you apply the reasoning capabilities of your mind to the Scriptures to figure out what they say. To do that effectively, you've got to have at least some familiarity with the Scriptures, and to gain that familiarity, do you remember what God told Joshua to do with the Scriptures before he entered the Holy Land?

---

[212] The story of St. Nicholas secretly placing gifts in stockings next to the fireplace of a poor family is at http://www.stnicholascenter.org/pages/three-impoverished-maidens/.
[213] It may have not been a punch but a "slap". For an account of the "slap" St. Nicholas purportedly gave to Arias, see http://www.stnicholascenter.org/pages/bishop-nicholas-loses-his-cool/.

C: Meditate on Scripture day and night.

T: Then finally, to determine whether these statements agreed with our Faith, we looked at the creeds drafted at the Councils of Nicaea and Constantinople. That is, we walked back into history to see what those who founded our Faith did when confronted with controversial issues. They made decisions in the fourth century that have stayed with us to the present day. Over time, that establishes a pattern or tradition, to which we looked for guidance. So we utilize three elements to decide important questions about our Faith:[214]

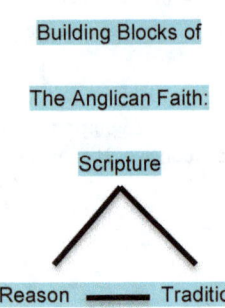

Building Blocks of

The Anglican Faith:

Scripture

Reason ——— Tradition

But, what did I list at the top?

C: Scripture.

T: Without the Bible, what would we use to reason with? Take away that book in front of you and what would you have to read to determine what Jesus or the prophets said?

C: Nothing.

T: The same with tradition: how would we know someone's tradition is more closely aligned with the Christian Faith without the Bible? So the Bible is critical to the other two elements. Without the Bible, we are simply left to guess. Look at the top of page 853 in the Book of Common Prayer and see what the Catechism says.

Q. How do we recognize the truths taught by the Holy Spirit?
A. We recognize truths to be taught by the Holy Spirit when they are in accord with the Scriptures.

---

[214] These building blocks trace back to the late-sixteenth century publication of Richard Hooker's *Laws of Ecclesiastical Polity*, in which he "denies the Puritan assertion that the Bible is the *only* source of authority; in his view Reason and Tradition are the other sources, and Reason serves to interpret both Scripture and Tradition." James Thayer Addison, *The Episcopal Church in the United States, 1789-1931* (Archon Books, 1969), p. 11.

T: So, if you hear some statement about our Faith made by anyone, regardless of his or her position, that statement should be in accord with what?

C: The Scriptures.

T: And where are the Scriptures found?

C: In the Bible.

T: Whether a statement is in accord with the Scriptures in the Bible, then, becomes the ultimate test of "truths taught by the Holy Spirit." Any statement that is not in accord with the Bible is not a Holy Spirit-taught truth.[215] Of course, in our Faith, we are free to argue over what the Bible says and means. If we argue, though, what do we use to analyze what Scripture says? [Hint: I'm talking about gray matter again!]

C: Our brains, that is Reason.

T: And if Christians have already argued over a specific issue in the past, we can look back to their discussions to enlighten our own. What do we call that look-back process?

C: Using Tradition.

B. The Apostles' Creed

T: Turn to page 66 in the Book of Common Prayer. What service are we looking at?

C: Evening Prayer I.

T: Services in the Book of Common Prayer frequently have two versions: the first in an older form of English dating back to the first prayer book; the second using a modern form of English. Below the Song of Simeon, what do you see?

---

[215] The concept of using Bible Scripture to refute incorrect doctrine was the reason cited for developing a comprehensive schedule of Bible readings in the first 1549 BCP. The preface to that prayer book, authored and/or approved by Archbishop Cranmer, is reprinted on p. 866 of our current BCP, and the relevant part states:

> For they so ordered the matter, that all the whole Bible (or the greatest part thereof) should be read over once in the year, intending thereby, that the Clergy, and especially such as were Ministers of the congregation, should (by often reading, and meditation of God's word) be stirred up to godliness themselves, and be more able to exhort others by wholesome doctrine, and to confute them that were adversaries to the truth.

Confirmand Reference Book First Edition

C: The Apostles' Creed.

T: Look at *Handout #11*, which has the Apostles' Creed, in a form similar to that on page 66, and the Nicene Creed.

Handout #11: Comparison of the Apostles' and Nicene Creeds

The Apostles' Creed; Received Text.	**The Nicene Creed, as Enlarged A.D. 381.**
(The clauses in brackets are the later additions.)	(The words in brackets are Western changes.)
1. I believe in God the Father Almighty,	1. We [I] believe* in one God the Father Almighty,
[Maker of heaven and earth].	Maker of heaven and earth,
	And of all things visible and invisible.
2. And in Jesus Christ, his only Son, our Lord;	2. And in one Lord Jesus Christ,
	the only-begotten Son of God,
	Begotten of the Father before all worlds;
	[God of God],
	Light of Light.
	Very God of very God,

	Begotten, not made,
	Being of one substance with the Father;
	By whom all things were made;
3. Who was [conceived] by the Holy Ghost,	3. Who, for us men, and for our salvation,
Born of the Virgin Mary;	came down from heaven,
	And was incarnate by the Holy Ghost of
	the Virgin Mary,
	And was made man
4. [Suffered] under Pontius Pilate, was crucified [dead], and buried;	4. He was crucified for us under Pontius Pilate;
	And suffered and was buried;
[He descended into Hades];	*　　*　　*　　*　　*
5. The third day he rose again from the dead;	5. And the third day he rose again,
	According to the Scriptures;
6. He ascended into heaven,	6. And ascended into heaven,

And sitteth on the right hand of [God] the Father [Almighty];

And sitteth on the right hand of the Father;

7. From thence he shall come to judge the quick and the dead.

7. And he shall come again, with glory, to judge the quick and the dead;

Whose kingdom shall have no end.

8. And [I believe] in the Holy Ghost;

8. And [I believe] in the Holy Ghost,

The Lord, and Giver of life;

Who proceedeth from the Father [and the Son];

Who with the Father and the Son together is worshiped and glorified;

Who spake by the Prophets.

9. The holy [catholic] Church;

9. And [I believe] in** one holy catholic and apostolic Church;

[The communion of saints];

*   *   *   *   *

10. The forgiveness of sins;

10. We [I] acknowledge*** one baptism for the remission of sins;

11. The resurrection of the flesh [body];

11. And we [I] look for the resurrection of the dead;

12. [And the life everlasting].

12. And the life of the world to come.

* The Greek reads the plural (πιστεύομεν), but the Latin and English versions have substituted for it the singular (credo, I believe), in accordance with the Apostles' Creed and the more subjective character of the Western churches.

** The Greek reads εἰς μίαν . . . ἐκκλησίαν, but the Latin and English versions, in conformity with the Apostles' Creed, mostly omit "in" before ecclesiam.

*** Here and in art. 11 the singular is substituted in Western translations for ὁμολογοῦμεν and προσδοκῶμεν.

Source: **Creeds of Christendom, with a History and Critical notes. Volume I. The History of Creeds, by Philip Schaff (public domain)**

T: Tell me, what is the difference between the Apostles' and Nicene Creeds?

C: The Apostles' Creed is shorter!

T: Some would say it is more succinct. Look at Articles 2 and 8 of *Handout #11*. How much does the Apostles' Creed say about Jesus and the Holy Ghost compared to the Nicene Creed?

C: One short phrase on each in the Apostles' Creed compared to several phrases on each in the Nicene Creed.

T: Now look at the right-hand column and find the places marked with asterisks across the line. What do you think those asterisks indicate?

C: Something is in the Apostles' Creed that is not in the Nicene Creed.

T: And what are the phrases in the Apostles' Creed not found in the Nicene Creed?

C: "He descended into Hades" and "The communion of saints".

T: On page 66, can you find those two phrases?

C: Yes, but the prayer book says "He descended into hell" instead of "He descended into Hades".

T: "Hades" was the Greek god of the underworld. By using the term in this context, the creed is referring to the physical place were Hades lived: Hell. The modern English version simply says "He descended to the dead."[216] When does the Apostles' Creed say Jesus descended to Hell?[217] [Hint: Read the preceding two phrases.]

C: After He was crucified, died and was buried.

T: And after He descended to Hell, what does the creed say happened?

C: "On the third day he rose again, He ascended into heaven"

T: So tell me when Jesus went to Hell? Since Jesus was crucified on Good Friday and rose on Easter Sunday, when did He descend to Hell?

C: Sometime on Saturday?

T: Jesus had died by about 3pm on Good Friday,[218] so He could have descended to Hell at that time. But why did Jesus descend into Hell[219] when He had lived a perfect life before God?

C: He had to pay for our sins [Sec. V.B.]

T: To see how St. Paul described Jesus' sacrifice, turn to II Corinthians 5:21:

C: "For he hath made him to be sin for us, who knew no sin; that we might be made the righteousness of God in him."

T: Remember the goat that was sent into the desert on the Day of Atonement? What was that goat called?

C: A "scapegoat".

T: When the high priest laid his hands on that goat, what did that represent?

C: He put the sins of Israel on the goat.

T: Had the goat sinned?

---

[216] Book of Common Prayer, p. 120.
[217] Hell is also referenced in the Creed of St. Athanasius. See BCP, p. 865: "For as the reasonable soul and flesh is one man, so God and Man is one Christ; Who suffered for our salvation, descended into hell, rose again the third day from the dead."
[218] Matthew 27:45-50. The "ninth hour" was three o'clock in the afternoon.
[219] For those who did not know that Jesus actually did go to Hell, we will soon read St. Peter's Pentecost speech at Acts 2:30-32 in which he quotes from Psalm 16:10: "For thou wilt not leave my soul in hell; neither wilt thou suffer thine Holy One to see corruption."

C: No.

T: The goat knew no sin, but the animal bore the sins of Israel. Now look at II Corinthians 5:21. Who was made to be sin for us who knew no sin "that we might be made the righteousness of God in him"?

C: Jesus.

T: So what did Jesus have in common with the goat on the Day of Atonement?

C: They were both scapegoats.

T: With one big difference: how often did the Israelites have to repeat the sacrifices on the Day of Atonement?

C: Once a year.

T: How many times did Jesus have to die on the cross and go to Hell to pay for our sins?

C: Once, for all time.

T: Put a bookmark in II Corinthians 5 and let's look at how St. Peter described Jesus' sacrifice in a speech he gave on Pentecost, soon after the Resurrection:

Acts 2

22 Ye men of Israel, hear these words; Jesus of Nazareth, a man approved of God among you by miracles and wonders and signs, which God did by him in the midst of you, as ye yourselves also know:

23 Him, being delivered by the determinate counsel and foreknowledge of God, ye have taken, and by wicked hands have crucified and slain:

24 Whom God hath raised up, having loosed the pains of death: because it was not possible that he should be holden of it.

25 For David speaketh concerning him, I foresaw the Lord always before my face, for he is on my right hand, that I should not be moved:

26 Therefore did my heart rejoice, and my tongue was glad; moreover also my flesh shall rest in hope:

27 Because thou wilt not leave my soul in hell, neither wilt thou suffer thine Holy One to see corruption.

T: We know from the last verse that Jesus went to Hell but did not stay there very long. From what you read in II Corinthians 5:21, why was it necessary for Jesus to go to Hell at all?

C: Jesus was made "to be sin for us".

T: And people burdened by sin go to Hell.[220] Now look at verse 24 in Acts 2: "Whom God hath raised up, having loosed the pains of death: because it was not possible that he should be holden of it." It was not possible for Jesus to be held by the pains of death. Tell me why, based on what we read in II Corinthians 5:21, Jesus could not be held in Hell.

C: Jesus "knew no sin".

T: If Jesus was without sin, did Hell have any right to keep Him?

C: No.

T: So, let's recap. Why did Jesus, as our Scapegoat, go to Hell after dying on the cross?

C: He carried our sins.

T: Why couldn't Hell hold on to Jesus after He got there?

C: Jesus himself was without sin.

T: Therefore, whose sins did Jesus leave in Hell?

C: Ours.

---

[220] As harsh as it sounds in today's no-fault culture, Jesus did not equivocate on the issue of who goes to Hell. See for example, Matthew 18:9 (also found in Mark 9:47 and Matthew 5:29): "And if thine eye offend thee, pluck it out, and cast it from thee: it is better for thee to enter into life with one eye, rather than having two eyes to be cast into hell fire." Luke, at 16:22-25, quotes Jesus discussing the parable of Lazarus, the beggar, and the rich man: "And it came to pass, that the beggar died, and was carried by the angels into Abraham's bosom: the rich man also died, and was buried; And in hell he lift up his eyes, being in torments, and seeth Abraham afar off, and Lazarus in his bosom. And he cried and said, Father Abraham, have mercy on me, and send Lazarus, that he may dip the tip of his finger in water, and cool my tongue; for I am tormented in this flame. But Abraham said, Son, remember that thou in thy lifetime receivedst thy good things, and likewise Lazarus evil things: but now he is comforted, and thou art tormented." We acknowledge Jesus conquering Hell in the liturgy of the Great Vigil of Easter (BCP, p. 287): "This is the night, when Christ broke the bonds of death and hell, and rose victorious from the grave." Finally, the Catechism states (BCP, p. 862): "By heaven, we mean eternal life in our enjoyment of God; by hell, we mean eternal death in our rejection of God." But read on; there is hope for those who have sinned!

T: And if Jesus paid for our sins by going to Hell,[221] will those of us who accept Jesus' sacrifice need to go to Hell to pay for our sins?

C: No!

C. The Sacraments

Learning Objectives

1. Confirmands will learn the origins of baptism and the related declaration of faith that was eventually codified in the Apostles' Creed.
2. Confirmands will understand the common elements of Holy Communion and Jewish Day of Atonement temple worship.
3. Confirmands will understand why there are Two Great Sacraments and five other sacraments.

a. Holy Baptism

T: We now turn to one of the most ancient of Christian ceremonies, called "Rites". This is the ceremony that would bring a person into the Christian Faith: Holy Baptism. This rite dates back to the baptism of Jesus by St. John the Baptist, but actually St. John had been baptizing people for some time prior to Jesus' arrival.

Mark 1

4 John did baptize in the wilderness, and preach the baptism of repentance for the remission of sins.

5 And there went out unto him all the land of Judaea, and they of Jerusalem, and were all baptized of him in the river of Jordan, confessing their sins.

---

[221] One question that may arise concerns those who died before the coming of Jesus and whether they had a chance to repent. I Peter 3:18-20 may address this issue:
> 18 For Christ also hath once suffered for sins, the just for the unjust, that he might bring us to God, being put to death in the flesh, but quickened by the Spirit:
> 19 By which also he went and preached unto the spirits in prison;
> 20 Which sometime were disobedient, when once the longsuffering of God waited in the days of Noah, while the ark was a preparing, wherein few, that is, eight souls were saved by water.

Verse 18 puts the setting in Hell, where Jesus had been "put to death" and then "quickened by the Spirit". Verses 19-20 state He "preached unto the spirits in prison; which were sometime disobedient," which implies that those sinners had a chance to hear His Word. The reference to God's "longsuffering" to allow Noah to attempt to warn others of the massive flood to come invokes the image of God's patience, allowing time for sinners to hear the message of salvation before His judgment.

6 And John was clothed with camel's hair, and with a girdle of a skin about his loins; and he did eat locusts and wild honey;

7 And preached, saying, There cometh one mightier than I after me, the latchet of whose shoes I am not worthy to stoop down and unloose.

8 I indeed have baptized you with water: but he shall baptize you with the Holy Ghost.

9 And it came to pass in those days, that Jesus came from Nazareth of Galilee, and was baptized of John in Jordan.

10 And straightway coming up out of the water, he saw the heavens opened, and the Spirit like a dove descending upon him:

11 And there came a voice from heaven, saying, Thou art my beloved Son, in whom I am well pleased.

T: Was Jesus the first person St. John baptized?

C: No.

T: What did St. John the Baptist say was going to be different when Jesus started baptizing people? [Hint: verse 8]

C: That Jesus will baptize with the Holy Ghost.

T: Then, when St. John the Baptist baptized Jesus, what did Jesus see when He came up out of the water?

C: He saw the Holy Spirit like a dove descend on Him. [Verse 10]

T: The Early Church followed Jesus' example and baptized its converts with water. Let's look at one of the earliest baptisms taking place after Jesus' Ascension into Heaven, involving Philip, one of the seven deacons that we discussed earlier [Sec. X.C.] who was chosen to help the apostles:

Acts 8

26 And the angel of the Lord spake unto Philip, saying, Arise, and go toward the south unto the way that goeth down from Jerusalem unto Gaza, which is desert.

27 And he arose and went: and, behold, a man of Ethiopia, an eunuch of great authority under Candace queen of the Ethiopians, who had the charge of all her treasure, and had come to Jerusalem for to worship,

28 Was returning, and sitting in his chariot read Esaias the prophet.

29 Then the Spirit said unto Philip, Go near, and join thyself to this chariot.

30 And Philip ran thither to him, and heard him read the prophet Esaias, and said, Understandest thou what thou readest?

31 And he said, How can I, except some man should guide me? And he desired Philip that he would come up and sit with him.

32 The place of the Scripture which he read was this, He was led as a sheep to the slaughter; and like a lamb dumb before his shearer, so opened he not his mouth:

33 In his humiliation his judgment was taken away: and who shall declare his generation? for his life is taken from the earth.

34 And the eunuch answered Philip, and said, I pray thee, of whom speaketh the prophet this? of himself, or of some other man?

35 Then Philip opened his mouth, and began at the same Scripture, and preached unto him Jesus.

36 And as they went on their way, they came unto a certain water: and the eunuch said, See, here is water; what doth hinder me to be baptized?

37 And Philip said, If thou believest with all thine heart, thou mayest. And he answered and said, I believe that Jesus Christ is the Son of God.

38 And he commanded the chariot to stand still: and they went down both into the water, both Philip and the eunuch; and he baptized him.

39 And when they were come up out of the water, the Spirit of the Lord caught away Philip, that the eunuch saw him no more: and he went on his way rejoicing.

T: Look back at verse 37. Before Philip baptizes the eunuch in verse 38, what did Philip do?

C: He said, "if you believe with all your heart, you may be baptized."

T: How did the eunuch respond?

C: He said, "I believe that Jesus Christ is the Son of God."

T: What does the eunuch's statement sound like? We just read through two creeds, take a look at the modern translation of the Apostles' Creed on p. 120 of the Book of Common Prayer.

C: The statement is close to a line in the Apostles' Creed, "I believe in Jesus Christ, his only son, our Lord."[222]

T: So before being baptized into the Christian Faith, Philip asked the eunuch to make a profession of his faith. That profession evolved into the Apostles' Creed. That creed is thought to have originated with Jesus' Apostles, which gave rise to its name.[223] Turn to page 301 in the Book of Common Prayer. What service are we looking at?

C: Holy Baptism.

T: After the sermon, what happens next in this service?

C: Presentation and examination of the candidates.

T: Who are the candidates?

C: People who will be baptized.

T: Now turn to page 304. What are you looking at?

C: The Baptismal Covenant.

T: Are you sure that's all it is? The Baptismal Covenant is in a question and answer format, with the priest asking the questions and the people responding. Let's look at the first three questions, then go back to page 120 of the Book of Common Prayer and compare the people's responses to the first three questions on page 304 to the Apostles' Creed. What are the people's responses?

C: They are saying the Apostles' Creed, just broken out into three sections!

T: So, on page 304, you see the ancient creed used in our service, in a question and answer format, as the first part of "The Baptismal Covenant". What is the first question?

C: "Do you believe in God the Father?"

T: The second?

C: "Do you believe in Jesus Christ, the Son of God?"

---

[222] There is an acceptable answer to this question from the Nicene Creed, but our focus here will be on the Apostles' Creed.
[223] For a comprehensive discussion of the origins of the Apostles' Creed, see http://www.newadvent.org/cathen/01629a.htm.

T: Finally, the third?

C: "Do you believe in the Holy Spirit?"

T: So, sum up how the questions are divided?

C: One on God the Father, one on the Son of God, and one on God the Holy Spirit.

T: Now turn to the part of the service where the actual baptism takes place on page 307. At the bottom of the page, in whose Name does the priest baptize the candidate?

C: In the "Name of the Father, and of the Son, and of the Holy Spirit."

T: So how was the Apostles' Creed related to the act of baptism?

C: Both refer to the Father, Son and Holy Spirit.

T: In our baptism service, which comes first, the declaration of faith through the Apostles' Creed or the baptism?

C: The Apostles' Creed. [BCP p. 304 then p. 307]

T: When Philip baptized the eunuch, which came first, the declaration of faith or the baptism?

C: The declaration of faith. [Acts 8:37 then 38.]

T: And that early declaration of faith eventually became a part of the Apostles' Creed. There are several ancient rites, such as that of Holy Baptism, that our Faith honors as "sacraments". Turn to page 857 of the Book of Common Prayer and tell me what the sacraments are.

C: "The sacraments are outward and visible signs of inward and spiritual grace, given by Christ as sure and certain means by which we receive that grace."

T: In the case of Holy Baptism, tell me what are the outward and visible signs of the act of baptizing someone? In other words, what do you see when you witness someone being baptized?

C: The priest pours water on head of the person being baptized.[224]

T: When you pour water on something that has dirt on it, what does it do?

C: It washes off the dirt.

T: If the water represents the Holy Spirit and the dirt represents our sins, what, then, does baptism do?

---

[224] While the confirmands should be able to figure this out for themselves, the sacramental elements of Baptism are described in the Catechism at BCP p. 858.

C: It washes off our sins.

T: That is the "inward and spiritual grace", because it is by God's grace that our sins are forgiven or washed away.

b. Holy Eucharist

T: Another sacramental rite is the Holy Eucharist, which our church celebrates every week [month], and sometimes more often. How did this service start? We go to the night of the Passover Feast when Jesus was betrayed and arrested:

> Luke 22
>
> 15 And [Jesus] said unto them, With desire I have desired to eat this passover with you before I suffer:
>
> 16 For I say unto you, I will not any more eat thereof, until it be fulfilled in the kingdom of God.
>
> 17 And he took the cup, and gave thanks, and said, Take this, and divide it among yourselves:
>
> 18 For I say unto you, I will not drink of the fruit of the vine, until the kingdom of God shall come.
>
> 19 And he took bread, and gave thanks, and brake it, and gave unto them, saying, This is my body which is given for you: this do in remembrance of me.
>
> 20 Likewise also the cup after supper, saying, This cup is the new testament in my blood, which is shed for you.

T: The Passover was a Jewish festival that represented an event that occurred in Jewish history. What was that event?

C: God passed over the houses of the Israelites when inflicting plagues on Egypt.[225]

T: What was the purpose of God sending the plagues?

C: To convince pharaoh to free the Israelites he held as slaves.

T: The Last Supper that Jesus had with His disciples was the Passover meal. In verse 19, Jesus takes bread and breaks it. What does He say it represents?

C: His body.

---

[225] Exodus 12:1-14.

T: Think back to our discussion of Jewish temple worship. On the Day of Atonement, what do the temple priests burn? [Section III.C.]

C: Animals.

T: Were the animals dead or alive?

C: Dead.

T: Who killed the animals before they were sacrificed?

C: The priests.

T: So the priests killed and then sacrificed the bodies of dead animals on the Day of Atonement. Look at verse 15: at the Last Supper, Jesus knew he was going to suffer; indeed, He knew He was going to be killed. So when Jesus said in verse 19, "This is my body which is given for you", what did He mean by saying His body is given for us?

C: His body was sacrificed.

T: Sacrificed, yes, but to what end? Why were animal bodies sacrificed on the Day of Atonement?

C: To pay for Israel's sins.

T: How many years' worth of sins did the animal sacrifices pay for?

C: One year's worth.

T: Then the ritual needed to be repeated. How many years' worth of sins did Jesus' sacrifice pay for?

C: Forever!

T: So, why was Jesus' body given for us?

C: To pay for our sins, forever.

T: In verse 20, St. Luke writes that after the supper, Jesus took the cup. What was in the cup? [Hint: verses 17-18.]

C: Wine.

T: What does Jesus say the cup represents?

C: His blood.

T: Again, going back to temple worship on the Day of Atonement, what did the High Priest do with the blood of the animals in the Most Holy Place?

C: He sprinkled blood on the Ark.

T: There's more to Jesus' sacrifice of His blood, though. Look carefully at verse 20. What does the cup represent?

C: The "new testament".

T: Or, the New Covenant between God and Man. Each of the sacraments has an "outward and visible sign" and an "inward and spiritual grace". What is the outward and visible sign of the Holy Eucharist? This is what you see the priest doing every Sunday at the start of Holy Communion.

C: The priest blesses the bread and wine.

T: Turn to page 334 of the Book of Common Prayer:

> *At the following words concerning the bread, the Celebrant is to hold it, or lay a hand upon it; and at the words concerning the cup, to hold or place a hand upon the cup and any other vessel containing wine to be consecrated*
>
> For in the night in which he was betrayed, he took bread; and when he had given thanks, he brake it, and gave it to his disciples, saying, "Take, eat, this is my Body, which is given for you. Do this in remembrance of me."
>
> Likewise, after supper, he took the cup; and when he had given thanks, he gave it to them, saying, "Drink ye all of this; for this is my Blood of the New Testament, which is shed for you, and for many, for the remission of sins. Do this, as oft as ye shall drink it, in remembrance of me."

T: Compare the first paragraph the celebrant speaks concerning the bread to the verses we just read in Luke 22. What verse from Luke most closely resembles what the priest says in our communion service?

C: Verse 19: "This is my body which is given for you: this do in remembrance of me."

T: Then look at the next paragraph. What verse from Luke does it most closely resemble?

Confirmand Reference Book First Edition

> C: Verse 20: "This cup is the new testament in my blood, which is shed for you."
>
> T: You will see shortly that the rest of that paragraph is taken from St. Paul's description of the Eucharist. But now let's figure out what is the "inward and spiritual grace" from the Holy Eucharist. What does the bread and wine represent?
>
> C: Jesus' Body and Blood.
>
> T: And there you have it: the inward and spiritual grace is the Body and Blood of Christ which we receive by faith.[226]

C. Other Sacramental Rites

> T: So far, we've covered two sacraments. What are those two?
>
> C: Holy Baptism and Holy Eucharist.
>
> T: They are called "the two great sacraments"[227] because Jesus personally gave those rites to the Church. But by saying Jesus "gave" the rite of Holy Baptism to the Church, did that mean He actually performed baptisms?
>
> C: Maybe?
>
> T: The answer may surprise you.

John 4

1 When therefore the Lord knew how the Pharisees had heard that Jesus made and baptized more disciples than John,

2 (Though Jesus himself baptized not, but his disciples,)

3 He left Judaea, and departed again into Galilee.

> T: So how did Jesus give the sacrament of Holy Baptism to the Church?
>
> C: He had His disciples perform the baptisms.
>
> T: Then Jesus, after His resurrection, instructed His disciples to keep on baptizing:

---

[226] BCP, p. 859.
[227] BCP, p. 858.

Matthew 28

16 Then the eleven disciples went away into Galilee, into a mountain where Jesus had appointed them.

17 And when they saw him, they worshipped him: but some doubted.

18 And Jesus came and spake unto them, saying, All power is given unto me in heaven and in earth.

19 Go ye therefore, and teach all nations, baptizing them in the name of the Father, and of the Son, and of the Holy Ghost:

20 Teaching them to observe all things whatsoever I have commanded you: and, lo, I am with you alway, even unto the end of the world. Amen.

T: What about Holy Communion? How did Jesus give us that rite?

C: Didn't He say, "this do in remembrance of me"? [from Luke 19:22 in the previous section]

T: Correct. We celebrate Holy Eucharist to remember Jesus' sacrifice for us.

T: There are five other sacraments that our Church observes that did not come from Jesus' direction but rather from the guidance of the Holy Spirit. They are:

Confirmation

Ordination

Holy Matrimony

Reconciliation of a Penitent

Unction

T: Let's discuss them in order. What is Confirmation?

C: Isn't that what we are going through now?

T: Right. Ordination?

C: That's for bishops, priests and deacons.

T: Through the laying on of hands by bishops. Think back to the ordination chart for bishops that we looked at earlier. What is the minimum number of bishops needed to ordain a new bishop? [Refer to *Handout #9*]

C: Three.

> T: Only one bishop is needed to ordain a priest or deacon. What is the difference between a priest and a deacon?
>
> C: Umm ....
>
> T: Look at page 510 of the Book of Common Prayer:

Preface to the Ordination Rites

The Holy Scriptures and ancient Christian writers make it clear that from the apostles' time, there have been different ministries within the Church. In particular, since the time of the New Testament, three distinct orders of ordained ministers have been characteristic of Christ's holy catholic Church. First, there is the order of bishops who carry on the apostolic work of leading, supervising, and uniting the Church. Secondly, associated with them are the presbyters, or ordained elders, in subsequent times generally known as priests. Together with the bishops, they take part in the governance of the Church, in the carrying out of its missionary and pastoral work, and in the preaching of the Word of God and administering his holy Sacraments. Thirdly, there are deacons who assist bishops and priests in all of this work. It is also a special responsibility of deacons to minister in Christ's name to the poor, the sick, the suffering, and the helpless.

> T: Who administers the holy Sacraments?
>
> C: Bishops and priests.
>
> T: Deacons assist. Therefore, only a priest, or bishop if present, may celebrate the Holy Eucharist.[228] The same is true for the other sacraments. What is Holy Matrimony?
>
> C: Marriage.

---

[228] In the absence of a priest, a bishop may authorize a deacon to distribute Holy Communion to a congregation; see BCP p. 408.

Preparation for marriage, including the solemnity of the marriage vows, is beyond the scope of this course. However, feel free to refer to the services in the Book of Common Prayer beginning on page 420, or, if you have access to the internet, look up the terms "Marriage" and "Celebration and Blessing of a Marriage" on the Episcopal Church's website glossary at http://www.episcopalchurch.org/library/glossary.

T: Next is Reconciliation of a Penitent. If you have done something wrong and are penitent, what are you doing?

C: Feeling sorry for what you did.

The Church website has a good discussion of how clergy address penance at http://www.episcopalchurch.org/library/glossary/penance.

T: Remember when we discussed sin and confession [Section V.B.b.]? We read the confession of sin from the Book of Common Prayer at page 360. What service is that found in?

C: Holy Eucharist II.

T: Now look at the service for Reconciliation of a Penitent on page 447. What is the difference in the confession at the bottom of page 447 and the confession at the top of page 360? Start with the basic differences: which uses the pronoun "we" and which uses the pronoun "I"?

C: The Holy Eucharist version uses the "we"; the Reconciliation version uses "I".

T: Which confession, then, is corporate in that several people speak the prayer at the same time and which confession is personal in that it is said by only one person?

C: The Holy Eucharist version is corporate; the Reconciliation version is personal.

T: So how many people, besides the priest, are involved in the Reconciliation rite?

C: One.

T: Right, it is a one-on-one discussion with the priest, guided by instructions in the Book of Common Prayer. Now focusing on the Reconciliation version of the confession at the bottom of page 447, what do you see at the end of the second sentence?

C: A blank line!

T: What do you think goes in the blank?

C: Sins?

T: Yes – specific sins that you, the penitent, remember and wish to confess. Now read the last sentence:

I firmly intend amendment of life, and I humbly beg forgiveness of God and his Church, and ask you for counsel, direction, and absolution.

> T: Once the priest hears specific sins, the priest may provide some counsel and direction, such as Scripture readings and devotional prayers. Then the priest gives the absolution: go to the top of page 448 and you will see two versions. Then, the priest adds:

> The Lord has put away all your sins.

T: What did we say happened when you confessed your sins? Think of our discussion of Jewish temple worship. Why can we enter into the Most Holy Place? [Section IV.A.]

C: Because Jesus' sacrifice washed away our sins.[229]

T: Correct, and that is exactly why the priest can say that your sins are absolved. Reconciliation is typically offered during the Church season of Lent and other times when Christians wish to inwardly examine and change their lives. Reconciliation is most helpful to those who desire to hear the priest say the words of absolution; in a sense, the penitent wishes to hear a verbal confirmation of the promises in Scriptures we have already studied. So if the outward and visible sign of Reconciliation is hearing the priest say, "The Lord has put away all your sins", what is the inward and spiritual grace of Reconciliation?

C: Jesus' blood washes away our sins.

T: As Episcopalians, are we required to go to a personal, one-on-one confession?

C: If we are, that's news to us!

T: There is a saying used in the Anglican Church applied to private confession: "All may, none must, some should".[230] Break it down by parts to see what it means.

C: "All may" means you can go to private confession, but "none must" go. "Some should" probably means some should go to confession because they need to!

T: Now let's look at Unction. Go to page 453 of the Book of Common Prayer. What is that service?

C: Ministration to the Sick.

T: "Unction" literally means "anointing the sick with oil".[231] Where in this service does that happen?

C: Part II. Laying on of Hands and Anointing.

T: Why anoint a sick person with oil? I can tell you that Jesus' disciples did it, but from a point of view of the sick person, what does it accomplish?

C: It makes the sick person feel better.

---

[229] Heb. 10:16-22.
[230] Some attribute the quote to Queen Elizabeth I, but there is no specific record.
[231] BCP, p. 861.

T: It is an outward and visible sign that people, and God, care about the sick person. So, what is the inward and spiritual grace of unction? Does God desire that the sick be healed?

C: Yes.

T: Then unction is God's grace "given for the healing of spirit, mind and body."[232]

---

[232] BCP, p. 861.

XII. Worship

Learning Objectives

1. Confirmands will learn the purposes underlying services for different times of day.
2. Confirmands will learn how readings from Scripture are selected and used in services.
3. Confirmands will understand the need to prepare to receive Holy Communion and the importance of Jesus' Body and Blood in the context of Jewish temple worship.

A. Rite One and Rite Two

T: When you walk into church on Sunday morning, what type of service do you usually attend? Is it Morning Prayer, Holy Eucharist, also called Holy Communion, or some other service?

C: Holy Eucharist.[233]

T: Did you know that there are at least two types of Holy Eucharist?[234] Look at page 323 in the Book of Common Prayer. What is the name of that service?

C: The Holy Eucharist: Rite One.

T: Keep your place there and flip to page 355. What service is that?

C: The Holy Eucharist: Rite Two.

T: Why do we have two different rites for the same type of service?

C: [Blank stares].

T: Look at the bottom of each of page 323 and 355.

Read each version of the prayer beginning "Almighty God":

Rite One	Rite Two
The Celebrant says	The Celebrant may say
Almighty God, unto whom all hearts are open, all desires known, and from whom no secrets are hid: Cleanse the thoughts of our hearts by the inspiration of thy Holy Spirit, that we may	Almighty God, to you all hearts are open, all desires known, and from you no secrets are hid: Cleanse the thoughts of our hearts by the inspiration of your Holy Spirit, that we may

---

[233] Some Episcopal churches hold Morning Prayer more frequently than Holy Eucharist; if that is the case with your church, simply begin with the second question in this section.

[234] There is another Order for Eucharist, found starting on BCP p. 400, that has the informal title of "Rite Three". It is closer to an outline that allows for significant creativity and flexibility, but starts with the admonition, "This rite requires careful preparation by the Priest and other participants."

perfectly love thee, and worthily magnify thy holy Name; through Christ our Lord. *Amen.*	perfectly love you, and worthily magnify your holy Name; through Christ our Lord. *Amen.*

T: Did you see the difference?

C: The Rite One prayer used old English words like "thy" and "thee". The Rite Two prayer used modern words.

T: Look back at *Handout #1*. Which version of the prayer was closer to the words used in Archbishop Cranmer's first prayer book?

C: The Rite One prayer.

T: Why?

C: The first prayer book used words like "thy" and "thee".

T: The use of Rite One or Rite Two is a matter of preference: those desiring the more traditional language of the earlier prayer books will opt for Rite One; those who want more contemporary language, opt for Rite Two.

B. Varieties of Services

T: Let's look at the Table of Contents to the Book of Common Prayer. Look at the list of services under the heading, "The Daily Office". Starting with Daily Morning Prayer: Rite Two, what comes next?

C: Noonday Prayer, then an "Order of Worship for the Evening".

T: [Interrupting] That Order of Worship is sometimes called "Vespers". It is usually held in the late afternoon or early evening, and it is a service for lighting the church candles. What's next?

C: Daily Evening Prayer: Rite Two, Compline.

T: Anyone know what Compline is?

C: [Silence]

T: Anyone say prayers before going to bed?

C: [Hopefully, a few hands go up]

T: Turn to page 133 let's look at some of the Compline prayers.

The Officiant then says one of the following Collects

Be our light in the darkness, O Lord, and in your great mercy defend us from all perils and dangers of this night; for the love of your only Son, our Savior Jesus Christ. *Amen.*

Be present, O merciful God, and protect us through the hours of this night, so that we who are wearied by the changes and chances of this life may rest in your eternal changelessness; through Jesus Christ our Lord. *Amen.*

Look down, O Lord, from your heavenly throne, and illumine this night with your celestial brightness; that by night as by day your people may glorify your holy Name; through Jesus Christ our Lord. *Amen.*

Visit this place, O Lord, and drive far from it all snares of the enemy; let your holy angels dwell with us to preserve us in peace; and let your blessing be upon us always; through Jesus Christ our Lord. *Amen.*

T: When you were young, was anyone afraid of monsters under the bed?

C: Or in the closet, etc.

T: I guarantee that the last prayer will get rid of those! If you have younger brothers or sisters, give these prayers a try, and, of course, feel free to use them yourself before you go to bed.

T: Now, back to the Table of Contents. We saw a service for:

Morning

Noonday

Early Evening

Evening

Nighttime

Several of these services were developed by Archbishop Cranmer during the sixteenth century, and the idea behind these services was innovative for the time in that they were structured around the workday to take advantage of when people may have time to come to a short church service. Look at the list: you can go in the morning before work, you can go during lunch break, and you can go after work. For that reason, these are services designed primarily for weekdays; for Sundays, what service does our church hold?

> C: Holy Eucharist[235]

C. The Word in the Holy Eucharist

T: Let's look at the Rite Two Holy Eucharist, beginning on page 355. The service is divided into two parts. You can find the names of the two parts on pages 355 and 361. What are they?

C: The Word of God and The Holy Communion.

T: Let's start with The Word of God. Looking at page 357, tell me the names of the important sections within The Word of God part, starting with "The Collect of the Day".

C: "The Collect of the Day"

       "The Lessons"

       "The Sermon"

       "The Nicene Creed"

       "The Prayers of the People"

       "Confession of Sin"

       "The Peace"

T: We've covered The Nicene Creed and Confession of Sin already. You should know what the Sermon is, as well as The Prayers of the People and The Peace,[236] so what is left is the Collect and The Lessons. Where do you find the Collect of the Day? Look in the Table of Contents.

C: Starting on page 159.

T: Those are Traditional Collects. We are looking at the Rite Two contemporary service, so where are the Collects for those?

C: Starting on page 211.

T: Keep your place on page 357 and flip to page 211. What is the first Collect you see?

---

[235] Some churches may hold Morning Prayer on Sundays along with (or occasionally in place of) Holy Eucharist. For our purposes here, simply note that, for at least some Sundays, Holy Eucharist is held.
[236] The Peace has a scriptural foundation in Matthew 5:21-26, where Jesus instructs that we reconcile first with our brothers and sisters who "hath ought against thee" before bringing "thy gift before the alter" of God. The Peace is placed before Holy Communion to remind us of that duty to reconcile.

C: "First Sunday in Advent".

T: Why do the Collects start with Advent? Why not Christmas or Easter?

C: Advent is the first season of the Church Year.[237]

T: So depending where you are in the Church Year, there is a Collect for that Sunday. The Collect pulls together themes for that Sunday. The first Collect for Advent, for example, talks about how "Jesus Christ came to visit us in great humility". What is the season after Advent?

C: Christmas.

T: So when this Collect says "Jesus Christ came to visit us in great humility", what is it talking about?

C: Jesus' birth.

T: What was humble about Jesus' birth?

C: He was born in a manger.

T: And not in a palace. So, on the First Sunday in Advent, we focus on Jesus coming "in great humility" by being born in a manger. The rest of the service will have readings that talk about Jesus' coming, and the hymns you sing likely will as well. <u>The Collect, then, is an introduction to what will come later in the service.</u> Speaking of the readings, that's the next section, called "The Lessons". Where do the Lessons come from?

C: The leaflet the usher hands you when you walk in to the church.[238]

T: The readings come from the Bible! The issue before us is: which verses will be read on a given Sunday? To find out look at page 888 in the Book of Common Prayer.[239] Read the first paragraph:

> The Lectionary for Sundays is arranged in a three-year cycle, in which
>
> Year A always begins on the First Sunday of Advent in years evenly
>
> divisible by three. (For example, 1977 divided by 3 is 659 with no

---

[237] Hopefully, you have covered the Church seasons in Sunday School before this course. If you need a refresher, the seasonal diagram at http://www.internetmonk.com/archive/church-year-spirituality is simple and easy to reference.
[238] Some churches do not provide leaflets. If your church does not, don't worry. Simply forge on!
[239] In 2007, the Book of Common Prayer was amended to use the Revised Common Lectionary ("RCL"). The Bible passages cited in this course are essentially the same under either the previous lectionary or the RCL, so there is no need to purchase more-current prayer books for this course. A version of the BCP with the RCL is available for free download at: http://www.episcopal-church.org/page/book-common-prayer.

remainder. Year A, therefore, begins on Advent Sunday of that year.)

T: So, a year whose digits are evenly divisible by three is Year A. What year are we in now? To figure it out, do the current year's digits add to a number evenly divisible by three?

Answer is "Yes"

C: Yes.

T: Then we will start Year A this year.

Answer is "No"

C: No.

T: Subtract one [or two] from the current year's sum. Does that get us to a sum that is evenly divisible by three?

C: Yes

T: Then Year A began in that year.

Continue here, after answering "Yes" or "No"

T: But when in our twelve-month calendar does Year A start? What is the first season of the Church Year?

C: Advent.

T: When on the calendar does Advent usually start? Advent consists of the four Sundays before Christmas, so count back four Sundays from December 25 and where are you?

C: Late November.

T: Or maybe early December, depending on what day of the week Christmas falls. So, when on the calendar does Year A Commence?

C: Late November or early December.

T: Right. Now look at page 889 under "Year A". What is the first line you see?

C: "First Sunday of Advent"

T: You'll notice that there is a psalm appointed to be read for that Sunday and then three lessons. What is the first lesson?

C: Isaiah 2:1-5

T: Is that from the Old Testament or the New Testament?

C: [Looking at Bible TOC] Old Testament.

T: What is next?

C: Romans 13:8-14 [Romans 13:11-14 in the Revised Common Lectionary]

T: Is that from the Old Testament or the New Testament?

C: New Testament

T: Is it one of the four Gospels or is it one of the epistles or letters written to someone?

C: Epistles.

T: The title gives it away: it is the Epistle to the Romans. Also, if you look through the rest of the Lectionary, you will see that all the second readings come from epistles, not the Gospels. Finally, what is the third reading?

C: Matthew 24:37-44 [Matthew 24:36-44 in the RCL]

T: Is that one of the four Gospels?

C: Yes.

T: Again, if you look through the rest of the Lectionary, you will see that all of the third readings are from the Gospels, not the epistles. For that reason, we usually refer to the third reading as the "Gospel reading". For all of Advent, which Gospel provides the Gospel readings for Year A?

C: Matthew.

T: For Christmas, which Gospel provides the readings?

C: Luke, and then John.

T: That's because Luke provides the most detailed account of Jesus' birth. If you have watched *A Charlie Brown Christmas*, Linus reads from Luke to tell the story of the nativity.[240]

---

[240] Actually, there was significant concern from network executives in 1965 when the special first aired that there would be a long, direct reading of Scripture. Fortunately, *Peanuts* creator Charles Schulz stood his ground and the network relented. See http://www.nationalreview.com/article/284093/gospel-according-peanuts-lee-habeeb for more details.

This is purely optional, but if you have time, you can watch Linus' monologue at: http://www.bing.com/videos/search?q=charlie+brown+christmas+movie+linus+reading+from+luke&view=detail&mid=26DF87BFD2A5323BFC7926DF87BFD2A5323BFC79&FORM=VIRE.

> T: Flip to Year B on page 900. Where do the Advent readings come from?
>
> C: Mark, then John.
>
> T: Flip to Year C on page 911. Where do the Advent readings come from?
>
> C: Luke.
>
> T: Then, after Year C, where do we go next?
>
> C: We go back to Year A.
>
> T: So, over three years, we see Advent readings from
>
> A: Matthew
>
> B: Mark
>
> C: Luke
>
> With a little John sprinkled in. This is true throughout each liturgical year. Year A draws heavily from Matthew for <u>all</u> church seasons; Year B from Mark; Year C from Luke. John is interspersed throughout. Anyone know why John is treated differently?
>
> C: [silence.]
>
> T: Because the Gospel of John is very different from the other three Gospels. Matthew, Mark and Luke are called "Synoptic Gospels" because they follow a similar outline, or synopsis, and appear to be drawn from similar sources. John is simply on a different plane of existence. While the Synoptic Gospels start out with John the Baptist and/or Jesus' birth, St. John's Gospel starts with Jesus being the Word of God in a passage we've read twice before [Sections VI.A. and XI.A.], and engages in an abstract, intellectual discussion right from the start.
>
> T: Now go back to page 357 and let's see where these readings come in the service. Under the heading "The Lessons", what are the instructions?

> *The people sit. One or two Lessons, as appointed, are read, the Reader first saying*
>
> *A Reading (Lesson) from_____.*
>
> *A citation giving chapter and verse may be added.*

After each Reading, the Reader may say

                    The Word of the Lord.
People   Thanks be to God.

or the Reader may say   Here ends the Reading (Epistle).

Silence may follow.

A Psalm, hymn, or anthem may follow each Reading.

T: How many lessons can there be in the service?

C: One or two.

T: So each church can choose whether to read the Old Testament lesson alone, the New Testament epistle lesson alone, or both. The Gospel reading is <u>not</u> optional, however! Continue reading from page 357:

Then, all standing, the Deacon or a Priest reads the Gospel, first saying

                    The Holy Gospel of our Lord Jesus Christ
                    according to_____.
People   Glory to you, Lord Christ.

After the Gospel, the Reader says

                    The Gospel of the Lord.
People   Praise to you, Lord Christ.

T: Look carefully. Who reads the Gospel reading?

C: "the Deacon or a Priest".

T: Any church member[241] can read the Old Testament lesson or the New Testament epistle lesson. Only ordained priests[242] or deacons can read the Gospel. Why do you think the service instructions require a priest or deacon for the Gospel reading?

C: The Gospels are important.

T: Correct. Also, the Gospel readings frequently quote Jesus in His role as a preacher or priest, so it is fitting to have an ordained person reading Jesus' words.

---

[241] Visitors may also read the lessons, but with some restrictions imposed by local rectors. For example, I find that requiring the reader to be a baptized or confessing Christian to be reasonable since the congregation would expect that the person reading from the Bible actually believes in the text being read.

[242] Bishops can read the Gospel as well, since they are also ordained priests.

T: Now jump to page 361. Where are we?

C: The Holy Communion.

T: What service are we in? [Hint: look at the bottom of the page.]

C: Holy Eucharist II

T: From page 355, the first part of the Holy Eucharist is what?

C: "The Word of God"

T: Where do the readings of the Word of God come from?

C: The Lectionary.

T: Trick question: the readings are from the Bible;[243] the specific verses for a given Sunday come from the Lectionary! After "The Word of God" section, we have "The Holy Communion", and the two parts constitute the Holy Eucharist. This service, more than any other, demonstrates the balance we have in the Episcopal Church between Word and Sacrament. We can trace the roots of this balance back to Archbishop Cranmer's first Book of Common Prayer published in the sixteenth century.

D. Preparation for Holy Communion

T: When we studied Jewish temple worship earlier [Section IV.A.], we read from the book of Hebrews that Christians could enter into the most holy place in God's Kingdom. Let's review that again.

Hebrews 10

10 By the which will we are sanctified through the offering of the body of Jesus Christ once for all.

11 And every priest standeth daily ministering and offering oftentimes the same sacrifices, which can never take away sins:

12 But this man, after he had offered one sacrifice for sins for ever, sat down on the right hand of God;

---

[243] Some of the readings in the RCL come from the Apocrypha, a collection of sacred texts that do not hold the status of canonical Scripture but, according to Article VI of the Articles of Religion, are "read for example of life and instruction of manners". So, the "Bible" referred to here is the expanded version with the Apocrypha.

13 From henceforth expecting till his enemies be made his footstool.

14 For by one offering he hath perfected for ever them that are sanctified.

15 Whereof the Holy Ghost also is a witness to us: for after that he had said before,

16 This is the covenant that I will make with them after those days, saith the Lord, I will put my laws into their hearts, and in their minds will I write them;

17 And their sins and iniquities will I remember no more.

18 Now where remission of these is, there is no more offering for sin.

19 Having therefore, brethren, boldness to enter into the holiest [place] by the blood of Jesus,

20 By a new and living way, which he hath consecrated for us, through the veil, that is to say, his flesh;

21 And having an high priest over the house of God;

22 Let us draw near with a true heart in full assurance of faith, having our hearts sprinkled from an evil conscience, and our bodies washed with pure water.

T: What allows us to enter into the holiest place and not get incinerated like Aaron's sons?

C: The blood of Jesus.

T: The blood of Jesus allows us to enter into a New Covenant with God. Look at verses 16 and 17 and tell me what happens to our sins under the New Covenant?

C: God no longer remembers them.

T: It is as if God erased them entirely; as if our sins never happened. Now look at verse 20. There is "a new and living way ... through the veil". Looking back at our diagram of the Jewish temple, where in the temple was the veil?

C: It blocked the view into the Most Holy Place.

T: Verse 20 says we have a way through that veil, and if you passed through the veil of the temple in Jerusalem, where would you be?

C: In the Most Holy Place.

T: Verse 20 also tells us what Jesus sacrificed to provide that way through the temple veil. What was that?

C: His flesh.

T: What do the bread and wine at Holy Communion represent?

C: Jesus' body and blood.

T: So Holy Communion is not just to help us remember Jesus' sacrifice; it reminds us that the purpose of His sacrifice is to bring us into the presence of God: to restore what Adam and Eve once had. Can we enter into God's presence burdened by sin?

C: No.

T: We have to confess our sins. Then, when we do, what does verse 17 say that happens?

C: God remembers them no more.

T: What we learned about Jewish temple worship has many similarities to Holy Communion. This passage from Hebrews sets out the case very clearly. St. Paul, though, added more.

I Corinthians 11

23 For I have received of the Lord that which also I delivered unto you, That the Lord Jesus the same night in which he was betrayed took bread:

24 And when he had given thanks, he brake it, and said, Take, eat: this is my body, which is broken for you: this do in remembrance of me.

25 After the same manner also he took the cup, when he had supped, saying, This cup is the new testament in my blood: this do ye, as oft as ye drink it, in remembrance of me.

26 For as often as ye eat this bread, and drink this cup, ye do shew the Lord's death till he come.

27 Wherefore whosoever shall eat this bread, and drink this cup of the Lord, unworthily, shall be guilty of the body and blood of the Lord.

28 But let a man examine himself, and so let him eat of that bread, and drink of that cup.

29 For he that eateth and drinketh unworthily, eateth and drinketh damnation to himself, not discerning the Lord's body.

30 For this cause many are weak and sickly among you, and many sleep.

31 For if we would judge ourselves, we should not be judged.

32 But when we are judged, we are chastened of the Lord, that we should not be condemned with the world.

T: Here, St. Paul gets serious about the impact of not confessing sins. In verse 30, what does he say has happened to those who have not confessed their sins but participated in Holy Communion?

C: Some are weak and sick; others are asleep.

T: Any guess on what "sleep" means here?

C: Dead!

T: So in verse 31, what does St. Paul want us to do?

C: Judge ourselves.

T: So that we will not be judged! This is the examination he talks about in verse 28 that should occur before receiving Holy Communion. Let's see what the Book of Common Prayer instructs on this subject. Turn to page 316.

An Exhortation

This Exhortation may be used, in whole or in part, either during the Liturgy or at other times. In the absence of a deacon or priest, this Exhortation may be read by a lay person. The people stand or sit.

1. Beloved in the Lord: Our Savior Christ, on the night before he suffered, instituted the Sacrament of his Body and Blood as a sign and pledge of his love, for the continual remembrance of the sacrifice of his death, and for a spiritual sharing in his risen life. For in these holy Mysteries we are made one with Christ, and Christ with us; we are made one body in him, and members one of another.

2. Having in mind, therefore, his great love for us, and in obedience to his command, his Church renders to Almighty God our heavenly Father never-ending thanks for the creation of the world, for his continual providence over us, for his love for all mankind, and for the redemption of the world by our Savior Christ, who took upon himself our flesh, and humbled himself even to death on the cross, that he

might make us the children of God by the power of the Holy
   Spirit, and exalt us to everlasting life.

3 But if we are to share rightly in the celebration of those holy Mysteries, and be nourished by that spiritual Food, we must remember the dignity of that holy Sacrament. I therefore call upon you to consider how Saint Paul exhorts all persons to prepare themselves carefully before eating of that Bread and drinking of that Cup.

4 For, as the benefit is great, if with penitent hearts and living faith we receive the holy Sacrament, so is the danger great, if we receive it improperly, not recognizing the Lord's Body. Judge yourselves, therefore, lest you be judged by the Lord.

5 Examine your lives and conduct by the rule of God's commandments, that you may perceive wherein you have offended in what you have done or left undone, whether in thought, word, or deed. And acknowledge your sins before Almighty God, with full purpose of amendment of life, being ready to make restitution for all injuries and wrongs done by you to others; and also being ready to forgive those who have offended you, in order that you yourselves may be forgiven. And then, being reconciled with one another, come to the banquet of that most heavenly Food.

6 And if, in your preparation, you need help and counsel, then go and open your grief to a discreet and understanding priest, and confess your sins, that you may receive the benefit of absolution, and spiritual counsel and advice; to the removal of scruple and doubt, the assurance of pardon, and the strengthening of your faith.

7 To Christ our Lord who loves us, and washed us in his own blood, and made us a kingdom of priests to serve his God and Father, to him be glory in the Church evermore. Through him let us offer continually the sacrifice of praise, which is our bounden duty and service, and, with faith in him, come boldly before the throne of grace [and humbly confess our sins to Almighty God].

T: The fourth paragraph ends with, "Judge yourselves, therefore, lest you be judged by the Lord." Where did you read that before?

C: In I Corinthians 11:31.

T: Paragraph five says, "Examine your lives and conduct by the rule of God's Commandments, ..." Where in the Bible do we find God's Commandments?

C: In the Old Testament.

T: Go to page 848 in the Book of Common Prayer.

> Q. What is the purpose of the Ten Commandments?
> A. The Ten Commandments were given to define our relationship with God and our neighbors.
>
> Q. Since we do not fully obey them, are they useful at all?
> A. Since we do not fully obey them, we see more clearly our sin and our need for redemption.

T: So sin is defined, partly, by not obeying what?

C: The Ten Commandments.

T: So the Old Testament provides us a guide to what is sin. Jesus summed up the Old Testament Law with two commandments. Look on page 851.

> Q. What are the commandments taught by Christ?
> A. Christ taught us the Summary of the Law and gave us the New Commandment.
>
> Q. What is the Summary of the Law?
> A. You shall love the Lord your God with all your heart, with all your soul, and with all your mind. This is the first and the great commandment. And the second is like it: You shall love your neighbor as yourself.
>
> Q. What is the New Commandment?
> A. The New Commandment is that we love one another as Christ loved us.

T: The New Testament as well as the Old Testament gives us guidance on what is sin. So, now that we know the importance of confessing sin before receiving Holy Communion, can you tell me where in the service for Holy Eucharist the Confession of Sin occurs? Is the confession before or after communion?

C: Before communion![244]

T: That was not by accident. God takes sin seriously; so should you when you reach that part of the service. What handout in this course could be helpful for you to review to see which sins you need to confess?

C: Handout #3.

T: Right. The handout summarizes Mark 7:21-22 and is a useful checklist.[245]

---

[244] For reference, in Holy Eucharist II, the Confession of Sin is found on BCP p. 359, Holy Communion starts on p. 361.
[245] Also, there is help available through clergy, as discussed on paragraph six of the Exhortation.

XIII. The Christian Hope

Learning Objectives

1. Confirmands will understand the importance of martyrs in Eschatology, and the nature of the Last Judgment.
2. Confirmands will understand the importance of their Baptism as the instrument of their salvation.
3. Confirmands will understand the Christian Hope: that nothing, including death, will separate us from the love of God.

T: We have reached the last section of the course before our review, and this is where we look at what is to come in the future. In the New Testament, there are many passages describing events to come in future periods, but which book of the New Testament is mostly dedicated to future events? [Hint: Some of you drew pictures from the New Jerusalem at the beginning of this course from that book.]

C: Revelation.

T: Where in the Bible do you find the book of Revelation?

C: The last book.

T: Fittingly, Revelation is at the end of the Bible to point us to the future. Much of Revelation is a vision, but who saw and recorded that vision? [The answer may be on the title page for the book in the confirmand's Bible, and the answer is also in Revelation 1:4.]

C: John.

T: This is likely the same John who wrote the Gospel of John.[246] Let's turn to the sixth chapter of Revelation. In this part of John's vision, he sees Jesus, as the Lamb of God, opening seven seals in a book during a period before Jesus returns to Earth from Heaven. If a document is sealed, like a letter or a book, what is the first thing you need to do before reading it?

C: Break the seal.

T: So Jesus here is breaking each of the seven seals in sequence. The first four seals talk about four men on four horses, each representing something bad [Revelation 6:1-8]:

Conquest

---

[246] The author of Revelation is also likely the author of I John as well. For a more detailed discussion on this topic, I recommend Leighton Pullan's commentary, which can be found at http://biblehub.com/library/pullan/the_books_of_the_new_testament/chapter_xxv_the_revelation_of.htm. As to the authorship of II John and III John, an elder named John who was associated with Jesus' ministry is a likely choice: see http://www.ncregister.com/blog/jimmy-akin/pope-benedict-on-the-mystery-of-john-the-presbyter.

War

Famine

Death

Here is a late-nineteenth century painting of the horsemen:

Four Horsemen of the Apocalypse, by Viktor Vasnetsov (1887). Public domain.

T: The sixth seal releases massive earthquakes and other physical calamities [Revelation 6:12-17]. The seventh seal, though, holds all these bad things back until God marks those who believe in Him so that they are not hurt [Revelation 7:1-8]. But I want to focus on what John saw when Jesus opened the fifth seal:

> Revelation 6
>
> 9 And when he had opened the fifth seal, I saw under the altar the souls of them that were slain for the word of God, and for the testimony which they held:
>
> 10 And they cried with a loud voice, saying, How long, O Lord, holy and true, dost thou not judge and avenge our blood on them that dwell on the earth?
>
> 11 And white robes were given unto every one of them; and it was said unto them, that they should rest yet for a little season, until their fellowservants also and their brethren, that should be killed as they were, should be fulfilled.

T: People who are killed for their religious beliefs are called what?

C: Martyrs.

T: What are the martyrs asking God to do in the tenth verse?

C: They wanted God to avenge their deaths.

T: And what were they told in verse 11?

C: To wait until the rest of the martyrs join them.

T: How do you think God avenges the deaths of the martyrs? [Hint: look at the painting.]

C: He releases the four horsemen.

T: Why are the martyrs singled out, from among all the Christian saints, and given special recognition?

C: They gave their lives for Christ.

T: They gave their lives instead of doing what? Usually, martyrs were offered a choice. What was that choice?

C: Renounce their faith or die.[247]

T: Did the martyrs that St. John saw renounce their faith in Jesus?

C: No.

T: We talked earlier about those who saw Jesus after His Resurrection. St. Paul placed the number at more than 500 [I Corinthians 15:6]. Some of those were later martyred by Roman authorities or others.[248] They all had a choice that could have saved their lives. What could martyrs, in the years before Christianity became legal, have done that would have saved their lives?

C: Renounce their faith in Jesus.

T: Yet, what they saw in the Risen Lord was so real that they chose death. <u>Indeed, the witness of these martyrs lives on with us today.</u> The testimony of the martyrs is the equivalent of a modern-day news video of an empty tomb on Easter morning followed by a meeting between the resurrected Jesus and His disciples walking along the road to Emmaus. That's how real the witness of the martyrs is! Given what I just said, do you now understand why

---

[247] We saw in the correspondence between Pliny the Younger and Emperor Trajan that those who recanted their belief in Christianity would be spared. This practice likely became common as Christianity become more widespread so as to avoid large-scale executions of persons willing to return to the pagan gods.

[248] Common belief is that all disciples, except St. John, were martyred. Others likely were during the reign of Nero.

the martyrs were given such a place of honor in the period before Jesus returns to the Earth?[249]

C: Yes.

T: And did you pick up on my statements that Jesus is coming again?

C: Yes.

T: What will Jesus do when He comes again? [Hint: we say what He will do in the Nicene and Apostles' Creeds]

C: "He will come again in glory to judge the living and the dead."

T: Turn to Revelation 20 and see.

> Revelation 20
>
> 11 And I saw a great white throne, and him that sat on it, from whose face the earth and the heaven fled away; and there was found no place for them.
>
> 12 And I saw the dead, small and great, stand before God; and the books were opened: and another book was opened, which is the book of life: and the dead were judged out of those things which were written in the books, according to their works.
>
> 13 And the sea gave up the dead which were in it; and death and hell delivered up the dead which were in them: and they were judged every man according to their works.
>
> 14 And death and hell were cast into the lake of fire. This is the second death.
>
> 15 And whosoever was not found written in the book of life was cast into the lake of fire.

T: So, on Judgement Day, when the Book of Life is opened, are you going to be with God or are you going into the Lake of Fire?

C: I hope I get to be with God.

---

[249] In addition to their recognition in the unsealing process of Revelation 6, the martyrs will serve as judges during a 1000-year period of evangelization following the apocalypse (Revelation 20:1-6) and prior to the final battle (Revelation 20:7-10).

> T: Well, the Good News is that you are going to be with God, and that issue was settled at your Baptism. Turn to page 858 in the Book of Common Prayer and see what the Catechism says about what your baptism accomplished.

> Q. What is the inward and spiritual grace in Baptism?
> A. The inward and spiritual grace in Baptism is union with Christ in his death and resurrection, birth into God's family the Church, forgiveness of sins, and new life in the Holy Spirit.

> T: So, if you are born into God's family with forgiveness of your sins and new life in the Holy Spirit, are you going into the Lake of Fire?
>
> C: No!
>
> T: Let's see what the Catechism says about Judgement Day. Turn to page 862:

> Q. What do we mean by the last judgment?
> A. We believe that Christ will come in glory and judge the living and the dead.
>
> Q. What do we mean by the resurrection of the body?
> A. We mean that God will raise us from death in the fullness of our being, that we may live with Christ in the communion of the saints.
>
> Q. What is the communion of saints?
> A. The communion of saints is the whole family of God, the living and the dead, those whom we love and those whom we hurt, bound together in Christ by sacrament, prayer, and praise.
>
> Q. What do we mean by everlasting life?
> A. By everlasting life, we mean a new existence, in which we are united with all the people of God, in the joy of fully knowing and loving God and each other.
>
> Q. What, then, is our assurance as Christians?
> A. Our assurance as Christians is that nothing, not even death, shall separate us from the love of God which is in Christ Jesus our Lord. Amen.

> T: So, we are going to have resurrected bodies and live among the communion of saints. Where will we be when that happens?
>
> C: Heaven.
>
> T: What if I told you that, by that point, Heaven and Earth had become one?

Revelation 21

1 And I saw a new heaven and a new earth: for the first heaven and the first earth were passed away; and there was no more sea.

2 And I John saw the holy city, new Jerusalem, coming down from God out of heaven, prepared as a bride adorned for her husband.

3 And I heard a great voice out of heaven saying, Behold, the tabernacle of God is with men, and he will dwell with them, and they shall be his people, and God himself shall be with them, and be their God.

4 And God shall wipe away all tears from their eyes; and there shall be no more death, neither sorrow, nor crying, neither shall there be any more pain: for the former things are passed away.

5 And he that sat upon the throne said, Behold, I make all things new. And he said unto me, Write: for these words are true and faithful.

6 And he said unto me, It is done. I am Alpha and Omega, the beginning and the end. I will give unto him that is athirst of the fountain of the water of life freely.

7 He that overcometh shall inherit all things; and I will be his God, and he shall be my son.

8 But the fearful, and unbelieving, and the abominable, and murderers, and whoremongers, and sorcerers, and idolaters, and all liars, shall have their part in the lake which burneth with fire and brimstone: which is the second death.

9 And there came unto me one of the seven angels which had the seven vials full of the seven last plagues, and talked with me, saying, Come hither, I will shew thee the bride, the Lamb's wife.

10 And he carried me away in the spirit to a great and high mountain, and shewed me that great city, the holy Jerusalem, descending out of heaven from God,

11 Having the glory of God: and her light was like unto a stone most precious, even like a jasper stone, clear as crystal;

12 And had a wall great and high, and had twelve gates, and at the gates twelve angels, and names written thereon, which are the names of the twelve tribes of the children of Israel:

13 On the east three gates; on the north three gates; on the south three gates; and on the west three gates.

14 And the wall of the city had twelve foundations, and in them the names of the twelve apostles of the Lamb.

15 And he that talked with me had a golden reed to measure the city, and the gates thereof, and the wall thereof.

16 And the city lieth foursquare, and the length is as large as the breadth: and he measured the city with the reed, twelve thousand furlongs. The length and the breadth and the height of it are equal.

17 And he measured the wall thereof, an hundred and forty and four cubits, according to the measure of a man, that is, of the angel.

18 And the building of the wall of it was of jasper: and the city was pure gold, like unto clear glass.

19 And the foundations of the wall of the city were garnished with all manner of precious stones. The first foundation was jasper; the second, sapphire; the third, a chalcedony; the fourth, an emerald;

20 The fifth, sardonyx; the sixth, sardius; the seventh, chrysolite; the eighth, beryl; the ninth, a topaz; the tenth, a chrysoprasus; the eleventh, a jacinth; the twelfth, an amethyst.

21 And the twelve gates were twelve pearls; every several gate was of one pearl: and the street of the city was pure gold, as it were transparent glass.

22 And I saw no temple therein: for the Lord God Almighty and the Lamb are the temple of it.

23 And the city had no need of the sun, neither of the moon, to shine in it: for the glory of God did lighten it, and the Lamb is the light thereof.

24 And the nations of them which are saved shall walk in the light of it: and the kings of the earth do bring their glory and honour into it.

25 And the gates of it shall not be shut at all by day: for there shall be no night there.

26 And they shall bring the glory and honour of the nations into it.

27 And there shall in no wise enter into it any thing that defileth, neither whatsoever worketh abomination, or maketh a lie: but they which are written in the Lamb's book of life.

Revelation 22

1 And he shewed me a pure river of water of life, clear as crystal, proceeding out of the throne of God and of the Lamb.

2 In the midst of the street of it, and on either side of the river, was there the tree of life, which bare twelve manner of fruits, and yielded her fruit every month: and the leaves of the tree were for the healing of the nations.

3 And there shall be no more curse: but the throne of God and of the Lamb shall be in it; and his servants shall serve him:

4 And they shall see his face; and his name shall be in their foreheads.

5 And there shall be no night there; and they need no candle, neither light of the sun; for the Lord God giveth them light: and they shall reign for ever and ever.

T: Anyone recognize this passage?

C: Didn't we use these verses to make drawings earlier?

T: Right, back at the early part of this course, the Revelation group created their drawings from these verses. According to Chapter 21, verse 1, what has happened to the Earth at the time of Judgment Day?

C: It is new, and there is no sea.

T: In verses 2 – 3, what does St. John see?

C: The New Jerusalem coming down from Heaven.

T: Where is the New Jerusalem going to rest?

C: Somewhere on the new Earth.

T: From verse 16, what can you tell me about the size and shape of the New Jerusalem?

C: It is a big cube.

T: You may remember from our earlier class that each edge will measure about 1,500 miles, and it will be so large that, if one edge was on the eastern coast of the U.S., the other edge could touch the Mississippi River. As to height, it will be several times taller than the current orbital height of the International Space Station.[250] From verse 22, tell me if there is going to be a church in the New Jerusalem?

---

[250] The International Space Station orbits at just over 400km, or about 250 miles above the Earth's surface. See http://www.heavens-above.com/IssHeight.aspx?lat=0&lng=0&loc=Unspecified&alt=0.

C: Not likely – there is no temple.

T: Why?

C: God and Jesus are the temple.

T: A temple, or church, is a place you go to worship God. If God and Jesus are the temple in the New Jerusalem, when you go to worship there, who will be standing in front of you?

C: God and Jesus!

T: Look at verses 23 – 25. What does the New Jerusalem have lots of?

C: Light.

T: Bonus points to anyone who can tell me why there is lots of light in the city where God dwells.

C: God is Light.

T: Hold your place there and flip to I John 1:5.

> I John 1
>
> 5 This then is the message which we have heard of him, and declare unto you, that God is light, and in him is no darkness at all.

T: FYI, this passage is likely written by the same John who saw the vision in Revelation. Since God is Light, and sin is darkness, can sin exist in His Presence?

C: No.

T: What does light do to darkness when you flip a light switch?

C: Light replaces darkness.

T: Light overcomes darkness; light obliterates darkness. God, at this point, has obliterated sin, and that will allow people like you and me to come into His Presence. Flip back to Revelation, Chapter 22, verses 1 – 2. When the Revelation groups drew this scene, what did it resemble?

C: It looked like the Garden of Eden.

T: What was missing in the New Jerusalem that was in the Garden of Eden?

C: The Tree of Knowledge of Good and Evil.

T: The Tree of Life is back, and we will have access to it. What do you think that means?

C: We will live forever?

T: Right. To confirm that, go to verses 3 - 5. In verse 5, who is John referring to when he says, "they shall reign for ever and ever"? [Hint: the answer is in verse 3.]

C: "His servants."

T: Are you one of His servants?

C: Yes.

T: Then that will be you. From verse 4, whose face shall you see?

C: God's.

T: When Adam and Eve were in the Garden of Eden, who could they see and talk to directly?

C: God.[251]

T: So, by the time the New Jerusalem arrives, what will we have that Adam and Eve had in the Garden of Eden?

C: The Tree of Life and being able to talk to God directly.

T: So, all is restored to the state in which God intended us to live in the first place.

---

[251] We see in Genesis 3:8 that, after eating the forbidden fruit, Adam and Eve "hid themselves from the presence of the Lord God". By inverse reasoning, therefore, we conclude that previously Adam and Eve could, and did, enter into the very presence of God.

XIV. Next Steps

A. The Baptismal Covenant in Action

The Baptismal Covenant, on p. 417 of the Book of Common Prayer, presents a series of questions the bishop asks regarding Christian commitment:

Bishop Will you continue in the apostles' teaching and fellowship, in the breaking of bread, and in the prayers?
People I will, with God's help.

Bishop Will you persevere in resisting evil, and, whenever you fall into sin, repent and return to the Lord?
People I will, with God's help.

Bishop Will you proclaim by word and example the Good News of God in Christ?
People I will, with God's help.

Bishop Will you seek and serve Christ in all persons, loving your neighbor as yourself?
People I will, with God's help.

Bishop Will you strive for justice and peace among all people, and respect the dignity of every human being?
People I will, with God's help.

Step through each of these questions and ask yourself how you intend to fulfill the commitments you made at your confirmation. Try to be as specific as possible. For example, if you are to "proclaim by word and example the Good News of God in Christ", then ask what will you do in your daily life to set such an example and how do you intend to proclaim the Good

News? One rector I worked with for many years had confirmands write out individual answers to these questions which she reviewed before agreeing to sponsor them for Confirmation. You can write your answers in the space provided under each question above.

B. Beyond This Course

If you are interested in further pursuing topics covered in this course, I recommend the following:

Archeological evidence of the spread of early Christianity

For those of you interested in learning about what archeology tells us about the growth of the Early Church, another book by Rodney Stark, *Cities of God,* not only discusses the archeological evidence of early churches, but examines how and to whom Christianity spread using statistical regression to test various hypotheses. However, you needn't be good at math to understand his points because Professor Stark summarizes his findings in the text of his book and puts the statistics in an appendix. His findings are quite interesting. Some are intuitive, such as the evidence that Christianity started in port cities along the Mediterranean before moving inland and spread first to cities within 1,000 miles of Jerusalem. Others are more surprising. His book examines the presence of pagan religions and their impact on Christianity and finds that cities with a temple to the Egyptian goddess Isis were more likely to have a Christian church by 100 A.D. than those without, and Stark posits that, due to certain similarities in the faiths, Isis worship prepared the way for pagans to convert to Christianity.

When bad things happen to good people

If you or a friend have had to grapple with some bad event that occurred, such as sickness, death or other loss, the C.S. Lewis book, *The Problem of Pain*, tackles the issue of pain caused by bad events head on. I especially recommend Chapters 5 through 7. A few good quotes:

> God saw the crucifixion in the act of creating the first nebula. The world is a dance in which good, descending from God, is disturbed by evil arising from the creatures, and the resulting conflict is resolved by God's own assumption of the suffering nature which evil produces.[252]

> A merciful man aims at his neighbour's good and so does 'God's will', consciously co-operating with 'the simple good'. A cruel man oppresses his neighbour, and so does simple evil. But in doing such evil, he is used by God, without his own knowledge or consent, to produce the complex good – so that the first man serves God as a son, and the second as a tool.[253]

Why Some Countries are Perpetually in Need While Others Have Plenty

---

[252] *The Problem of Pain* by C.S. Lewis © copyright CS Lewis Pte Ltd 1940, p. 80. Extract reprinted by permission.
[253] *The Problem of Pain* by C.S. Lewis © copyright CS Lewis Pte Ltd 1940, p. 111. Extract reprinted by permission.

If you are looking for reasons why bad things, such as poverty and famine, persistently happen in some countries but not others, an excellent and thoroughly researched book addresses this issue. In *Why Nations Fail* by Daron Acemoglu and James A. Robinson, the authors explain how autocratic governments establish extractive economic regimes to funnel wealth to the privileged elites while impoverishing the people they govern. Through numerous and interesting examples, the authors show how the extractive institutions are set up and operated. More importantly, they explain how inclusive political institutions that allow for pluralism in government also allow for creative destruction that paves the way for innovation. Hence, they explain why some nations fail while others succeed.

Lewis' Space Trilogy and the "Progressive Element"

Even C.S. Lewis weighed in on elitism. *Chronicles of Narnia* was not the only fiction series C.S. Lewis wrote. From 1938 - 1945, he published an adult fiction series of books that takes the reader to Mars in *Out of the Silent Planet*, then to Venus in *Perelandra*, and finally back to Earth in *That Hideous Strength*. The main character in the trilogy, Dr. Elwin Ransom, was modeled after Lewis' good friend, J.R.R. Tolkien, who wrote the *Hobbit* series. The last book of the trilogy is most pertinent to issues of today and can be read without reading the previous two books. In *That Hideous Strength*, Lewis explored the beliefs and methods of what he called the "Progressive Element" in academia, which resembled the early origins of today's progressive movement in that academics believed they could and should exert control over less-enlightened individuals to bring about a society that the intellectuals believed to be superior, with a small group of intellectuals in charge and given dictatorial powers.

That Hideous Strength is an excellent companion to the George Orwell works on socialism that you will likely encounter in high school: *Animal Farm* and *Nineteen Eighty-Four*. Even more relevant to today, though, is that Lewis in 1945 presciently labeled the entity that would implement the progressive agenda in *That Hideous Strength* as the "National Institute of Co-ordinated Experiments" or N.I.C.E. Ironically, today, Lewis' homeland of Great Britain has a government agency named N.I.C.E., the National Institute for Clinical Excellence (now called the National Institute for Health and Clinical Excellence) that was founded 54 years after Lewis' book was published. Today's N.I.C.E. rations healthcare under Britain's socialized medicine regime and tells Britons whether their health system will pay for mammograms and other health services. This book is a must-read!

All these books are available through on-line retailers and at many bookstores.

One final thought: If you found some sections of this course of interest and you want to learn more, seek out your church youth ministry leader or a priest and ask to incorporate some of this course's topics that interested you into the curriculum for high school teenagers. If Confirmation is offered for eighth grade thirteen-year olds in your church, for example, you may wish to suggest a course for ninth graders that explores extra-Biblical sources, such as Josephus and others that I could not fit in. I think you will find that your youth leader or priest will be most receptive. God bless you in all that you undertake!

www.ingramcontent.com/pod-product-compliance
Lightning Source LLC
Chambersburg PA
CBHW071956070526
44583CB00015B/1219